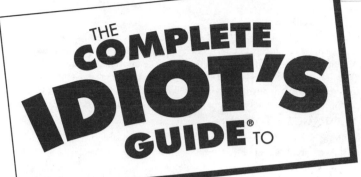

THE COMPLETE IDIOT'S GUIDE® TO

Restoring Collector Cars

by Tom Benford

ALPHA

A member of Penguin Group (USA) Inc.

Copyright © 2004 by Tom Benford

International Standard Book Number: 1-59257-234-0
Library of Congress Catalog Card Number: 2004105320

06 05 04   8 7 6 5 4 3 2 1

Interpretation of the printing code: The rightmost number of the first series of numbers is the year of the book's printing; the rightmost number of the second series of numbers is the number of the book's printing. For example, a printing code of 04-1 shows that the first printing occurred in 2004.

Printed in the United States of America

Note: This publication contains the opinions and ideas of its author. It is intended to provide helpful and informative material on the subject matter covered. It is sold with the understanding that the author and publisher are not engaged in rendering professional services in the book. If the reader requires personal assistance or advice, a competent professional should be consulted.

The author and publisher specifically disclaim any responsibility for any liability, loss, or risk, personal or otherwise, which is incurred as a consequence, directly or indirectly, of the use and application of any of the contents of this book.

Most Alpha books are available at special quantity discounts for bulk purchases for sales promotions, premiums, fund-raising, or educational use. Special books, or book excerpts, can also be created to fit specific needs.

For details, write: Special Markets, Alpha Books, 375 Hudson Street, New York, NY 10014.

Publisher: *Marie Butler-Knight*
Product Manager: *Phil Kitchel*
Senior Managing Editor: *Jennifer Chisholm*
Senior Acquisitions Editor: *Renee Wilmeth*
Development Editor: *Ginny Bess Munroe*
Production Editor: *Janette Lynn*
Copy Editor: *Drew Patty*
Illustrator: *Chris Eliopoulos*
Cover/Book Designer: *Trina Wurst*
Indexer: *Brad Herriman*
Layout/Proofreading: *Rebecca Harmon, Mary Hunt*

I dedicate this book to the memory of my son, Tom Benford, Jr., who passed away while I was writing it. He's gone on to cruise in a better place. Until we meet again, son.

Thomas A. Benford, Jr.
September 20, 1968–October 21, 2003

Contents at a Glance

Contents

Foreword

When I was a punk kid starting out in this business sometime in the Dark Ages, collecting and restoring old cars was about as popular as surfing on Lake Winnebago. A few nuts like Henry Austin Clark, Tiny Gould, and William Harrah thankfully saved hundreds of rare automobiles from the crusher, but for the most part old cars were considered piles of useless scrap. I can recall my father telling me how his prized Stutz had been hauled off to the junkyard in the middle of the Depression—a worthless used car of no value.

In the middle fifties, as I was searching for a '32 Ford coupe to build my first hot rod, I came across a rare Duesenberg Model-J close coupled sedan rusting away in an Upstate New York scrap yard. It was doomed, causing me to puzzle in retrospect about how miraculous it is that so many wonderful machines like it managed to avoid a similar fate.

A half-century later we are experiencing a complete turnabout. Everything is now collectible, including crocks that have little or no value, other than to their owners. Plymouths, Chevrolets and Fords that were produced by the tens of thousands during their heyday are now included in the collectible ranks, along with the aristocratic marques that bring hundreds of thousands of dollars—if not millions—at the numerous, high-buck auctions run by RM, Barrett-Jackson, Christies, and so on.

What was once a miniscule and obscure past time has been elevated to a wonderful, worldwide hobby engaged in by millions of mildly demented car lovers. Thanks to them, a significant component of our twentieth century heritage has been preserved.

At the same time a lusty business for restoration shops, NOS components, publications, parts suppliers, and the afore-mentioned sales and auction houses has been created. I have no idea regarding the magnitude of commerce involved in the collection and restoration of old cars of all types, but I am sure it totals in the tens-of-billions of dollars annually.

Now comes Tom Benford to give the hobby yet another dose of adrenalin with his wonderful *The Complete Idiot's Guide to Restoring Collector Cars*. He has artfully combined useful tips with a light, eminently readable style that offers value to both the hardcore restoration enthusiast and to the novice who might be considering the resurrection of his uncle's clapped-out Hudson Hornet.

We can confuse these efforts with the flinty world of investment and finance, but in reality they embody a source of passion and satisfaction for those of us who love old automobiles, be they Brahmin Bugattis or bourgeois Buicks. Within these pages Tom offers both prized advice and amusement for enthusiasts everywhere.

—Brock Yates

Wyoming, New York

Brock is Editor-at-Large and featured columnist for *Car and Driver* magazine. He is also an award-winning journalist and commentator for the Speed Channel Cable Network. He has written several well-known books on cars, hotrods, racing, and motorcycles including *Outlaw Machine* (1999, Little Brown). He has been an active radio and television program host and a CBS Sports color commentator on cars and car sports since 1976. He also wrote the screenplays for *The Cannonball Run* and *Smokey and the Bandit II*, both starring Burt Reynolds. Yates is also the originator and organizer of the famed Cannonball Sea-To-Shining-Sea Memorial Trophy Dashes and the more recent internationally recognized One Lap of America endurance event.

Introduction

When I was seven years old, my dad, Timothy B. Benford, Sr., purchased a 1933 Pierce-Arrow seven-passenger sedan for $100 and he worked for several years in his spare time restoring the car. I guess that's when I first got the "warm and fuzzies" over old cars. I remember sitting behind the huge steering wheel on a couple of occasions imagining that I was tooling this three-ton tank down the road in high style.

My dad acquired several other collector vehicles and they were all in various stages of restoration when he passed away in 1961. I was 10 at the time, and my mom sold off the collection.

During my teens and early '20s, I "busted my knuckles" working on my various cars and I became a fairly good wrench in the process. However, owing to mounting financial and parenting responsibilities, I settled down with "normal" cars that didn't require much under-the-hood time from me, and that's pretty much the way it stayed for the next two and a half decades. In all that time I really didn't give too much thought to getting back into working on cars, and collector cars were the furthest thing from my mind.

In the mid-1990s my wife, Liz, and I were spending the Memorial Day weekend in Hyannis, Massachusetts, where we happened upon a 1933 Dodge 5-Window Coupe street rod for sale. Both of my children were grown and out on their own, we had some "disposable income" to play with, and—literally on a whim—we bought this outrageous vehicle.

We put over eight thousand miles on this car the first year we owned it, which we dubbed "Screaming Mimi" after an expression that my mom used to use occasionally. We went to every cruise night and car show we knew of, sometimes going to as many as five in one week. On the nights when there was nothing happening, we'd just jump into the car and go for a cruise on our own. To say we were car crazy would be a safe description. We couldn't get enough of this collector car stuff—the flame had not only been rekindled in me, but now it was burning brighter than ever before!

The following year we purchased a 1948 Dodge Sport Coupe and a 1935 Nash Aeroform. The Dodge was in decent condition when I bought it for $1,000, and although I did some restoration work on it, it was pretty much a driver right from the get-go. The Nash was another story altogether, and you'll find out more about this bucket of rust that we paid good money for elsewhere in this book. Suffice it to say that buying the Nash was a mistake of major proportions. We got involved with vintage Corvettes and I also bought a 1967 Buick Riviera to restore along the way.

We became members of a car club and met folks who have become our oldest and dearest friends. We've been to more car shows than you could shake a stick at, we have hundreds of trophies adorning the rafters of our two-car garage, we have two 45-foot cargo trailers on our property to store our seven collector vehicles and the whole experience we've had with the collector car hobby over the last decade is something we wouldn't trade for anything in the world.

I guess my late son, Tom, Jr., also inherited the "gasoline in the veins" gene from me, since he started working on cars as soon as he was old enough to drive. His pride and joy was a Dodge Charger that he owned, followed by a Z28 Camaro. My daughter, Adina, on the other hand, has no interest in wrenching around under the hood of her truck, but, like her dad, she has a penchant for writing and playing the guitar.

As I'm writing this introduction I'm looking around my home office and there's automobilia all over the place—stained glass automotive sun catchers in the windows, the chrome script emblem from a Corvette perched on a window frame, a clock that looks like a disc brake, die-cast models up the wazoo, photographs of our cars on the wall, a paperweight made from a piston and even a framed advertisement for a Benford Golden Giant spark plug from 1917 along with two actual Benford spark plugs with their original packaging. Yeah, I guess you could say I'm a car nut.

There's a lot to learn when you're new to this hobby, and what I've tried to do here is to share the knowledge and experience I've gained over the last decade with you. I made a lot of mistakes along the way, and I hope that this book will save you from making the same ones I did. Experience is the best teacher, but you don't have to have the bad experiences, so I certainly hope I've succeeded here in helping you to avoid these mistakes and the problems they can produce.

This is definitely a fun hobby, and that's the biggest dividend you'll get from it—fun by the ton! Your entry and education in the collector car hobby begins as soon as you turn the page, and I sincerely hope you have fun reading this book and enjoying the collector car hobby!

How to Use This Book

The Complete Idiot's Guide to Restoring Collector Cars is a book that builds on material already covered as it progresses through its five parts.

Part 1, "In the Eye of the Beholder," explains the differences between the many genres of collector cars, and it helps you to analyze both your motivations and your expectations. It also explains what makes a good potential restoration candidate and provides some caveats on what to avoid getting involved with, along with giving you pointers on the various ways you can locate a collector car.

Part 2, "Preliminary Considerations," explains the differences between domestic and foreign vehicles and special things you should know when considering the restoration of an imported car. Everything you'll need to know about buying a collector car at auction is also covered here, as well as your various restoration options, where to get parts and more.

Part 3, "Getting the Project Underway," is the actual game-plan for a restoration project. Here's where you'll learn how to map out everything for the project including parts, services, labor, time, and money. Tips are also provided for getting the best value for every dollar spent, as well as ways to save money.

Part 4, "Let's Get Down and Dirty," gets you involved hands-on with your project vehicle. Detailed information on documenting the vehicle and disassembling it in an orderly fashion is covered, as are the elements and functions of the seven basic categories: frame, running gear, power, body, brakes, electrical and interior. This part also covers tips for restoring and refurbishing the various parts and components of the vehicle, grouped into these seven basic categories.

Part 5, "Ready to Roll," explains your options when it comes to insuring and registering your collector vehicle, having it appraised, and making the decision to trailer it or drive it. The fun and social side of the collector car hobby is also covered with information on cruise nights, car shows, and car clubs as well as advice on protecting your investment.

Extras

The Complete Idiot's Guide to Restoring Collector Cars also has little gems of information sprinkled throughout each chapter in boxed sidebars. These sidebars provide additional tips, definitions of terms/slang/jargon, warnings of potential dangers, and additional information that you may find helpful or even amusing. (Rule #1 is to have *fun* in the collector car hobby; Rule #2 is to always remember that it is a *hobby!*) We call these sidebars:

Brake It Down
The collector car hobby has its own jargon, so here's where you'll get the skinny on what it all means.

Pit Stop
These sidebars are warnings on things to be avoided for the sake of safety, saving money, or courtesy.

Overdrive

These sidebars will give you tips, shortcuts and other interesting information on how to make things easier, safer, or more fun.

4-Wheel Jive

These are the juicy "bet you didn't know" tidbits that are interesting—little known and often amusing facts and trivia pertaining to automobiles that serve to lighten things up a bit while being informative.

Acknowledgments

Numerous people have generously given their support, advice, labor, and talents to help me with this book, and I'd like to take this opportunity to acknowledge them now.

Carl Bessey, my good buddy, has helped me with difficult projects, has acted as my "hands model" while I shot photos and has unselfishly shared his considerable knowledge, experience, labor, and advice.

My close friends, Ken McBrearty and the late Roy Merkel, were my cohorts, co-conspirators and often provided comic relief while I worked on various automotive projects including this book. We'll always be the "three amigos."

John Sloane at The Eastwood Company is the tool expert and his recommendations on specific and special-purpose tools have made my life easier on many occasions. Ken Keuter is my man at Craftsman Tools and he went above and beyond the call of duty to make sure everything needed arrived on time. Mike Trueba at Auto Chic, Carl Sprague at Custom Autosound, Mike Stallings at Wheels Vintique and Scott Sonnier at Oxlite Manufacturing also deserve a big round of applause.

Kudos also go out to Bob and Ibi Nathans at Ibiz, Ted Busch at Busch Enterprises and John Helgren at Milweld/Hobart Welders.

I would most certainly be remiss if I didn't acknowledge all of the research, scheduling, tracking, proofreading, and other hard work done by my best friend, buddy, fellow car nut, soul mate, and wife, Liz. Her encouragement, optimism, sense of humor and undaunting support in all of my undertakings made putting this book together easier than it otherwise would have been.

I also owe a very special thank you to my literary agent, Michael Snell.

Another very special thank you is in order to Rick Carey for his excellent technical editing. His insight and suggestions were right on target and I feel privileged to have had him as my technical editor. I certainly hope we have the opportunity to work together again in the future.

Lastly, my sincere gratitude goes to Renee Wilmeth and Ginny Bess, the two major editors at Alpha Books who worked with me, for their belief that I was the right guy for this project.

Trademarks

All terms mentioned in this book that are known to be or are suspected of being trademarks or service marks have been appropriately capitalized. Alpha Books and Penguin Group (USA) Inc. cannot attest to the accuracy of this information. Use of a term in this book should not be regarded as affecting the validity of any trademark or service mark.

Part 1

In the Eye of the Beholder

Welcome, pilgrim, to the wild, wonderful, and sometimes wacky world of the collector car hobby. The restoration process is a major part of the hobby, because virtually every collector car, no matter what genre, has undergone a restoration to some extent. That's just the nature of the animal when you're dealing with older vehicles, and it's all part of the game.

Without a doubt, one of the nicest things about the collector car hobby is that it offers something for just about every automotive taste. Whether you're into antiques, classics, vintage cars, customs, street rods, military or special interest vehicles, or even professional cars like hearses, for sure you'll find it in this hobby and that's one of the many things we'll explore in this part of the book.

Chapter 1

Collector Car Differences

In This Chapter

◆ Considering collector car genres

◆ Rising restoration prices on rare vehicles

◆ Making modifications that reflect your personality

◆ Checking out other peoples' collector vehicles

There are many genres of collector cars. What is a "collector car" you ask? Generally speaking, a collector car is one that, for a number of reasons, is regarded as more than utilitarian transportation. It may be a vehicle's age, rarity, unique styling, mechanical innovation, historic significance, oddness, or other qualities that set it apart from everyday cars.

The apple of your eye might be a 50-plus year old vintage classic, a sexy little European number, it might be that gorgeous '57 Chevy convertible the guy down the block had when you were a kid, or a Hemi 'Cuda like the one Nash Bridges drove.

Even fairly recent vehicles can be regarded as collector cars. The Plymouth Prowler, Dodge Viper, and PT Cruiser are good examples. Knowing about each genre and what sets it apart from the rest will help you to determine what it is about a particular car that really rings your bell.

Beauty or Beast?

To a surprisingly large number of people, cars are more than just vehicles; they are rolling works of art. Many people feel strongly, even passionately, about their cars and believe that their particular automobile makes a personal statement about who they are, what they like, and how they prefer to move around.

While this can just as validly apply to the guy next door who babies and pampers his pre-owned Lexus, it is far more dramatically demonstrated and prevalent when it comes to collector cars. Indeed, the guy with a 1965 Mustang convertible probably feels as strongly about his ride as the fellow with the $100,000-plus Aston-Martin like James Bond drove in *Goldfinger*.

One thing is certain: Collector vehicles can take many forms, from a *classic car* to a street rod, and some will appeal to you more than others. So let's take a few minutes to explore the various genres that compose the collector car world.

Antique Cars

Antique cars represent the very beginnings of the automobile. Cars manufactured from the mid-1880s through 1916 generally fall into this category. During this pioneering era of automotive development, many different ideas and mechanisms were experimented with. In addition to the gasoline internal combustion engine, other forms of power included steam and electricity.

Many of these early vehicles were literally horseless carriages that were quite crude. Resembling buckboard carriages, steering was usually accomplished with a tiller rather than a steering wheel. Brass kerosene lanterns were used for nighttime illumination, and the motors had to be started using a hand crank. Typically, these were exposed vehicles without a roof or windshield. The driver and passengers would wear "duster" coats and goggles. The frames of these cars were made of wood, and they were usually outfitted with all-white tires. Body styling, for the most part, was non-existent: Slab sides and square fenders were the norm for these cars.

These cars are still around today, but they are generally difficult to find. Obtaining parts for these early vehicles can be a real challenge, because virtually all the parts were hand made and were rarely interchangeable between copies of the same model. Because much of this vehicle is wood, restoring one of these antique autos is more of an exercise in woodworking than in mechanics.

> **4-Wheel Jive**
>
> You could get a Model T Ford, also known as a "Tin Lizzy," in any color you wanted—as long as it was black! In his quest to make an affordable car, Henry Ford restricted the production color of the Model T to black because black paint dried faster, thereby speeding up production. He sold millions of them.

Vintage Automobiles

Vintage automobiles generally encompass cars that were manufactured between 1916 and 1924. By this time, electric starters had been introduced, eliminating the dangerous hand crank; it's estimated that by 1917, 97 percent of all American-made automobiles had electric self-starters. Electric lighting had also replaced the kerosene lanterns for night driving illumination.

Styling considerations also entered the picture. Bodylines became less boxy and more flowing; enclosed bodies in coupe and sedan configurations afforded more protection from the elements, and they were equipped with windows that could be raised and lowered. The evolution of the automobile was gaining momentum.

Mechanical advances continued at a speedy clip during this period, too. Packard developed a V-12 engine, and other manufacturers produced "straight-8s." Soon after, V-8, V-12, and V-16 configurations were offered in various marques.

4-Wheel Jive
Charles Kettering invented the electric automobile starter, which is one of the most important advancements the auto industry has ever known. The electric starter first appeared on Cadillacs in 1912, and cars equipped with electric starters enjoyed spectacular sales over those with hand crank starters.

These vintage autos included the Model T Fords, the Model A Fords, the Chevrolets, Chryslers, Dodges, Plymouths, Buicks, Oldsmobiles, Studebakers and other makes that were priced to be affordable for the common man. Rather than receiving handcrafted coach work, these vehicles were mass-produced on assembly lines. These early cars made automobiles and the ability to traverse the country accessible to anyone who could afford to buy one.

The young automotive industry was booming and, by the end of the vintage era in America, thousands of automobile names were listed; these entrepreneurial manufacturers frequently only produced a single car. Experimentation was still quite prevalent, and the car-buying public could choose from motorized buggies, electric-powered vehicles, motorized cycle cars, steam-powered vehicles and even sports cars from marques like Stutz and Mercer.

Because vintage cars are still fairly abundant and easy to find (at least those produced by major manufacturers like Ford, Chevrolet, Dodge, etc.), they are considerably more affordable than a high-end classic. Typically, these cars were built to be very durable, and they lived up to that expectation surprisingly well.

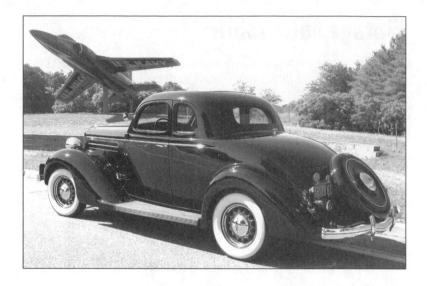

This nicely restored 1935 Dodge DU Coupe still manages to cruise along at 60 mph without a problem.

Thanks to their high production numbers, parts for vintage cars are also usually easy to locate and frequently quite reasonably priced. Several manufacturers are also reproducing many parts for vintage cars, so you have a choice between purchasing original parts or reproduction units. Restoring a vintage car can be a fun proposition that won't break the bank in most cases—especially if you elect to do the lion's share of the work yourself.

Classics

Classic automobiles were typically manufactured between 1925 and 1948 and, in most instances, represent the golden age of motoring. This period of time in automotive history is known as the coach-built era because the bodies of these Classics were handmade by coachbuilders.

Brake It Down

The Classic Car Club of America (CCCA) defines a **classic automobile** as "a fine or distinctive automobile, either American or foreign, built between 1925–1948 in limited numbers. They are also sometimes called full classics or Classic with a capital 'c'".

Generally, a Classic was high-priced when new and was built in limited quantities. Other factors, including engine displacement, custom coachwork and luxury accessories, such as power brakes, power clutch, and "one-shot" or automatic lubrication systems, help determine whether a car is considered a Classic.

American-made Classics include such names as Auburn, Duesenberg, Cadillac, Lincoln, Packard, and Pierce-Arrow. Classics manufactured in Europe include such marques as Hispano-Suiza, Minerva, Aston-Martin, Bentley, and Rolls-Royce. These expensive vehicles were owned by the rich and famous of their day.

This pristinely restored 1924 Packard is a vintage, American classic. Restored cars of this caliber routinely fetch prices in the high 6-figure bracket.

It was a common practice to purchase a Duesenberg, LaSalle, Packard, or other marque from the manufacturer as a *running chassis* and then have a private coach works build a custom body for it. Those who could afford such ostentatious vehicles could also afford to have distinctive, one-of-a-kind bodies fabricated for them to further underscore their wealth and social status.

Because these Classics were produced in very limited numbers, they are rare and, consequently, are still very expensive. A pristinely restored Classic can easily cost well over $500,000, with some exceptional examples fetching seven- or even eight-figures. Because of the high level of skill and expertise required to do a restoration on a Classic, it is a job best left to a professional restoration facility that is properly equipped to do the restoration correctly. It is not uncommon for the restoration of such a vehicle to exceed $150,000. In fact, that would be a real bargain in most cases.

> **4-Wheel Jive**
>
> The word "marque" (pronounced "mark") is used to designate a model or brand of automobile, such as Lincoln or Rolls-Royce.

> **Brake It Down**
>
> Also sometimes called a "rolling chassis," **running chassis** refers to an automobile's frame, engine, transmission, suspension, gas tank, steering system, drive train, brakes, wheels and tires, and cooling system. In effect, it is the complete car without the body attached to it.

World-Renowned Marques

Around the globe, several automobiles have been recognized as world-class cars because of their distinctive appearance, performance, or features and innovations. These marques include the Duesenberg, Packard, Cadillac, Lincoln, Rolls-Royce, Jaguar, Bugatti, Ferrari, Porsche, Mercedes-Benz, Corvette, and many others.

Not all world-renowned marques are beauty contest winners, however. To this list you can also add the original Mini-Coopers, the Morris Minor, the Volkswagen Beetle, the Fiat Abarth, the MG roadster, and others. These, too, are cars known and recognized throughout the world. These utilitarian vehicles made low-priced transportation affordable to the masses, even though their styling cues weren't exactly stunning.

Depending on the particular marque you select, the restoration can range from easy and inexpensive to very difficult and costly. Depending on the car, finding parts can be a walk in the park or a quest for the Holy Grail. These are serious things to consider if you're thinking of restoring one. For example, finding a radiator cap for a Model A Ford is relatively easy, while locating the famous "kneeling archer" radiator cap for a Pierce-Arrow is a difficult and very expensive proposition.

Modern Classics

Some cars have been so innovative in their styling or engineering that they can rightly be called modern classics. Without a doubt, the most popular trend in the collector car hobby is restoring "nostalgia" collector cars rather than true classics.

For instance, the 1953 Corvette became America's first true sports car with its two-seat configuration, the 1955 Thunderbird was innovative with its removable hardtop with "porthole" windows, and the Lincoln, offered the only four door convertible, and it had *suicide doors* on the rear.

Modern classics are cars produced in the 1950s, 1960s, 1970s, and even the 1980s and later that have a panache all their own. When they were new, they stood out in a crowd, turned heads, and made bold styling statements. They were the breaths of fresh air in an automotive industry that had grown stodgy and musty. These modern classics were significant evolutionary building blocks in the history of the automobile.

Some examples of modern classics include:

◆ 1955–1957 Thunderbirds

◆ 1955–1957 Chevrolets

◆ 1955–1958 Chevy Nomad Station Wagons

- 1957 Chrysler 300C

- 1959 Cadillac

- 1957–1959 Ford Skyliners

- 1963 Corvette Sting Ray Split Window Coupe

- 1954–1962 Nash Metropolitans

- 1957 Studebaker Golden Hawk

- 1964–1966 Pontiac GTO

- 1949–1953 MG TD Roadster

- 1965 Ford Mustang

- 1950–1965 "Bathtub" Porsche 356s

- 1981–1982 DeLorean DMC-12

- 1961–1967 Jaguar XKE

- 1953–1954 Buick Skylark

- 1953 Oldsmobile Fiesta

- 1953–1958 Cadillac Eldorado

Brake It Down

A **suicide door** has the hinges at the rear of it, rather than at the front. Suicide doors were popular during the 1920s and 1930s. They derived their name from the fact that anyone trying to exit a moving vehicle through a one of these doors was committing suicide.

Depending on the individual make, model, and year, the prices for modern classics vary quite a bit. Another thing that greatly affects the price for a modern classic is its condition. For example, an original, unrestored 1965 Pontiac GTO that has been garage-kept its entire life, has under 80,000 original miles and has never been in a collision will sell for ten times more than one that has been laying around in someone's yard under a tarpaulin for the last thirty or so years.

When looking for a modern classic or any collector car, remember that the vehicle's overall condition has a direct influence on the price. The better the condition of the car, the less work it will require for restoration, and the higher its purchase price will be.

4-Wheel Jive

Amber-colored front turn signals were first adopted as standard in 1962.

The Corvette: America's Sports Car

In 1951, Harley Earl was the head of styling at General Motors. After World War II, sports cars were quite popular with returning GIs who had become acquainted with the low, nimble, and fast two-seaters during their tours of duty in Europe. Earl was determined to create a new breed of American car that could compare favorably with Europe's Jaguars, MGs, Alfa Romeos and Ferraris. His goal was to have a stylish two-seat convertible design ready for the company's January, 1953 Motorama Exhibit at the prestigious Waldorf Astoria Hotel in New York City.

> **4-Wheel Jive**
>
> Myron Scott gave the Corvette its name. Scott worked for Campbell-Ewald, Chevrolet's advertising agency, and discovered the name while looking through his home dictionary under "C." The word corvette described a small, fast battle cruiser used during World War II by the British navy. Scott was also the father of the Soap Box Derby.

The prototype Corvette roadster was secretly developed in Earl's private studio. It was such a hit at the Motorama show that GM management gave the green light to start manufacturing the car at Chevrolet's plant in Flint, Michigan. On June 30, the first Corvette rolled off the assembly line with a sticker price of just over $3,000 and it has been America's sports car for over a half-century now.

Corvettes are favorites to restore, but restoring a Corvette is different from restoring a "regular" car in many ways. The most significant difference is that the Corvette's body is made of fiberglass rather than metal; working with fiberglass requires very specialized skills. Another thing to consider is the Corvette's electrical system; because the body is nonconductive, it can't be used to ground electrical connections like metal-bodied cars can. And on some years, there are some other differences like fuel-injected engines and independent rear suspensions, which make restoring a Corvette a very specialized job, indeed.

Also bear in mind that most Corvettes have had difficult lives. Because they were conceived and produced as performance cars, they have generally received a beating along the way with countless jack-rabbit starts, clutch-dropping at high RPMs to spin the rear wheels and, more often than not, a collision or two with an immovable object like a fire hydrant or a telephone pole while being piloted by an irresponsible driver.

> **Pit Stop**
>
> When viewing collector cars at a cruise night or a car show, remember not to touch the vehicle. Proper collector car etiquette dictates that you look with your eyes, not your hands.

Working on a Corvette restoration can easily become a Zen thing as you become immersed in the project—working on the car can be a way of "zoning out" and concentrating completely on the task at hand. Fortunately, res-toration parts are readily available for every year from a variety of sources. However, be aware that restoring a Corvette can be a very expensive proposition.

Other Sports Cars

Sports cars are nimble two-seaters that are loads of fun to drive and perennial favorites for restoration. MG Roadsters, MG Midgets, and MG-Bs are frequently available at very reasonable prices, as are Triumphs, Sunbeam Tigers and Austin-Healeys, to name just a few.

Saab Sonnets and Bricklins, because of their scarcity, are excellent projects for restoration. Jaguars and Mercedes SLs are also quite popular sports cars for restoration, although their prices are a bit higher. Porsches and Alfa Romeo Spiders are also sports cars you might want to consider. Of late, the Datsun "Z" has come into its own and is sought after by collectors for restoration projects.

Some sports cars are really high-end, and the original Shelby Cobras and Aston-Martins fall into this category. Dubbed the "Corvette Killer" in its day, an unrestored Shelby Cobra from the early 1960s would cost a minimum of approximately $150,000, and a fully restored Cobra with racing history can approach the one million dollar range. Even the replica Cobras and kit Cobras are $50,000 or more. Aston-Martins, Lamborghinis, and Ferraris are also quite pricey.

Sporty Cars

Unlike the Corvette, the Ford Thunderbird was never intended to be a sports car. Outfitted with a V8 engine and comfortable suspension, the 1955 through 1957 Ford Thunderbirds are more accurately called sporty cars rather than sports cars. In 1958, the T-Bird became a four-seater, and any existing misconceptions about it being a sports car were once and for all quelled. There's no such thing as a four-seat sports car, but there are plenty of four-seat sporty cars out there—including BMWs, Saabs, and others. Older "beamers" (BMWs), Karmann-Ghias, Datsun "Z" series and other such "sporty" cars are relatively easy to find, they're affordable and they are generally restorations that won't break the budget.

Ground Shakers: American Muscle Cars

One of the segments of the collector car hobby that has enjoyed unprecedented resurgence is the current popularity and interest in American muscle cars. The term was first used in the late 1960s to designate a mid-sized car with a large-displacement V8 engine that was built for speed.

Some examples of American muscle cars include:

- Pontiac GTO (the 1964 GTO was the original muscle car)
- Chevrolet Camaro SS396
- AMC AMX
- Chevrolet Chevelle SS396
- Dodge Challenger R/T 440
- Plymouth Barracuda Hemi and Hemi 'Cuda
- Dodge Charger RT
- Ford Fairlane
- Ford Torino GT
- Dodge Dart 383 and 440
- Ford Shelby Cobra Mustang
- Dodge Super Bee
- Chevrolet Nova SS
- Buick GS

Because muscle cars are currently so hot on the collector car scene, their prices are way up there. Even rusted-out hulks from the late 1960s and early 1970s are going for big bucks, and restoring them is an expensive prospect. However, the allure and appeal of a piece of Detroit iron with a huge, fire-breathing mill under its hood, ladder traction bars and slicks at the rear, and aggressive looks make a muscle car difficult to resist.

Pony Cars

The term "pony car," which originated in 1964 with the Ford Mustang, describes affordable, performance-oriented American vehicles that were sporty in appearance and popular during the 1960s and 1970s. In addition to the Mustang, the Mercury Cougar, Chevrolet Camaro, Pontiac Firebird, Plymouth Barracuda, Dodge Challenger and AMC (American Motors Corporation) Javelin were considered pony cars.

Pony cars are also enjoying a lot of popularity and they're very desirable collector cars. Prices are currently on the high side, although, with a bit of diligence, you can still find a desirable pony car for restoration at a reasonable price. Parts are available from a number of catalog houses, reproduction manufacturers, and salvage yards. A well-equipped pony car with top-of-the-line performance equipment can be considered a junior muscle car.

Customs

Customs are cars that have been designed and modified to be truly one-of-a-kind vehicles. Almost any car (or truck, for that matter) ever made can be a candidate for customization.

Customs can range from mild to utterly wild, and there's a slot for just about everything in between the two extremes. Older cars like the 1950 Fords are favorites of customizers who frequently shave the door handles, *french* the headlights and radio antennas, cover the rear wheels with skirts, and smooth all of the body seams. Customs such as these are frequently called *leadsleds* because molten lead was traditionally used as body filler in the early days of customizing.

The nice thing about customs is that there are no rules; virtually anything goes. It's not uncommon to see that an owner who had his own vision of what he wanted his car to look like has customized even the most unlikely cars.

Restoring an older custom can be difficult and expensive, depending on what was originally done to the vehicle and its state of disrepair or neglect. In many cases, those who desire a custom car are better off starting from scratch with a sound base vehicle and transforming it to match the image in their mind's eye rather than trying to bring back what someone else originally had in mind.

Brake It Down

Recessed head or taillights that are smoothed into the body panels are **frenched**. If they are deeply frenched, they are said to be tunneled.

Brake It Down

A **leadsled** is a lowered, late 1940s to early 1950s car with molded body seams that are traditionally done with lead solder.

4-Wheel Jive

Ragtop is a slang expression for a convertible.

Street Rods and Street Machines

A street rod is a street-legal American car manufactured from 1925 through 1948 that has been saved from the crusher, rebuilt (from the ground up, literally) and customized to the individual owner's tastes. It is a high performance vehicle that is also an art form, an amalgam of components joined together harmoniously to make a very personal statement.

Following are some of genres of street rods:

◆ **Resto-rods.** These look original on the outside, but are anything but original under the hood.

◆ **Nostalgia rods.** These resemble the hot rods of the past. These are sometimes finished in black primer with wide whitewalls, painted steel wheels, discs or spinner wheel covers, a pair of fuzzy dice hanging from the mirror, a lady luck or eight-ball shift knob and roll-and-pleat upholstery.

◆ **Techies.** These are professionally-built turn-key rods.

◆ **Highboys.** These are fenderless and ready to rock 'n' roll.

◆ **Labor-of-love rods.** Although they may never take a trophy or win public recognition, these are unabashedly the pride and joy of the build-it-and-drive-it street rod set.

On the other hand, a street machine is essentially a street rod that was originally manufactured from 1949 or later, but has still undergone performance modifications and body alterations. A few quick examples of popular street machines are the 1956 Ford Crown Victoria, the 1957 Chevrolet, the 1965 Pontiac LeMans, and the 1962 Chrysler Newport.

> **4-Wheel Jive**
>
> The Chevrolet "bowtie" logo was inspired by the pattern on the wallpaper in a French hotel bedroom that was occupied by William Durant in 1908; Durant went on to become the president of Chevrolet and the founder of General Motors. The bowtie logo first appeared on Chevrolet cars in 1913.

Street rods and street machines appeal to many people because, like customs, there are really no rules. The vehicle is a reflection of your own particular taste and vision. You can take something as mundane as a 1965 Studebaker Lark, drop in a modified Chevrolet small block engine, give it a snappy paint job with a custom interior, and you have a cool street machine. It is the fact that modifications are not only allowed but are the order of the day that make street rods and street machines so appealing, popular, and fun.

Sleepers and Ugly Ducklings

Sleepers are loosely defined as mundane family sedans, economy cars, and basic transportation vehicles—the cars that your parents may have had while you were growing up. Some typical examples of sleepers include a four-door Chevrolet Biscayne, a Ford Country Squire Station Wagon, a Nash Rambler, a four-door Mercury Marquis—I think you get the idea here.

Sleepers earned that moniker because there's nothing visually exciting about them, and they usually offered lackluster performance compared to other cars of their day. It's amazing that cars like these that weren't that sexy when they were new are popular restoration prospects today. They're fairly easy to find and can be generally inexpensive. Restoration parts aren't too difficult to come by, so you may want to consider a sleeper restoration project. They're economical to restore and own, and still popular for car club events, a low-priced entry ticket into the collector car world.

Ugly ducklings are like homely sleepers. Think of the bubble-shaped AMC Pacer or the wedge-shaped AMC Gremlin and you start to get the idea of what an ugly duckling looks like. Other cars that easily fall into this category are the Ford Pinto, Chevrolet Vega, Ford Maverick, Chevrolet Chevette and others of similar size and appearance. Like sleepers, they can still be found in sufficient numbers and at prices low enough for them to be seriously considered as restoration projects. Parts are also affordable and easy to come by.

SIVs: Special Interest Vehicles

This is kind of a catch-all category for oddball and exotic vehicles such as police cars, military vehicles, fire engines, Amphicars (a hybrid car that drove on land and functioned as a boat in the water) and just about anything else that doesn't comfortably fit within the framework of the other genres. You're just as likely to find a WWII half-track truck as an Excalibur, Lotus Elan, or Meyers Manx in the special interest genre, too.

Locating a special interest vehicle depends largely on what you're looking for. The restoration process may be more demanding and expensive than working on vehicles in the other genres because they were produced in comparatively small quantities, so give that some extra consideration as you search for that special interest vehicle that appeals to you.

Professional Cars

What's a professional car, you ask? A professional car can be loosely defined as a custom-bodied vehicle that is based on passenger car styling and used in the funeral, rescue, or livery services. Professional cars can be hearses, flower cars, service cars, ambulances, limousines, or cars that are specially built to combine two or more of these different functions, such as combination hearse-ambulances, sedan ambulances or invalid coaches.

Like virtually every other aspect of the collector car hobby, the interest level in professional cars has risen considerably over the last decade. Once considered a "fringe element" of the hobby, these vehicles are being seen more frequently at cruise nights and car shows.

The fact that these are not mainstream vehicles could work in your favor, because most people aren't too interested in parking a hearse in their driveway or garage, even if the price is right. However, because these vehicles are built in limited numbers and held by their professional owners for many years of service, they aren't always readily available. They're out there, however, if this type of vehicle appeals to you and you're willing to do some digging (pardon the pun).

Trucks

Restoring old trucks has become more popular in the last 10-15 years, and there are no signs that it will wane any time in the near future. Favorite candidates for restoration are Ford, Chevrolet, and Dodge pickups, but such oldies-but-goodies like a 1948 Studebaker Pickup or a 1956 Chevrolet Sedan Delivery are also very viable contenders. The light-duty trucks like those mentioned are usually sought after for restoration projects, but it isn't unheard of for someone to set about restoring a 1948 Mack dump truck.

You can find an old truck in many places, and these vehicles have proven their durability through decades of hard work. The price is often right, and restoring an old truck can be loads of fun. If you can't locate a replacement part in a boneyard, restoration parts suppliers may have what you need, or you can often make a part yourself.

The Least You Need to Know

- There are many collector car genres that you should consider for a potential restoration project.

- Rarity and demand drives up the price of a restorable vehicle and increases the cost for restoration parts.

- You don't have to do a "perfect" restoration; you can elect to make modifications and customizations that reflect your tastes.

- Take the time to check out the collector cars other folks own and have some fun while you're doing it.

Chapter **2**

What's Your Motivation?

In This Chapter

- ◆ Remembering the good ole days
- ◆ Investing in collector cars
- ◆ Discovering the hobby of restoring cars on your own
- ◆ Understanding the business side of collector cars

What would possess a person to purchase a 40-year-old car, take it all apart, restore, refurbish, or replace all of the worn parts, have it repainted and re-plated, and then put it all back together again, especially when the restored vehicle will be mechanically and technically inferior to today's cars? The answer is surprisingly simple. People restore cars for fun and fulfillment.

There are several motivating factors that attract people to the collector car hobby, and that's what we'll explore in this chapter.

So Why Do It?

Take a few minutes and analyze why you want to restore a collector car. Is it whimsy or a deep-rooted desire? Are you prepared to dedicate lots of time, effort, and money to a project that may take several years to complete? Are you interested in preserving a piece of automotive history or are you just looking for a new challenge for your spare-time hours? This is the time to recognize and understand your motivation for getting involved in the collector car hobby and restoring a vehicle.

The Nostalgia Trend

The 1950s, 1960s, and even the 1970s were "special" decades. The 1950s ushered in television, strip housing developments, hula-hoops, Davey Crockett hats, and the Mickey Mouse Club. V8 engines, Corvettes, T-Birds, tail fins, and automatic transmissions were but a few of the new "modern jet-age" symbols that enriched our automotive experiences.

In the 1960s we were introduced to folk music, followed by The Beatles and the ensuing British invasion in music. JFK was assassinated, the Pontiac GTO started the muscle car movement, and the Ford Mustang single-handedly inspired the term "pony car." Flower power and psychedelic experiences influenced students, and space flight had advanced to the point that we had our first manned landing on the moon by the end of the decade. Cars with large displacement engines pumping out gobs of horsepower made motoring fun at home while the Vietnam War was in full swing on the other side of the world.

The psychedelic 1970s continued, while the oil crunch caused gasoline shortages and lines at the pumps. The Sony Beta Max made it possible to videotape a TV show and view it at a more convenient time, and microwave ovens made cooking food faster and easier. Nixon resigned, reminding us that he was "not a crook," and cars were equipped with catalytic converters and used unleaded gas to protect the environment. Smaller cars manufactured overseas that were economical to operate started to come onto the scene like gangbusters while American automakers tried to cut weight and power on their vehicles to meet EPA requirements.

Those Were the Days

The nostalgia trend is prevalent and it continues to gain momentum; there is a deep-rooted desire among many people to remember a simpler time when family values were upheld, the streets were safe, respect was given to elders and authority figures, and mom's apple pie, baseball, a warm home, a stable job, and a good car were just a few of the things that made the United States the best place to live on the entire planet.

The automobile had a major influence on our lives during the twentieth century, and because it was with us all along the way, it has an important place both in history and nostalgia. Restoring a collector vehicle is a way of making history come alive through the preservation of a conveyance from yesteryear. For many, the restoration process is as much fun as driving the car when it is finished. This yearning for a hands-on project to give a venerable vehicle a second chance at life motivates many people, and it may be your own reason for getting into this hobby.

Reliving Your Youth

I remember being a freshman in high school when I first saw the Corvette Sting Ray split window coupe in 1963. I was crossing the boulevard and there it was, waiting for the light to turn green. Its red paint job, knock-off wheel spinners, sleek lines, and snappy whitewall tires absolutely transfixed me, to the point that I just stood there staring after the light had changed and cars were honking at me. I fell in love with that car at that instant and I promised myself I would own a Corvette just like that one someday when I could afford it.

Some 32 years passed before I made good on my promise to myself. Along the way my two kids had grown into adults and moved out on their own, I made a few career changes, and had many, many cars along the way. None of them were Corvettes, just practical transportation vehicles.

Well, I finally got my Corvette and the day I went to look at it, I got goose bumps and butterflies in the stomach exactly the way I did as a teenager when laying eyes on it for the first time. What a rush! When I got behind the wheel and put it in gear it was 1963 all over again.

Brake It Down

CID is an abbreviation for cubic inch displacement, which is a measurement of the volume of an engine's cylinders. Essentially the larger the CID, the more horsepower the engine can produce.

The 1963 Corvette Sting Ray coupe became an instant collector classic, because it was only produced for one year. The strip that separates the two rear window panels was eliminated for 1964, never to return again.

In retrospect I had a few other cars in my late teens and early twenties that I wish I still had now. My 1964 Chevelle Malibu SS with its small-block 283 *CID* engine and 4-speed trans was a very fast little car. I later owned a 1965 Mustang 2+2 Fastback with a 289 CID engine, 4-speed trans, factory styled-steel wheels, and the "rally

Brake It Down

A Carson top is a solid, removable roof usually covered in a soft material and used on some roadsters, cabriolets, and phaetons.

pack" tachometer/clock combo. (I traded this one in on a Ford Country Squire station wagon due to family obligations.)

I'm not the only person who, even if in only a small way, wishes he could relive the glory days of his youth. Reliving your youth through the restoration of a collector car isn't a bad thing, and if that's your motivation, then more power to you!

Collector Cars as Investments

Are collector cars good investments? That's a question I've been asked very often and the answer is: maybe yes and maybe no. There are many factors to consider.

Certain collector cars are inherently more valuable than others. Rarity, desirability, and the level of restoration all affect the value of a collector vehicle, as well as the state of preservation and maintenance the vehicle is kept in. Certain genres of collector cars, such as muscle cars, are enjoying a very hot market currently and the prices they command are absolutely astronomical. I know of a 1970 Chevelle SS 454 coupe owned by a magazine editor who is a friend of mine that sold recently for $100,000! He bought and restored the car because he had one just like it while he was in high school. It was a hobby restoration that took him several years to complete in his spare time, and he never intended to sell it while he was restoring it. He entered it in a local car show and someone who "absolutely had to have it" offered him $80,000 for it, which he declined. Within a half-hour this fellow offered him $100,000 as a final offer, to which he finally said yes.

Considering that this car sold for less than $4,000 brand new, I'd say that was an enormous amount of appreciation, wouldn't you? This story had a happy and profitable ending, albeit serendipitous, because he never considered the car to be an investment. It was a hobby vehicle that he enjoyed restoring and driving and, subsequently, made a good deal of money from.

On the opposite side of the coin, I'm friendly with a car collector who owns a 1941 Plymouth that she calls "Harry." This car has garnered the Mayflower Award from Plymouth for several consecutive years and is regarded as the most perfectly restored 1941 Plymouth in the entire world.

My friend jokingly comments that it only cost her about $37,500 to restore a car that has a value of $7,500 on the collector car market. Luckily for her, the restoration was a labor of love.

Finding a Comfort Level

If you intend to restore collector cars for investment, you have to determine what level of restoration you'll feel comfortable doing. Basically, there are three ways to go here, so let's take a look at your options:

This 1937 Ford Cabriolet is in reality a street rod that retained much of the original look and "flavor" of the stock vehicle.

- ◆ **Refreshing an Older Restoration.** This is by far the easiest way to go and, in most cases, offers the fastest turnaround opportunity. Essentially what you will be doing here is "freshening up" a restoration that was done perhaps 10–15 years ago. This entails light derusting where required, touch-ups or repainting, replacing visibly worn items, cleaning and detailing the engine compartment and polishing all the bright work (chrome, stainless, and aluminum trim). Often, after a restoration is complete and the owner has enjoyed the car for a few years, he starts to yearn for another project and subsequently puts his restored collector car up for sale. This frequently presents a good opportunity to acquire a car that only needs minimal work to put it back in top condition. At that point you can enjoy the car or put it up for sale at a higher price than you paid for it.

- ◆ **Picking Up an Abandoned Project.** More often than you'd think, people will start a restoration project and, for some reason, never complete it. Sometimes people simply don't have the time to work on the project, they've lost interest in doing it, they have realized they are in way over their heads, or they are tired of having an old clunker take up space in the garage. Such project abandonment frequently occurs after the car is first brought home and a frenzy of disassembly has taken place. Now, with parts scattered all over the garage floor, it dawns on the hapless owner that he hasn't documented anything, he doesn't have a clear plan for doing the restoration, and he has no clue as to where all these disassembled parts belong on the vehicle.

Because of these factors, you can usually get an abandoned project vehicle very inexpensively. However, there are a few trade-offs for the cheap price: You can't be sure that all of the parts that were taken off are still with the car, you probably don't have documentation of the work that was done thus far, and putting everything back together will be much like doing a jig-saw puzzle. If you like a challenge and you are not in any great hurry to finish the restoration, this can represent an excellent investment opportunity.

Overdrive

If you have a specialty vehicle dealer in your area that carries and sells collector cars, pay his car lot a visit to get an idea of what these cars are selling for. Take along a camera and a notepad. Snap some pictures of the cars and note their make, model, year, and the general condition of restoration. These pictures and data on the vehicles will come in handy as you compare prices for similar vehicles on the Internet or at auctions. Due diligence is the keyword here, so don't be a slacker.

◆ **The Total Restoration.** Your third option for doing a collector car restoration for investment purposes is to do a complete restoration from the ground up. For most people, this will be a spare-time project that will span several years. To maximize your equity in the vehicle and keep the restoration costs minimal, you should plan on doing the majority of the work yourself. Having a game plan in place is the way to embark on such an enterprise. Follow this outline as a basis for your plan, and use it to determine whether the project might be a profit-producing undertaking:

1. Decide on a car for restoration.

2. Locate several possible candidates.

3. Compare the prices and condition of the candidate vehicles.

4. Locate perfectly restored vehicles of the exact same year, make, and model with similar equipment and learn what they are currently worth in today's collector car market.

5. Establish delivery charges, if any, from the seller's location to the restoration location.

6. Estimate the costs of parts that will be required for the restoration, using catalogs and Internet sources.

7. Inflate the parts estimate by 30 percent for unexpected expenditures.

8. Estimate how many hours of labor the restoration will require. Double this estimate.

9. Figure out about how many hours per week you can devote to the restoration and divide that into the labor hour estimate to determine how long the project will take until it is completed.

10. Get estimates for outside vendor services, such as paint and bodywork, engine work, and/or transmission rebuilding, upholstery, and other things you don't want to do yourself.

11. Add up the estimates including the purchase price of the car.

12. Compare your total to the figure you established in step 4.

Now, it goes without saying that some collector cars are going to continue to appreciate regardless of other factors in the market. The reason for this is that these cars are truly unique and scarce because they were produced in very limited numbers. When restored, such vehicles will fetch top dollar. But restoring such a collector car is only the first half of the journey; after the restoration is complete the vehicle must be preserved and maintained to hold its value, which is another item to consider if you're doing the restoration as an investment exercise.

Restoring It Yourself as a Hobby

Restoring a collector car is an enjoyable hobby and is undoubtedly the biggest motivating factor for most people involved in restorations. Making something nice from something shoddy using your own two hands and knowing that you are doing a good job is satisfying and something you can be proud to tell others about. There's a sense of fulfillment preserving a piece of motoring history and giving this vehicle a second shot at life rather than seeing it go to a crusher in a junkyard.

Many folks I know who've done their own restorations, myself included, relate the task to going back to a slower, simpler time. I know I've often wondered while working on my collector cars what tales they could tell me if they could talk. I've often marveled at the underside of my cars while working on the suspension or other chassis components and thought about how many roads and miles this metal has traversed, what the weather and driving conditions were like, and what was going on in the previous owners' minds while they were piloting the vehicle. Flights of fancy like this are common and welcomed "mental oases" when working on your restoration, particularly some of the more tedious and boring tasks. You can really get lost in what you're doing and the hours just wile away without your notice.

Restoring a collector car doesn't have to be a solitary activity. The whole family, or at least part of your family, might want to become involved and there are plenty of small jobs that will have to be done so there's something for everyone to do. Encourage your spouse and kids to participate in the project and have some quality family time while working on it.

The Business End of Collector Cars

While our main focus in this book involves the hobby aspects of collector car restoration, it is indeed a business as well for many others. Because this is a motivating factor, we will spend some time looking at what's involved in the business end.

Restoration Facilities

Restoration facilities are service garages that only do restoration work on collector cars and light trucks. They are staffed with experienced professionals who are well versed in all aspects of restoration. This is definitely not the corner garage guy who does your oil changes. Such specialty houses charge rates commensurate with the skill of their personnel and the quality of their work. I know an older gent who had his 1941 Packard Darrin restored at a well-respected restoration facility in northern New Jersey. The finished car is absolutely gorgeous and, when I asked him how much the restoration cost, he candidly commented, "I didn't get much change back from $200,000." But he got what he paid for and he's happy with it.

Specialty Paint and Body Shops

Most body shops make their money doing "insurance jobs," or repairs from collisions that are being paid for by the vehicle owner's insurance. The payments for these jobs are calculated by the insurance adjuster using a time and parts costing method. If the body shop can complete the repair in less time than the adjuster has allocated for it, the shop makes extra money which means additional profit. This is the bread and butter of the body shop, so it's no surprise that most body shops don't want to get involved in doing restoration work; it simply isn't as clean, fast, or profitable as doing insurance jobs.

Like dedicated restoration facilities, there are specialty paint and body shops that do custom work. In addition to working on restorations, these shops also cater to other specialty automotive markets like finishing race cars and show vehicles. Also like the restoration facilities, they are usually staffed with highly skilled people using state-of-the art materials and equipment to come as close to perfection as humanly possible. As you can imagine, these services don't come cheaply. But then again, you wouldn't really want your pride and joy restored collector car to wear a $99.99 Earl Scheib paint job, would you? It's like the old adage about oats: The fresh, clean oats cost a lot more than the ones that have already been through the horse.

Rebuilding Facilities

If you're very lucky, your collector car's engine and transmission will be in good working order, but that usually isn't the case. Removing, rebuilding, and reinstalling a motor and/or transmission require special equipment and tools that most folks don't have sitting in their garage, and it also requires skill and knowledge not possessed by the Average Joe. Jobs such as these are best handled by outside vendors who specialize in such rebuilding services. It is usually important to most collector car hobbyists to maintain the correct *matching numbers*—that is, matching the engine and transmission that were originally installed in their vehicle rather than trading them in for a replacement motor, so be sure the mechanic knows you want your original engine rebuilt. In some genres, such as customs, street rods, and street machines, number-matching components are totally irrelevant, because the vehicle was never intended to be a correct restoration in the first place.

Brake It Down

Matching numbers means that a car's vehicle identification number (VIN) matches with the partial VIN on the engine and the one on the transmission. To be a true "matching numbers car," the engine identifier and the transmission identifier also match the options on the build sheet. The codes for the other major components such as the rear end, radiator and alternator should also match. Many other items plus individual components (for example, heads, block, intake manifold, etc.) also have date codes either cast or stamped into them and these should match as well.

Catalog Parts Suppliers

Almost without exception, there is at least one catalog parts supplier that has what you need regardless of what collector car you're restoring. Some suppliers have catalogs that cover an entire range of cars, such as "everything for the Camaro, Chevelle and Nova restorer." Others are more specific, like "Your one-stop source for 1955–1957 Thunderbird parts." These are great resources for ordering replacement, reproduction, or used parts for your restoration. If there are several parts suppliers for your particular restoration project, you're in the lucky position of being able to shop among them for the best price.

Salvage Yards

When I was a kid, *salvage yards* were known as junk-yards or boneyards, but these days salvage yards and auto parts recycling yards are the preferred monikers they carry. Depending on your restoration and location, these can be a terrific and cost-effective resource for getting the parts you need. There are also several large salvage yards in Arizona, California, and Texas that specialize in "rust-free" used vintage replacement parts and they will ship anywhere in the United States. These are definitely worth checking out to save some cash and they may be the only source for some parts.

Reproduction Parts Manufacturers

Some parts just can't be found in usable original or restorable condition. The pot-metal hood ornaments and trim on older cars that get pitted with age exemplify this. More often than not, these pieces can't be restored and rechromed with good results. For this reason, many of these parts are being reproduced by several specialty manufacturers, often under license from the original manufacturer if they are still in business. These reproduction parts manufacturers sell their parts through catalogs and over the Internet, and they're an invaluable resource when doing a restoration.

Restoration Tool and Shop Supply Houses

These houses carry all kinds of wonderful tools, aids, and shop supplies specifically for restoring collector vehicles. Many of these are specialty items you can't get at the local Sears or NAPA store. These houses sell their wares via mail-order catalogs and the Internet. It's a good idea to keep a few catalogs on hand because when you're doing a restoration sooner or later you're sure to need something that you won't be able to get anywhere else.

Collector Car Magazine, Periodical, and Book Publishers

No doubt, you've probably bought and read some of these already. Magazines and periodicals are terrific resources for learning more about a particular collector car that you own or you're interested in. The local Barnes & Noble or Walden Books usually have a better selection of these specialty publications than the local candy store or smoke shop. Don't forget the Internet as a source for buying or subscribing to these publications as well.

Collector car books are another great informational resource. Chances are pretty good that someone has written a book about your particular collector car and it's well worth searching Amazon.com on the Internet or taking a trip to the local bookseller to see what's available.

Collector Car Writers, Photographers, and Authors

Although I thoroughly enjoy the collector car hobby, I don't work for free. There are lots of other professional magazine writers, automotive photographers, and book authors out there like me who are very happy and privileged to earn income from sharing information on topics they genuinely love with readers like you. Yes, it's a business and it is hard work, but it's also fun, too. On behalf of all of us, thanks!

Collector Car Auctions and Auctioneers

Collector car auctions often provide the opportunity to get that dream car you've always wanted and couldn't find anywhere else. Collector car auctions are big business and often attract world-class cars from all over the globe. The auction is a business that charges the seller a fee to put the car up on the block and, if it sells, receives a percentage of the selling price. The auctioneers spark enthusiasm for the car and build the bidding momentum up to a frenzy pitch so that when the gavel finally comes down they've gotten the highest price for the seller and a bigger slice of the pie for the auction house.

Collector and Specialty Car Dealers

These are car dealers that specialize in collector and exotic vehicles. Depending on where you live, you may have several within an hour's driving distance or there may be none for several miles. More often than not, the cars available at these dealerships are on consignment, which means the owner will pay the dealer a predetermined commission when the vehicle is sold. Caution should always be the watchword when dealing with used car dealers, and this applies to collector/specialty dealers as well. While many are legitimate and honest, there are also those who are unscrupulous and are only interested in parting you from your money.

Collector Car Locator Services

For a fee, these services will locate a particular year, make, and model for you. Usually you can specify the geographical area you want them to use, or they can provide listings for each "hit" they find across the country. Some of these services also provide proxy buying for which they will waive the location fee and charge a commission for handling the sale transaction.

Brake It Down

A kit car refers to a reproduction of an existing automotive design (for example, 1932 Ford Coupe), sold in various stages of production to allow for completion and customization by the builder. Kit cars are very popular with the street-rodding set.

Proxy Inspectors and Buyers of Collector Cars

Proxy inspectors and buyers will travel to inspect a car you may be interested in for a fee. They will give you a report on the car's condition, any modifications or repairs that can be detected, as much of the particular vehicle's history as possible, and an overall assessment of whether the asking price is reasonable. If previous arrangements have been made to do so, the proxy inspector can then purchase the car for you and arrange to have it delivered.

Appraisers

To you the car may look like a million bucks, but it's the appraiser who puts in the reality check. Appraisers are usually experts in their field and they keep their knowledge of current values, market trends, and auction sale prices for collector cars up-to-date. A good, accurate appraisal is very important in determining the purchase or sale value of a collector vehicle as well as how much to insure it for.

Specialty Vehicle Insurers

The same company that insures your 1999 Volvo probably won't want to give you coverage on your 1934 Ford Coupe. That's why there are specialty vehicle insurers. These companies specialize in collector vehicle insurance and often will insure the vehicle for its full appraised value, or even its agreed replacement value, for probably a lot less than you're paying for your Volvo's coverage.

Specialty Vehicle Transporters

Let's say you're on vacation in California and you spot a collector car for sale at a price that's right and it really turns you on. The problem is that you live in Maine and you don't want to drive the car all the way back (perhaps it couldn't be driven anyway).

Here's where a specialty vehicle transporter can save the day. These enclosed 18-wheelers are designed specifically for transporting collector and specialty vehicles, and they usually make frequent coast-to-coast trips moving various cars back and forth to and from shows. You can have your California jewel-in-the-rough shipped back to Maine at a very reasonable price, and be assured that it will arrive without damage.

Specialty Vehicle Storage Facilities

While storage of a collector vehicle isn't a major concern or problem for the majority of folks in this hobby, owners of very high-end vehicles often prefer to have their precious marques stored in a climate- and humidity-controlled facility to keep the car fresh and pristine. Such storage isn't cheap, but if you have a car worth a lot of money, then you'll want to consider this.

Car Care Products Manufacturers

Car care products are a big business in the collector car world. Everything from feather-duster brushes to chamois and sponges to tire glaze, car washes and polishes, and more are sold in high volume to collector car buffs. Interior car products like leather and vinyl cleaner, engine degreasers, chrome and aluminum wheel cleaners, metal polishes, and more come into play. And let's not forget the manufacturers of car covers, portable automobile shelters, battery trickle-chargers and a plethora of other products that all generate income from sales to the collector car enthusiasts.

4-Wheel Jive
The Indianapolis Motor Speedway opened in 1909 to provide a rigorous competitive testing ground for new automotive components, systems, and designs. It was resurfaced shortly after opening with 3,200,000 bricks and is has been known as "The Brickyard" ever since. The annual Indianapolis 500-mile race is held there every Memorial Day weekend.

The Least You Need to Know

- Nostalgia is very big among baby boomers as well as other age groups in American society. There is a collective yearning to remember those simpler, uncomplicated times in the past.

- Restoring a collector car can be a walk down memory lane and a chance to relive your youth.

- You can restore a collector car as a hobby activity, as an investment or as a profit-generating activity.

Chapter 3

What Are Your Expectations?

In This Chapter

- ◆ A perfect restoration
- ◆ Detroit didn't build it that way
- ◆ Compromises along the way
- ◆ Good looks and reliability
- ◆ Deviations from pure stock
- ◆ Creature comforts

There are many levels of restoration, and the restoration level that's right for you depends entirely on your expectations. Herein we'll try to determine how perfect is too perfect, how a collector vehicle can sometimes be over-restored, and how to strike a comfortable balance that will produce a finished car that you'll be happy with.

As you probably expected, it's time to get the show on the road, so away we go!

What Do You Expect?

It's time to do a bit of soul-searching now to establish your expectations. Your expectations will be the basis for achieving your restoration goal, so it's important to know what you're going for right from the start.

> **Brake It Down**
>
> **Mill** is an old slang term for a car's engine. **Binders** is a slang term for a car's brakes.

> **Brake It Down**
>
> **Frame-off restoration** is a restoration project in which the entire vehicle is completely disassembled with all parts cleaned or replaced as necessary, so that the restored car meets the original factory specifications as closely as possible.

Here are some very legitimate questions to ask yourself. What exactly is it that you want to achieve in restoring a collector car? What level of perfection do you want? Do you want it to be 100 percent correct in every way? Do you want to trailer the car to shows or do you expect to drive it and have fun with it? Would you like it to have the original "retro" look while enjoying some creature comforts while you drive it? How about power and handling? Do you want to swap out that puny six-cylinder *mill* it came with from Detroit for some V8 muscle? And, with the extra power, do you think the stock *binders* will be enough to stop it safely and surely?

These are questions you should give some serious thought to. There are many levels of restoration, and understanding these levels will help you establish how far you want to go with your collector car.

The Quest for Perfection

A perfect restoration results in a vehicle that is absolutely correct and flawless in every respect; essentially it is as good (or in many cases, better) as it was sitting on the showroom floor. Every nut, bolt, clamp, hose, and belt is absolutely correct and exactly like the ones used on the assembly line when the car was built. For many folks, this is the level of restoration they strive for and they'll spend several years and lots of money to achieve perfection of this caliber. Doing such a restoration requires meticulous attention to detail, a tenacity to stick with a project that will have many tedious and boring aspects to it, and a commitment to staying true to the cause without taking any shortcuts or making any compromises. If this is what you want, then I encourage you to go for it.

CAUTION

Pit Stop _____

A common mistake many people make is over-restoring their collector car. What this means, simply, is that it is too perfect—it wasn't this pristine when it came off the assembly line in Detroit the day it was made. Original factory imperfections such as some overspray on the firewall or grease pencil inspection marks that were on the car originally are "fixed" during the restoration. In serious judged car shows, such over-restoration can cause you to lose points, which is something to keep in mind if you expect to be showing the car.

There are some downsides that you should take into consideration if you plan for a perfect restoration. When a perfect level of restoration is achieved, everything becomes a threat to the vehicle. It's a fact of life that we live in an imperfect world, so a collector car that is perfect is at odds with the natural order of things. By "things" I mean tree sap, acid rain, road grime, road salts, pebbles and sand, pigeon droppings—in short, the everyday things in life that turn new cars into old ones over time. To keep the perfect restoration perfect, the car must be protected, babied, and pampered. This usually means keeping it in a climate-controlled environment or, at the very least, covered with a fleece-lined car cover in an enclosed, heated garage. It will have to be transported in an enclosed trailer to various car shows and exposition events that you enter it in. Driving it on and off the trailer is about as much action as it's going to see with its engine running.

I have a friend, Bill, who did a meticulous restoration on a 1967 Corvette 427 Coupe. This car was perfect in every way, right down to the correct inspection marks on the chassis. He even had the hang tags on the tuner dial of the radio. When the car was done, he took it to a car show sponsored by the local chapter of the National Corvette Restorers Society (NCRS) to have it judged. The car scored a very impressive 99.7 out of a perfect 100 points. (He lost the .3 points because the judges couldn't get all of the AM radio stations in clearly without static on some.)

Bill entered his Corvette in five other local shows that season, driving it to and from each event, probably sixty miles for the round trip to the most distant of these shows. At the end of the season he put the car on a lift to clean up the chassis, and he confided to me that if the car was to be judged by the NCRS again in that condition he would be lucky to achieve a score of 90 points. Pebble nicks, road grime, heat and moisture had already taken a visible toll on the frame and paint job. While it was no major disaster, it was still visible upon close inspection.

I include this true story to give you a very realistic example of what happens when you drive a perfect restoration. Of course, you can drive the car if you wish, but you'll have to do a lot of cleaning and detailing to it after each road trip to maintain its show-quality condition. Just bear in mind that from the very first mile, the restoration starts to deteriorate and the car will not remain perfectly restored if it is driven.

Deviating from Detroit

Restorations are largely a matter of taste, and you should do what's going to make you happy. Remember, this is your car and it should reflect your visions and expectations, and yours alone. That having been said, you may want to do things to the car that weren't originally done on the assembly line.

Replacing the stock steel wheels with *mags* or styled aluminum wheels may be the way to go. If the vehicle is a pre-1965 car, you might want to consider replacing the stock drum brakes with disc brakes for added safety. If the car has manual steering, upgrading it to power steering may be something you'll want to do. The point is that you don't have to keep the car at the same level of comfort and technology it was manufactured with. It's okay to make modifications. It's your car, remember?

> **Brake It Down**
>
> **Mags** is an abbreviation for magnesium wheels. Mags are lightweight wheels, usually having a 5-spoke design, made of magnesium or magnesium/aluminum alloy. These wheels are attractive and give the car a custom look. The first factory mag wheels were introduced by Pontiac in 1962.

The factory also installed trim moldings that you may elect to keep or eliminate, depending on your tastes. Some people completely lose the outside door handles, opting for solenoid-operated doors controlled by key-fob remote controllers. For certain, Detroit didn't build them that way, but that doesn't mean that you can't follow the beat of your own drum.

Making Compromises

As your restoration project progresses, you might want to make some compromises. These can involve saving time or money, or might involve the addition of comfort and convenience items to the vehicle, or performance and safety improvements. Compromises are great if they meet your expectations.

For the absolute perfectionist, the car's motor will have to have the original, date-coded *alternator*. If you're not quite that rigid, opt for a replacement unit from the local auto parts store rather than spending a small fortune having the original unit rebuilt. That's a compromise, but it's one that many folks can live with.

Let's take it a step further. You know the alternator has to be replaced, so you decide to purchase a chrome-plated unit to give the engine some additional eye-candy under the hood. Another compromise, but it's not necessarily a wrong one. If it's what you want, then it's a good one.

Brake It Down

The **alternator** is a device that converts rotational energy to AC current, provides energy for the vehicle's electrical system, and also recharges the battery. The alternator uses the principle of electromagnetic induction to produce voltage and current. Prior to the advent of the alternator around 1963, DC generators were used on automobiles.

Reliable and Lookin'

A very popular trend in collector car restoration is to put lots of emphasis on the car's appearance and utter reliability. I confess that I am not a purist and I'm all in favor of driving a collector car that will get me where I'm going and back again without having to call AAA for a tow.

In doing your restoration, repainting the car will most certainly be a part of the overall project. When your collector car was made, let's say in 1965, *nitrocellulose lacquer* was the paint used by the factory and that was the state-of-the-art automotive paint at that point in time. Lacquer looked good when it was new, but it was prone to dulling and cracking over time due to UV exposure and the elements.

In 1981 the base coat/clear coat paint system was introduced and it is used almost exclusively today. The base coat/clear coat paint system is also known as a two-stage paint system; some high-end automobiles manufactured today use a three-stage system for additional effects like pearl and metallic in the finish color.

Brake It Down

Nitrocellulose lacquer is a type of automotive paint that was used through the early 1980s. Because of its noxious vapors and high toxicity, it was outlawed for use in the United States by the Environmental Protection Agency (EPA).

Due to EPA restrictions, nitrocellulose lacquer is not legal for use in the United States any longer, although acrylic lacquer is legal and available.

While lacquer would be the correct way to go, many restorers would opt, with good reason, to use the two-stage base coat/clear coat paint. It's more durable, easier to apply, costs less and certainly looks much better than the equivalent paint job done with lacquer. Is this "correct"? No. Is it acceptable and attractive? You bet.

> ### 4-Wheel Jive
>
> The oil shortage of the 1970s caused the cost of manufacturing tires to skyrocket; it takes at least six gallons of oil to make one tire.

And here's one more thing about the paint. We have a much wider selection of colors, hues, and specialty automotive paints today than we had even a decade ago. Why stay with the Matador Red of forty years ago when you can bathe your restoration in Firethorn Red Metallic available today. You might even add some pin striping or even flames.

Rollin' Down The Roadway

The cars of the 1960s used bias-ply tires, but today we roll on high performance radials. Bias-ply tires were thin, had a harsh ride and tended to squeal during turns if the tire pressure was slightly low. There's an old joke about driving a car with bias-ply tires, running over a dime and being able to tell if it was heads or tails by the way the tires felt when they went over it. While this yarn is a bit of hyperbole, suffice it to say that tire technology has come a very long way in the last 40 years. While radials aren't the "correct" tires for your collector car restoration, they are certainly safer and more reliable than the old bias-ply tires. For those reasons, I'd give them the thumbs-up on my restoration, and a lot of other people would, too.

Cells and Such

Battery technology has evolved as well. I remember the old Delco "magic eye" sealed batteries that had a viewing window or "eye" built into the top. Supposedly, when this "eye" looked green, everything was okay with the battery. Unfortunately, this was a sealed battery—there was no way to add water, so if you had a black "eye" and it wouldn't accept a charge, the battery was dead. Purists will go for the "correct" battery, whether it's a Delco "magic eye," an Exide or whatever, and that's okay. I want my collector car to start when I turn the key, so I go with a nice modern battery that permits me to check and replenish the water level as required. Reliability is important to me, and I know I'm not alone here.

> ### Brake It Down
>
> In customizing terms, a decked car is one that has had the chrome details and trim removed from the trunk and hood, then smoothed over.

The mag wheels on this restored 1963 Pontiac Catalina put it in the "street stock" class at judged car shows. Such minor modifications like these that can be taken off in less than one hour are allowed at many judged shows.

My friend Ken has a 1963 Pontiac Catalina that he enjoys taking to judged Pontiac shows. He keeps the "correct" battery in the trunk, but uses a modern battery for driving. When he gets to the show, he swaps the modern battery for the correct one in the trunk, and by so doing, he doesn't lose points for having an incorrect battery. A simple, yet crafty, solution.

Going Your Own Route

In addition to the acceptable modifications and improvements I mentioned earlier, there are further, more radical deviations from pure stock that many people will opt for during their restorations.

For example, I have a friend named Bobby who's a real car nut. I mean, this guy is really off the deep end—he eats, drinks, sleeps, and breathes cars. Bobby spent almost five years restoring a 1967 Chevrolet Camaro Coupe. Because he works as an auto body repairman full-time, this was a spare-time project for evenings and weekends. (When he's not working on cars, he's glued to cable TV's SPEED Channel watching NASCAR.)

Cosmetically, the car is pristine in every respect. The paint, racing stripes, emblems, material lining the trunk, interior, door handles, everything looks exactly as it should. When you pop the hood, things are a bit different, though. Instead of seeing the small-block Chevy engine with a 4-barrel carburetor you expect to find, therein resides a late-model fuel-injected LT1 Corvette engine with a computer control module and plenty of chrome plating.

4-Wheel Jive

Nitrous Oxide (N_2O), also simply called nitrous, is commonly known as laughing gas. Nitrous is often used in drag racing to boost engine performance for short periods. When burned, N_2O releases nitrogen and oxygen; the released oxygen permits more gasoline to be burned, resulting in the boost in power. Unfortunately, this extra power boost puts a strain on all of the engine's components, so nitrous should be used very sparingly.

And to give this little Camaro an extra jolt, he has a nitrous oxide boost system installed. Says Bobby of his Camaro, "I wanted it to look exactly as it did when it was new, but I wanted a lot more performance than it had when it came from the factory. The 'Vette engine and the nitrous pack did the trick for me." For sure, this is Bobby's idea of what a restored Camaro should be. Good for him.

Such deviations from stock are purely a matter of personal preference and should be incorporated into the restoration if this is what you expect of your finished project.

Cruising in Comfort

The range of creature comforts and options wasn't all that broad 40 or 50 years ago. While you could get a radio in the car, it was probably only able to receive AM broadcasts and play them through an anemic speaker, usually mounted in the center of the dashboard. Crank-out side vent windows were used to keep the passenger compartment ventilated during hot summer days, as air conditioning wasn't available on all models or at all with some makes in those days. Power steering and brakes were also luxury items that weren't installed in many cars of the era because of the added cost. But that doesn't mean that your restored ride has to be spartan by any means.

Road Music

Just about everyone wants a good music system in their car with AM/FM stereo reception and a cassette player at the minimum; most folks want the whole nine yards with a 12-disc CD changer, too. "Stealth" stereo systems are available that can be hidden in the glove box or under the driver's seat. The nice thing is that the original radio stays in the dash where it was installed at the factory for cosmetic purposes. But you get the benefit of today's audio technology from the stealth system and its hidden kick-panel or under-dash speakers. It looks like retro, but it sounds like today. What's not to love here?

You can also get direct-fit replacement radios that have a retro look to them but modern electronics. As the name implies, these units fit directly into the same original factory dash opening that the original radio mounted in, so you don't have to cut your dash up to make them fit.

Multidisc CD changers are also available that can be mounted in the trunk, out of sight. Some of these are FM-modulated, which means that you tune the car's FM radio to a specified frequency and the CD audio is played through that channel on the radio. Generally, an infrared remote control unit is used to select the disc and track and to pause, stop, or play the music. A number of manufacturers offer these FM-modulated CD players.

There are also multidisc CD changers that are controlled directly through buttons located on their mating radios, so no remote controller is necessary.

4-Wheel Jive
The radio was first offered as an option on the 1923 Chevrolet Superior and it cost about $200, or roughly one-fourth the total price of the car.

Satellite Radio Systems

Satellite radio systems are increasing in popularity and, as one would expect, they're starting to find their way into the interiors of collector cars. Often they can be mounted out of sight and controlled via wired or wireless controllers with LCD displays.

There are currently two satellite radio standards in operation and they each offer 100 channels of digital, near CD-quality audio that is either completely or almost completely commercial-free, depending on the channel, in a wide variety of formats to suit all tastes.

The two standards are XM (www.xmradio.com) and Sirius (www.sirius.com). Unlike home satellite TV systems like DirectTV or the Dish Network that require 18-inch dish receivers, the satellite radio systems use a small, low-profile roof-mounted antenna and some other hardware the antenna connects to that can easily be concealed in the car's interior in a number of locations, such as under the passenger seat.

The XM and Sirius systems are not currently compatible with each other and no single component receives both systems, although the way they work is similar. XM has its studios in Washington, D.C., and Sirius operates studios located in New York City's Rockefeller Center. They both bounce their broadcast signals off satellites in orbit over the United States.

XM uses two satellites they call "Rock" and "Roll," and these are positioned over the east and west coasts to provide coverage for the lower 48 states. The service costs

$9.95 per month and offers 101 channels of digital programming. Of the 60 music channels, many have no commercials at all and those that do only have about two minutes of commercial time per hour.

Sirius has their satellites positioned in a lower elliptical earth orbit and, although their service is $12.95 per month, all of their channels are completely devoid of commercials.

Keeping Your Cool

Air conditioning is considered essential by many collector car hobbyists and, if the original car wasn't equipped with A/C, they make sure it gets installed while the restoration is being performed.

There are a few companies who offer after-market air conditioning systems for vintage, collector, and custom vehicles including street rods. The majority of these systems are direct-fit units that use the vehicle's original ventilation duct system.

Having had experience installing one of their systems, I can attest that they fit like a glove and throw lots of good, cold air. The systems come with everything you need to install the compressor, condenser, fan/heater/defroster unit and all the lines, *O-rings* and fittings required. The only additional items you'll need are a compressor belt of the appropriate length (all applications are different) and R-134A refrigerant to charge the system.

> **Brake It Down**
>
> An **O-ring** is a type of sealing ring, usually made of rubber, silicone, or a similar flexible material, shaped like the letter "O." The O-ring is compressed into adjoining grooves to provide a seal. O-rings are commonly used to seal the fittings of automotive air conditioning systems.

> **Overdrive**
>
> One of the best ways to learn about collector car restoration is to talk with people who have already been down the road. Go to car shows and cruise nights and ask questions. You'll find that "car people" are gregarious and are quite happy to talk about their cars and what it took to get them to the state of restoration they're currently in. Just as important as the tips and advice you'll get from them, you'll also get a handle on the pitfalls, difficulties, and mistakes they encountered along the way. Ask intelligent questions, be a good listener, and remember to thank them for sharing their information with you.

Lost in the '60s

There's no good reason to be lost in the '60s, or the '50s, or '70s, for that matter, unless you want to be. Like other creature comforts, Global Positioning Systems (GPS) are finding their way into more and more collector vehicles.

If you're not familiar with GPS, it is basically a receiving device that can be mounted in the car (some can be carried in your pocket) which utilizes satellite tracking to precisely locate and report the position of an object, such as your car. While it was originally developed by the Department of Defense, GPS systems are now widely available for civilians to navigate on roads, through the woods, in the air, or at sea.

"Frenched" headlights like these are popular with collectors who customize their cars. The dark center is a "blue dot"—another popular item on 1950s and 1960s customs.

A GPS will report your latitude, longitude, and altitude. Many have regional map graphics already installed in them or that can be downloaded into the receiver to show your position relative to known landmarks or roads. Others allow you to enter the coordinates of the destination and will visually track the progress of your journey.

Overdrive

It's always a good idea to keep a fully charged fire extinguisher in your collector vehicle. Be sure to get an extinguisher that is rated and intended for use on oil/gasoline fires. A good extinguisher can quell a problem in seconds, thus avoiding a

The system uses a satellite antenna receiver to determine the location and velocity by triangulation from multiple satellites, and it is accurate to within about twenty feet. GPS systems are particularly popular with collector car buffs who like to take their vehicles on rallies, poker runs, or other road events sponsored by car clubs.

> **4-Wheel Jive**
>
> Pontiac introduced its Firebird in 1967 to compete with the Ford Mustang.

There are several compact, portable GPS receivers available and the prices for these have come down considerably over the last couple of years. If you envision taking your restored classic on road trips, you may want to consider getting a GPS receiver. And don't forget, that you can also use one of the portable units in your "normal" car, too.

Pit Stop

If someone is selling a collector vehicle for considerably less than the current market average price and the deal seems too good to be true, it probably is. Shop around for similar vehicles to get a handle on prices, and then do some serious inspection work on the suspect car. Don't hesitate to bring along a knowledgeable person who knows what to look for. Generally, if a seller tells you about a lot of small faults or things wrong with the car, he's trying to dissuade attention from a major problem that may go unnoticed by an unwary buyer. As always, let the buyer beware.

The Least You Need to Know

- There are many levels of restoration, and you should decide on the level that will come the closest to meeting your expectations of the restored vehicle.

- The restoration doesn't have to be "100 percent correct." It should result in a car that you're happy with.

- It's perfectly okay to use the advantages today's technology has to offer for the sake of safety and improved performance.

- Additions of creature comforts like air conditioning, stereos, and GPS systems can make driving your collector vehicle more enjoyable and comfortable.

Chapter 4

What to Restore— So Many Decisions!

In This Chapter

- ◆ Determining what type of car is right for you
- ◆ Determining your preferences: big, small, roadster, coupe …
- ◆ Deciding what you can afford
- ◆ Funding and financing your car
- ◆ Storing your car

Deciding what collector car you want to restore is only one of many decisions you'll have to make. You will also need to determine what you can afford, how you are going to finance it, where you will store it, and so on. To make these decisions, you'll have to strike a balance between whimsy and practicality. You'll also have to balance your fantasies with reality. You have plenty of choices and options, so it's highly likely that you'll decide on a vehicle that you'll be happy with—before, during, and after the restoration is complete.

So Many Decisions To Be Made

Just about everyone has a favorite car in mind that they'd like to own, and the reasons they favor this particular vehicle are personal and can be based on a number of factors. So first, let's establish why you find certain cars appealing. Take a look at this list and select the reason(s) why you are keen on a particular car:

- ◆ Your dad had one
- ◆ Childhood memories
- ◆ It was your first car
- ◆ Great times with your girlfriend/boyfriend in this car
- ◆ You had great times with your buddies in this car
- ◆ You love how it looks
- ◆ You love how fast it is
- ◆ You love the huge engine
- ◆ You think it impresses people
- ◆ You like its classic lines
- ◆ You just like it and can't put your finger on why

Now that you know why you want what you want, let's see if this particular car is going to work in the overall scheme of things.

Pit Stop _____

Avoid buying an incomplete car for restoration. The time and money you will spend searching for parts to replace those that are missing may equal or exceed the price you paid for the car itself. It's much wiser to find a car that has all of its parts because then if a part needs to be replaced, you know what it looks like.

What Car Is Right for You?

How do you choose a car? Sometimes, the car seems to choose you. Other times, you'll have to make your mission to find the car you want. The following stories should help you find what you want.

Sandy's Project Car Found Him

Sometimes the right car will "find" you. A friend of mine, Sandy, owns a service station. Over the years, Sandy has restored tow trucks from the 1920s and 1930s, an old fire engine, and an old dump truck. He confided that while he enjoyed doing the restorations, he was never able to fully enjoy these vehicles as he always trailered them to car shows. He had a yearning for a collector car he could cruise in and enjoy.

Heavily recessed tail lights like these are said to be tunneled. Doing custom metal work like this takes a lot of skill and tunneling was a customizing trick popular in the 1950s and 1960s; it's making a comeback these days.

Quite by accident he came upon a Studebaker Lark convertible that was for sale in fair shape with very little rust and the price was right. While he never had any great affection for Larks, he didn't dislike them either. Sandy felt this was a car he could restore over the course of a year in his spare time and it wouldn't cost him too much to do the job properly. He was just casually looking for another project so this car filled the bill nicely.

Now the car is finished and Sandy enjoys driving it to cruise nights and car shows. Because his total outlay was only a few thousand dollars including the purchase price of the car, he drives it quite a bit without fretting about getting nicks or chips.

Brake It Down

Three deuces is a slang term for an engine equipped with three two-barrel carburetors. This configuration is also called a tri-power setup (on GM products) or a six-pack on Chrysler Corporation cars (collectively known as Mopars).

For Sandy, this was the right car, and it found him. His criterion was simply having a restoration project that would result in a collector car he could enjoy driving. This car could have just as easily been a Mustang or a Javelin or whatever. Because he was open-ended and didn't have any particular make or model in mind, it all worked serendipitously for him. And, yes, he's as happy as a Lark with the way it all turned out.

If you're like Sandy and want to get involved in doing a restoration without a particular car in mind, try to find a car that …

> **4-Wheel Jive**
>
> The first three-color, four-way traffic signal was installed in Detroit, Michigan, in 1920.

- You like.
- Is in the best condition you can afford.
- You think you'll enjoy working on.
- You'll be happy with when it is finished.

Ken's Catalina Quest

I have another friend, Ken, who specifically hunted for a definite make and model like the one he had in his youth. As Ken tells it, in April, 1963 he decided to purchase a new car. Many of his friends were buying Fords or Chevrolets but because he was never a "me, too" kind of guy, his choice was a 1963 Pontiac Catalina convertible in powder blue with a matching blue top. To Ken, this car was a dream come true. But, like all dreams, they come to an end when it's time to wake up.

> **Brake It Down**
>
> Tudor is what Ford called its two-door cars in the 1930s and 1940s.
>
> Fordor is what Ford called its four-door cars in the 1930s and 1940s.

Ken's wake-up call came in May of 1966, when his daughter was born. The Catalina, with well over 100,000 miles on it by then, was starting to "nickel and dime" him to death. He sold the Catalina and purchased a 1966 Pontiac Ventura, "a real family man's car," as he put it. But he missed his powder blue Catalina so much so that he promised himself some day, when he was financially able, he would again purchase the car of his dreams.

Ken and his wife, Terry, searched for many years with no luck, rejecting over 50 cars in several different states, passing them over because of the extensive work that would be required to get them back in decent condition.

Ken's perseverance paid off, however, in March of 1993. While driving down a country road in Kokomo, Indiana, he noticed a 1963 Catalina convertible sitting in a yard with a for sale sign in the window. This car had a good, solid body with very little surface rust and great potential for restoration. Ken and Terry flew out to Indiana the following weekend and drove the ragtop home to New Jersey, where the restoration project began immediately. Ken did the engine rebuild himself, farming out the paint and frame restoration to a local Pontiac dealer's body shop, and he had a local upholstery shop do the interior restoration.

Ken's original Catalina was powder blue with the optional blue factory top and the tri-blue interior, so that's what he went for when he restored this car. He calls the car "Second Time Around" and he really enjoys driving the car to shows and cruise nights.

Here are two true stories that both have happy endings. Sandy was looking for a project that would give him an enjoyable cruise car, and was open to just about anything. Ken had a definite target in mind and he kept searching until he found the perfect car for his restoration. I relate these two stories to illustrate the point that there are different approaches to choosing a collector car that's right for you.

If, on the other hand, you're like Ken and you have a specific year, make, and model in mind, try to find a car that …

- Matches exactly or very closely what you have in mind.

- Is priced fairly.

- Is in fair to good condition.

- Won't require lots of rust repairs.

- Will live up to your expectations when it is finished.

There are also some very practical considerations that enter into choosing a car that's right for you. Let's say, for example, that you always wanted a 1970 Cadillac Eldorado, and that's the car you'd like to get and restore. While this is what you desire, make sure this 18.4-foot long vehicle will fit into your garage. If it won't, you might want to consider something a bit smaller that will fit.

> ### 4-Wheel Jive
>
> The Oscar Mayer "Weinermobile" was first used as an advertising vehicle in 1936 and it still performs that function today.

> ### Brake It Down
>
> The crankshaft is the main shaft in the engine with one or more cranks, or "throws," in it that are coupled by connecting rods to the engine's pistons. The combustion process creates reciprocating motion in the rods and pistons, which in turn is converted to a rotating motion by the crankshaft as it revolves.

> ### Brake It Down
>
> The camshaft is the shaft in the engine that is driven by gears, belts, or a chain from the crankshaft. The camshaft has a series of cams, or lobes, that open and close the intake and exhaust valves as it turns.

What Would You Like? Big, Small, Roadster, Coupe, What?

There are many factors to consider when choosing your car. How big or small should it be? What body style suits you best? This section explores all of the choices.

Size

Collectors cars come in as many sizes as SUVs of today do. The following categories will help you sort them out.

Land Yachts

Land yachts are large luxury cars, typically the chromed, finned, oversized vehicles of the late fifties to early sixties. The 1959 Cadillac Sedan DeVille, the Lincoln Premieres, and the Buick Roadmasters of the 1950s are typical land yachts.

Full-Sized Cars

Full-sized cars are also cars capable of transporting a driver and five passengers, but they are lighter and less flashy than land yachts. The Chevrolet Impala, Pontiac Catalina, and Ford Galaxie 500 are typical full-sized cars.

Intermediates

Also known as mid-sized cars, intermediates are smaller than full-sized cars but larger than compacts. Examples include the Chevrolet Chevelle, the Ford Torino, the Dodge Coronet, and the 1970s Volvos.

Compact Cars

These are very small cars that usually can only seat four people at maximum. Examples include the Volkswagen Beetle, the Renault Dauphine, Chevrolet Chevette, Ford Maverick, AMC Pacer, and the Pontiac Sunbird.

Body Styles

If you thought cars came in more sizes than you could imagine, take a look at the body styles you will find.

Coupes

A coupe is a two-door closed body type that is typically distinguished from a two-door sedan by a sleeker, shorter roof, and longer trunk. An example of a coupe is the 1956 Ford Crown Victoria.

Business Coupes

Business coupes are simple two-door coupes, without a back seat or a rumble seat, built between the mid-1930s and early 1950s. These are also sometimes called a businessman's coupe. The 1946 Chevrolet Style-master Model 1504 Business Coupe is an example.

> **Brake It Down**
> A cooling system is the system that removes heat from the engine by the forced circulation of coolant and thereby prevents the engine from overheating. It includes the water jackets, water pump, radiator, and thermostat.

Club Coupes

A club coupe is a two-door coupe with a rear seat and no windows behind the doors (known as blind rear quarters) from the mid-1930s to early 1950s. An example would be the 1948 Dodge Club Coupe.

Convertibles

These are open-top cars with a folding roof and roll-up side windows. Examples would include the 1957 Chevrolet "ragtop" and 1965 Mustang convertible.

Roadsters

A true roadster is a two-seat convertible without side windows. The 1953–1955 Corvette and MG TD are examples of roadsters. The term is often used (incorrectly) to describe two-seat convertibles like the Mazda Miata, the BMW R3 and the Porsche Boxster.

Sedan Deliveries

Popular during the mid-1950s, a sedan delivery is a two-door station wagon with solid body panels instead of windows on the sides at the rear of the car. The 1956 Ford Sedan Delivery is an example.

> **4-Wheel Jive**
> The Edsel is generally regarded as one of the biggest flops in automotive history due to ugly styling cues and poor marketing strategy. The car simply never caught on with the public.

Touring Cars and Phaetons

Popular during the 1920s and early 1930s, touring cars were six- or seven-passenger open cars without windows. A phaeton was a more luxurious touring car. The 1928 Ford Phaeton is an example.

Cabriolets

Cabriolets are convertibles with more luxurious padded tops that usually are exposed and sit on top of the rear deck when folded. Most cabriolets have two doors but in fact some have four doors. The 1937 Ford Cabriolet is an example.

Woodies

This usually refers to a station wagon that incorporates natural finished wood for the structure of exposed body panels, although it can also be a passenger car that has exterior wooden panels or trim. The 1949 Ford Station Wagon is an example of a woody.

Sedans

Typically a sedan is a four-door car with a *B-pillar* behind the front doors, although some sedans have only two doors. The Lincoln Town Car is a sedan example.

Hardtops

A hardtop is a closed body car with no B-pillar. The 1955 Chevrolet Bel Air four-door hardtop is an example.

Station Wagons

A station wagon is usually a four-door vehicle with a rear door or gate and seats that fold down for additional cargo room (although the 1955–1957 Chevrolet Nomads were two-door wagons). Station wagons can usually transport six to nine people, depending on their seat configurations. The 1969 Ford Country Squire is an example.

> **Brake It Down**
>
> A **pillar** is a post supporting the roof (also known as the "greenhouse") of a closed body car. Pillars are described in shorthand by their location: "A-pillar" at the windshield; "B-pillar" behind the front door; "C-pillar" at the rear.

> **Brake It Down**
>
> The cylinder block is the basic part of the engine containing the engine cylinders and to which other engine parts are attached. It is usually an iron casting and often also functions as the crankcase.

These are the basic body styles that are available for collector cars. If you have a couple of kids or grandkids and you want to take them along with you and your spouse on cruise nights or to car shows, a 1932 Ford Deuce Coupe, an MG roadster, a 1955 T-Bird or other two-seater isn't going to be a good choice for you. Instead you might want to consider a Ford Model A Sedan or a 1958 or later T-Bird that can accommodate four people.

How Deep Are Your Pockets?

You may have heard the expression, "a champagne taste with a beer budget," to describe someone who longs after something that's beyond their means. Collector cars can be like that, for sure.

Right from the outset you have to realistically decide how much you can spend to purchase and restore a project car. Notice that I didn't say decide how much you *want* to spend; how much you *can* spend is the key element here. For most of us, if we spread the project out over a few years we'll be in a better position to spend more than if we try to get everything done in a shorter period of time, say a single year. Spreading the project out over more time gives you the opportunity to compare prices on parts from a number of sources and make purchases in a more leisurely fashion. It also gives you more time to evaluate service providers for things you'll have to farm out. You'll also have more time to check out references for these providers and for looking at pictures or examples of their work.

Sure, you may very well want to spend $20,000 on a restoration but, realistically, your budget won't let you spend more than $15,500 on a project this year. So you have to be practical and use some common sense in determining how long you're willing to spread the project out and what you can actually spend on it.

Now, using this $15,500 figure as an example, let's say you see a restorable 1965 Chevrolet Impala Super Sport for sale. The car is in running condition, but it is certainly showing its age. The upholstery is pretty well shot as is the carpeting, and the inner door panels have seen better days, too. The motor blows a little blue smoke, but nothing too bad. The tires are in bad shape and will have to be replaced, along with the exhaust system. The paint is not original and it's pretty bad and the front and rear bumpers are rusted. There's also some rocker panel rust. The guy who's selling it wants $5,000 for the car.

Now, let's do a very conservative estimate on what it's going to cost to put this car in respectable condition:

- ◆ $1,800—new interior & carpeting components
- ◆ $1,000—top-end motor rebuild

- ◆ $600—tires

- ◆ $400—exhaust system

- ◆ $1,000—bodywork/rust repair

- ◆ $5,000—paint job

- ◆ $800—rechrome bumpers

That comes to $10,600 plus the $5,000 for the car itself, for a total outlay of $15,600. Remember that your total budget for this year is $15,500, so you've already exceeded your budget by $100.00. There are other expenses such as shipping and handling charges, taxes, miscellaneous items such as fasteners and shop supplies along with possible towing costs to get the car from the seller's location to yours. I also told you earlier to "take parts costs and double them." If you want to go through with this project, it will have to span two or more years.

That's not only okay, it's good. Consider that the average restoration takes about 2,000 hours. That works out to a 40-hour week for a full year. Certainly, if you're like most folks, you already have a full-time job so you're only going to work on the restoration some evenings and weekends. Because of this, the project will indeed take several years to complete. On the upside, that means you won't have to spend a lot of money all at one time—you can spread your expenditures out by only purchasing the particular parts or services you need for each stage of the project.

Do Your Homework

Now, before you part with any money and make any commitments, do some research to find out basic facts about the 1965 Impala SS. Here's what a quick search on the Internet produces:

- ◆ There were 746,800 V8 Impalas made in 1965 but only 239,500 V8 (and 3,600 6-cylinder) Impala SSs.

- ◆ Impala Super Sports listed in very good restorable condition have asking prices of $8,000 to $9,000.

- ◆ A show-quality restored Impala SS can be purchased for $13,000 to $18,500.

I found all of this valuable information in less than 10 minutes by searching "Chevrolet Impala SS" on Google.com. Now we know that with over 1,000,000 Impalas produced that year, the 1965 Impala was a popular car and it certainly can't be considered rare. Because standard Impala parts will fit on the Impala SS as well, used and reproduction parts will be easy to get. The seller's $5,000 price for the car is certainly reasonable compared to competitive asking prices for vehicles in similar condition. And when the car is finished you should be able to get your original investment out of it if you decide to sell it. Now you're in a position to make an intelligent decision about whether you want to buy and restore this car or continue looking.

But wait a minute! A show quality restored Impala SS can be bought for $13,500. Even if the seller is firm, firm, firm, that still leaves $2,000 of your $15,500 budget to fix things the seller might have felt were acceptable but you don't, time to do them and the opportunity to enjoy the car, *right now*. Remember we said earlier, "Buy the best car you can afford. And that applies to any type of collector vehicle, from an antique Model T to a monster truck and everything in between."

 Overdrive

Consider restoring a car from the 1970s. They're more plentiful, parts are easier to get and they're relatively inexpensive because they're generally regarded as "old cars" rather than modern classics.

The collector car hobby gives you plenty of latitude to create something different like this monster truck that started life a half century ago as a daily work vehicle.

Funding and Financing

There are several lending institutions that will finance collector vehicles, and they're listed in Appendix A. You may also want to consider opening a home equity line of credit. With a home equity credit line you can borrow up to the full amount you've been approved for, and you only pay the interest on what you've actually borrowed rather than the full amount of your credit line.

Pit Stop

Don't let your desire to get a collector car get in the way of your better judgment. For example, don't purchase a vehicle using your credit card—the interest payments will be astronomical. The same holds true for using a home equity loan—factor in the interest costs to get a handle on what the vehicle is really going to cost you when all is said and done.

Frequently, you're given a checkbook that is connected to your credit line, so making a purchase is as easy as writing a check. Some banks issue a special credit card that you use for purchasing things on your credit line as well.

The nice part about a home equity line of credit is that you don't have to divulge what you're using the money for. Once your credit line is approved, you can buy a collector car, a swimming pool, or a new kitchen; it doesn't matter what you spend it on to the lending institution. Speak with your local bank to learn more about the available options.

Overdrive

You might also want to start a special fund for your collector car right now as you start to look around for a vehicle. In my friend Ken's case, he started saving money a little at a time and, eight years later when he finally found that 1963 Catalina for restoration, he not only had enough money for the car but he had saved up enough to pay for the full restoration as well, with change left over.

Where Will It Live?

Another decision you should make up front is where the car is going to be stored while it is being worked on as well as when it is finished. Usually the pat answer is "I'll work on it in my garage." Really? Let's give this some thought.

Brake It Down

Catalytic converters are emission control devices filled with platinum or palladium that continue combustion to finalize burning and reduce emissions in the exhaust stream. Catalytic converters first appeared in 1975 and mandated the use of unleaded gasoline.

You have a two-car garage, so there's plenty of room for your collector vehicle as well as your "normal" car. That's true as long as your collector vehicle is still in one piece. What happens when you start taking parts off and have to store them while the restoration is going on? Where are you going to store the hood, fenders, bumpers, doors, and other large parts? It is a law of physics that a disassembled vehicle takes up much more room than one that is intact, so your everyday driver may well spend its winters out in the driveway.

Realistically, you'll need triple the space that the fully assembled car occupies to have enough working room and storage for take-off parts. An option you might want to consider is renting a spot at a self-storage facility to use as a temporary holding area for parts and assemblies you're not going to be working on for some time to come.

Also keep in mind that from the day the restoration starts until the day it is finished your garage isn't going to be a garage any more. It will be a mechanic's bay, a body shop, a re-upholstery shop, a restoration facility and, in some cases, a paint shop as well.

Overdrive

Even though your collector car may not have been equipped with seatbelts when it came from the factory, they are important safety items you should consider installing, especially if you're going to cruise in the vehicle. Check with your state's Division of Motor Vehicles to learn what laws your collector vehicle will have to comply with.

Pit Stop

Beware of buying a collector vehicle manufactured from 1975 or later that doesn't have its stock exhaust system with catalytic converters. It is illegal to drive any vehicle, collector or otherwise, without catalytic converters if they were originally installed on the car by the manufacturer. Even if you have special historic license plates on the car, you will be subject to getting a summons if your exhaust system doesn't comply with federal emissions laws.

Depending on the rarity and value of your finished restoration, you may decide to garage the vehicle at a climate-controlled storage facility. This is a worthwhile investment to keep the restoration from deteriorating over time.

The Least You Need to Know

- Occasionally the right collector car will find you. Other times, it might take you years to find just the right one.

- Consider how you want to use your collector car once it is restored and make that an important consideration in the body style you look for.

- Determine what you can spend on the project and try to spread the expenditures over time.

◆ You have several ways of funding and financing the car and its restoration expenses. Be sure to research the options and consult with experts if you need help.

◆ Storing the car and its parts will take up a lot of garage space; consider an alternate storage facility.

Chapter 5

Where Do You Find a Collector Car, Anyway?

In This Chapter

- ◆ Searching magazines, newspapers, the classifieds, and the Internet
- ◆ Spreading the word
- ◆ Dealing with specialty car dealerships
- ◆ Going to car shows, cruise nights, and car clubs
- ◆ Saving a car from the crusher
- ◆ Using finders and paying their fees

When it comes to finding collector cars, the world is literally your oyster. There may be one lurking in someone's garage just around the corner, or one may be sitting somewhere in Europe waiting for a new American home. Collector cars are out there in abundance, and there are numerous ways to find them.

Turn the page and let's go collector car hunting.

Looking for a Collector Car in All the Right Places

Collector cars are all over the place. Whether you're looking for a restoration project, a street rod, a boulevard cruiser, a muscle car, or some sort of special interest vehicle, they're all out there in various states of condition and price ranges. But knowing where to look can help you zero in on exactly what you want in the shortest amount of time. Here's an excellent selection of things to search in your collector car quest.

Magazines, Newspapers, and Classifieds

The next time you're in the local Barnes & Noble or other bookseller store, check out the automotive magazine section. That's where you'll find lots of "trader" magazines that consist entirely of ads placed by people who have cars and parts for sale.

There are different genres of these magazines available, such as *Mopar Trader*, *Corvette & Chevy Trader*, and *Mustang Trader* to name a few. There are also generic magazines, such as *Old Car Trader*, that are not marque-specific. These trader magazines are usually regionalized with separate editions for the East Coast, mid-America and the West Coast. The downside is that, even with the regional issue, the car you're interested in might still be several hundred miles away from you.

Then there are the marque-specific consumer magazines such as *Corvette Enthusiast*, *MG Enthusiast*, *Mustang Works*, *Super Chevy*, *VW Trends*, and many others that also have classified sections for buying and selling vehicles and parts.

Be sure to check the automotive section of your local newspapers, too. Frequently you'll see ads for collector vehicles and project cars in them. The real advantage in finding a car in the newspaper is that it will usually be located in your immediate area, and that makes it easy and convenient to check the vehicle out in person. The downside here is that the selection of cars available will be very limited and you may never find what you're looking for in the local paper. But it's worth taking a look, anyway.

Without a doubt, the best printed resource for locating collector cars, parts, accessories, and memorabilia is *Hemmings Motor News*. *Hemmings* is known as the bible of the collector car hobby, and with good reason. Published monthly, every edition contains over 800 pages of classified ads for collector cars of every make, model, description, and condition. There are also sections for trucks, special interest vehicles, parts, manuals, literature, owners manuals, sales brochures, and much, much more. In short, if it has anything at all to do with collector cars, you'll find it in *Hemmings*.

As a matter of fact, the first two vintage Corvettes my wife and I bought were found in *Hemmings*.

Pit Stop

Ninety-nine percent of the time a basket case is an abandoned project that was deemed to be hopeless by the person who started it and now it is chaos. Regardless of how good the price is, you are probably much better off walking away from a basket case.

You'll be getting into something that's going to cost you a lot of time and money. Doing a restoration on a complete car is difficult enough, even when you fully document where all the parts came from. If you buy a basket case you have no way of knowing if all the parts are there or where they go. Buying a basket case is just asking for a lot of aggravation and frustration.

There are also "cars wanted" and "parts wanted" sections that you can run your own ad(s) in to help you locate that dream vehicle or, once you have it, to get the parts you need. It's a most worthwhile resource and it's available at the local newsstand or bookseller as well as by subscription.

Old Cars Weekly is another excellent publication in tabloid newspaper format that carries lots of ads for cars, parts, accessories, and *automobilia* in general for sale, as well as having "wanted" sections, too. Available by subscription, it is a good resource that arrives in your mailbox every week, or you can purchase individual copies at the newsstand or from your bookseller. As with *Hemmings*, the downside with *Old Cars Weekly* is that cars from all over the country are advertised, so there's a potential distance factor to keep in mind if you find something you're interested in.

Brake It Down

Automobilia is a catch-all term that encompasses accessories, advertising specialties, brochures, or other memorabilia items specifically relating to the automobile. These can include sales brochures, owners' manuals, key chains, ashtrays, tin signs, gas pump globes, and other items of similar nature.

Overdrive

When scanning *Hemmings, Old Cars Weekly,* or other such publications, remember that the early bird catches the worm. Get a new issue as soon as it hits the stands because the really good deals always go fast.

The advertisement for Benford's Golden Giant Spark Plugs (no relation to the author) came from a 1917 issue of Motor Age *magazine. It's a good example of automobilia.*

The Internet: A Classic Car Treasure Trove

The Internet has made the entire world accessible to anyone with a computer and a web connection. Regardless of what you're looking for, it's on the World Wide Web, and collector cars are certainly no exception.

Use your favorite search engine to search the key words "collector car" and you'll be absolutely astounded by the number of hits it returns. Narrow the search down a bit using key words to find the particular make and model or genre of car you're interested in, such as "Ford Mustang" or "street rod" or "muscle car" and that will help to zero in on what you're looking for.

There are websites dedicated to collector car sales, like www.collectorcartraderonline.com, which features over 148,000 collector vehicles for sale at any given time. This is just one example; you'll find a listing of some additional online collector car sites that feature vehicles for sale in Appendix A, but this is only a small portion of the hundreds (perhaps thousands) of sites of this type. Because new sites are cropping up all the time, searching the web frequently will give you the best shot at finding what you're looking for. The same downside applies to finding a car on the Internet as it does with *Hemmings* or *Old Car Weekly:* The car could be on the other side of the country, so even though it may be perfect, there's the distance factor to consider again.

Word of Mouth Works, Too!

Don't underestimate the power of word of mouth when it comes to broadcasting that you are trying to find a collector car. Tell the local garage mechanic what you're looking for and he'll help to spread the word. Mention that you're looking for a collector car to your friends and the folks at work. You never know who may have an aunt with that all-original 1962 Buick sitting in her garage with under 100,000 original miles that she might be willing to sell because she doesn't drive anymore.

In the section of New Jersey where I live there are many senior citizen developments. These are excellent hunting grounds for collector cars, many of which are still in the possession of the original owner. These senior villages have community halls with bulletin boards, so posting a sign that says you're looking for an older car to purchase for restoration is another word of mouth venue to consider pursuing. Be sure to have tear-off strips on the bottom with your phone number for potential sellers to contact you.

Very often, these villages put out a monthly newspaper for the residents. Generally, advertising space is very inexpensive in these papers, so running a small ad could be very cost effective in helping you to find a car worth restoring at a good price.

Also consider posting your signs in the local auto parts stores, speed shops, automotive machine shops, car washes, and even supermarkets. You never know who's going to see your little notice and pass the word along to someone they know who has a car they want to sell.

> **Brake It Down**
>
> Four on the floor is a colloquial term for a four-speed manual transmission with the shifting lever mounted on the floor rather than on the steering column.

> **4-Wheel Jive**
>
> The Volkswagen Beetle was the brainchild of Adolf Hitler.

Specialty Car Dealers

There are numerous specialty car dealers all over the country who handle collector cars, *exotics*, and special-interest vehicles exclusively. Very often, these dealers offer a full range of services including financing and insurance for the vehicles they sell.

More often than not, the cars you'll find at a specialty car dealership will be on consignment. What this means is that the person selling the car consigns it to the dealer, who displays it on his lot or in his showroom. When the car is sold, the dealer gets a percentage of the proceeds as his commission for handling the car. In rare instances the dealer will charge a flat fee for a given time period

> **Brake It Down**
>
> *Exotics* are usually high-priced foreign two-passenger roadsters, coupes or convertibles, such as the Lamborghini Countach and the Ferrari Testarossa, among others.

to hold the car. For example, he may charge $1,000 to keep the car on his lot for six months. If and when the car is sold, he doesn't get any additional money.

A very important thing to remember is that the specialty car dealer is, at the very root of it all, still a used car salesman. If he doesn't sell the cars on his lot, he doesn't get any commission, so he has a vested interest in moving these vehicles. This may very well motivate him to put some extra spin on how good the car is and embellishing the truth is a big part of the sales pitch. While this will undoubtedly be the case even when purchasing a car directly from a private owner, the likelihood of it happening with a specialty car dealer is almost a given certainty.

On the other hand, specialty car dealers are businessmen with fixed locations. They have an investment in their business and their reputation, just like Wal-Mart and the local hardware store. As used car dealers, they are subject to state laws. These include statutory warranties of fitness, which they cannot avoid. If you buy from a dealer and find sawdust in the transmission, you can take it back and get a refund. You don't have that recourse with a private seller.

Brake It Down

A replicar is a replica of a real car that was made at an earlier time. Popular examples include the Shelby Cobra replicars produced by several companies. While these replicars are often expensive, their price is frequently just a drop in the bucket compared to what an original version of the vehicle is worth in the current market.

You can locate a specialty car dealer in your area by consulting the phone book under automobile dealers. You can also search the Internet, as several of the larger and more reputable dealers will offer a satisfaction guarantee that the car is all that it is represented to be. Many will also arrange transportation to have the car delivered. In most of these cases, the car is pretty well done, and may only need some minor "freshening."

Pit Stop

Be sure that what you're considering buying is the real thing and not a replicar or a modification of another car to make it look like something it is not in reality. Examples of this would include adding the appropriate striping and badges to a standard production Chevrolet Chevelle to make it look like it's a Chevelle Super Sport (SS). Another example would be selling a fiberglass-bodied 1932 Ford Deuce Coupe as the real thing, when in fact it is a replicar.

There are also dealers that sell only project cars. These cars can vary greatly in condition, completeness, and price. A few years back I purchased a 1935 Nash Aeroform sedan from a dealer in Black Falls, North Dakota, who only sold project vehicles from 1949 or earlier. The car looked decent in the photos he sent me, and he told me the interior was nonexistent and the car had no glass. The original six-cylinder engine and transmission was still in the car, but it didn't run. The dealer had given the car a coat of red lead primer to inhibit further rusting. The car cost $1,700 to purchase, and then it cost me another $900 to have it shipped from North Dakota to New Jersey.

When the car was delivered to our home, and as it rolled off the flatbed, my wife and I both looked at the car, then at each other, and wondered what had been going through our minds when we bought this heap. The fact that it didn't have an interior, any glass or a nonrunning engine didn't bother me, because I wanted to make a street rod out of it anyway. What did bother me, however, was that the dealer neglected to tell me there was no floor in the car; it had totally rusted out. It also had a fairly large gash on the rear quarter panel of the driver's side, a view that he didn't provide a photo of and I, in my naiveté, neglected to ask for.

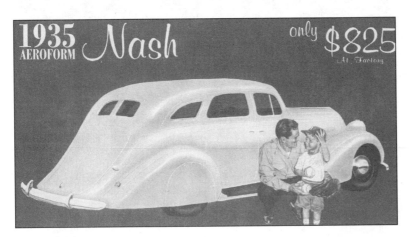

Here's an advertisement for the 1935 Nash Aeroform, which sold for only $835 in its day. The car the author purchased from North Dakota didn't look anything like this, however.

This Nash was a huge car, and it sat in my yard for about three years without me doing anything to it. This was too big a project that was going to require a lot of metalwork and welding, so I sold the car at a considerable loss to another wide-eyed masochist who had big plans for this car. Unlike me, this fellow saw the car physically before he gave me his money and he knew exactly what he was buying. Go figure—it takes all kinds.

Brake It Down

Fat fendered is a nickname for 1935–1948 Fords that were wide and rounded in appearance.

Belly of the Beast: Cruise Nights, Car Shows, and Car Clubs

In better than a decade of being involved in the collector car hobby, I honestly don't think I've ever gone to a cruise night or a car show without seeing at least one vehicle with a "for sale" sign on it. Both of these events are excellent venues for locating a collector vehicle. While these are frequently finished vehicles, you can also find projects that need freshening or are original and need restoring.

Cruise nights are great events to see restorations other folks have done and generate ideas for your own project.

People sell collector cars for various reasons, so talk with the owner and ask him why he's selling the car. Typical reasons will include:

Overdrive

Foldable canvas chairs with metal tubing frames make sitting around at cruise nights and car shows more comfortable. These chairs are inexpensive and readily available, they don't take up much room, and they come with their own storage pouches.

- Selling the car to buy something different.
- This car is done and he/she wants another project.
- Moving and won't have suitable storage for it or doesn't want to store it.
- Spouse says it's either the car or me.
- Baby on the way and wants to buy a house.
- Needs to raise money for some personal reason.

In my experience, these are by no means all the reasons, but they are the ones you'll hear most often.

Finding a car you like that's for sale at a car show or a cruise night has some real advantages:

- Unless it was trailered, the car made it there under its own power, which is a good sign.

- You can hear the engine run.

- You can inspect the vehicle.

- You can ask the owner questions.

- You can find out how negotiable the price is.

4-Wheel Jive

The Chevrolet Corvair was the first American mass-produced rear-engined car. Corvairs were produced from 1960 to 1969. Ralph Nader's book, *Unsafe At Any Speed*, sealed the fate of the Corvair and provoked strict governmental safety regulations for the automobile industry.

There are also many large, regional car shows throughout the country that have "car corrals" as a central feature of the show. Two of the bigger regional events are held several times a year at the Carlisle, Pennsylvania fairgrounds and also in Hershey, Pennsylvania. For a set fee, usually around $50–$100, folks enter their cars into the corral for sale. Eager prospective buyers with money in hand visit these car corrals looking for the car that's just right for them, so this is also an excellent place to find that dream car or project you want.

Additionally, there are indoor car shows and sales held in major cities throughout the year. Here in New Jersey there is a huge show and auction held at the Atlantic City Exposition Center in February of every year. Because it is held indoors, weather is never a problem and the car corral is always huge with hundreds of vehicles of all descriptions, conditions, and price ranges for sale. Check with your local and state exposition authorities to find one in your area.

Ascertain when and where local car clubs have their meetings and plan on attending a few. These are great opportunities to do networking and get the word out that you're looking for a project car. Collector car folks, for the most part, are gregarious and friendly, so don't be surprised if a couple of club members decide to take you under their wings and offer you the benefit of their experience. This is, in most instances, sage advice that will help to get you on the fast track in a hurry. Keep in mind, though, that they love their cars and they will try to convince you, the novice, that you should buy what they own.

Boneyards

At first blush, you might not think that a boneyard (also called a junkyard or auto salvage yard) would be a likely location to find a project car for restoration, but it is actually etty good place to go hunting. Not all the cars that end up in boneyards were in collisions. Many of them were simply junked because they were old and not worth much on the used car market. Others may have had mechanical problems like a seized or blown engine or perhaps the owner didn't want to spend money on repairing an old car.

Often you can find a complete car that hasn't been cannibalized yet, or you can get whatever it's missing by taking the parts off another car in the yard that's the same year, make, and model.

Brake It Down

Gullwing doors are hinged to open vertically rather than horizontally. The name came about because the doors, when open, resemble a seagull in flight with wings spread.

4-Wheel Jive

There were only about 1,400 1954–1956 Mercedes Benz 300SL gullwing coupes produced.

The boneyard makes most of its money by selling used parts—things like brake rotors, transmissions, engines and engine parts, fenders, rear ends—in short, just about any part that someone needs. Most people mistakenly think these yards make their money by crushing the car and selling it to a metal recycler, but this is not the case. In most boneyards the car is only crushed and recycled after everything that can be sold has been removed from it.

Understandably, the owner of the yard might not be too keen on selling you the whole car, because by parting it out he can probably get more for it, but that will take time. Working in your favor, though, is the fact that selling you a whole car can be fast, clean money for the yard owner. No disassembly, no cutting torches and no storing this hulk in the yard until it is picked clean.

If you find something you're interested in at a salvage yard, be bold and ask the owner what he wants for the car, and don't be shy about haggling. If your target vehicle is missing parts, negotiate to have the owner throw in the missing components from another car as part of the deal. And try to get him to include delivery of the vehicle as well, because it likely won't be in drivable condition.

There's one more very important point when buying a project car from a boneyard. Make sure that title to the vehicle is the correct one and that the VIN on the car matches the number on the title. If the yard owner doesn't have the title for the car, either tell him there's no deal or get him to concede big-time on the price, because you'll have to lay out about $100–$300 to procure a title for the vehicle. As a general rule of thumb, if there's no title there should be no sale.

If you read publications like *Old Cars Weekly* you'll see several boneyards located in Arizona, California, Texas, and other dry-climate locales advertising rust–free restorable vehicles and parts. While these boneyards are excellent for finding that vintage car or truck you want, there are caveats. Unless you're within traveling distance of the boneyard, you're pretty much buying a pig in a poke. Make sure you request photos of the candidate vehicles or, better yet, a videotape that shows all four sides as well as the engine compartment, trunk, and interior spaces. In addition to the price of the vehicle, you'll also have to add in the shipping costs (remember my experience with the 1935 Nash from South Dakota). While rust-free is good, it generally doesn't come cheaply when the additional shipping is figured into the equation.

And what I said earlier about getting a title with the vehicle applies here too, especially because you're getting an out-of-state vehicle. Lack of a title will complicate registering and licensing it in your state.

> **Overdrive**
>
> If you need additional storage space for stowing parts and assemblies such as the fenders and nose of the car while you're doing the restoration, consider purchasing a shed or round-roofed outdoor shelter as an alternative to renting space in a self-storage facility.

Finders and Fees

Car finders and vehicle locator services are other sources for getting a restorable project vehicle. You can check your local phone book under automotive locators and you can also check the Internet by searching key words like car finders or vehicle locator.

In all cases you'll have to provide a specific year or range of years for the make and model vehicle you want the locator to find. The more specific you are about what you're looking for, the better they'll be able to target their search efforts on your behalf.

The range of services these companies provide and the fees they charge can vary quite a bit. Some companies require an up-front subscription fee and they levy a small charge for every "hit" they find that matches your wish list. Others will charge you a monthly rate and provide you with a list of all the vehicles and their locations that they find over the course of the month.

4-Wheel Jive

Preston Tucker unveiled the Tucker Torpedo in July of 1947. Among the car's innovative features were fuel injection, pressurized water cooling, aerodynamic design, pop-out safety windshields and a cyclops third headlight that turned in the direction the car was moving. Only 51 Tucker Torpedoes were built and sold for about $2,400 each. The 49 remaining cars today are worth $400,000 to $1,000,000 each. The Tucker couldn't compete on a level playing field due to political pressure resulting from the lobbying of the Big Three carmakers (GM, Ford, and Chrysler).

Still others will provide you with a list of hits that matches your list, but will only charge you for providing the specifics about hits that you are interested in learning more about. Usually the way this works is that they provide you with the hits for your desired year, make, and model and they give you the general location (for example, Staten Island, New York) and the asking price. If the vehicle sounds like a prospect to you, it's within your acceptable distance and in your price range, you can request additional information, for which you will be charged. The expanded information will give more detailed information about the vehicle's overall condition, mileage, color, optional equipment and, if available, how many previous owners it has had. Any damage or nonfunctioning equipment will also usually be noted, and the better services will also supply photos and/or a videotape of the vehicle.

Often these companies will offer additional services if you're interested in a particular vehicle. These services can include a physical inspection of the vehicle by one of their staff members, shooting videotape and detailed photos of the vehicle, an appraisal, and comparison of the asking price with other comparable vehicles. Frequently, they will also act as your purchasing agent and arrange transport of the vehicle from the seller's location to you.

The fees these companies charge may be very well worth the cost when you consider the amount of time and leg work you'll save trying to locate that dream car of yours, so it's definitely something to think about.

4-Wheel Jive

Al "Scarface" Capone had a 1930 V16 Cadillac custom-built to his specifications. The car had bullet-proof glass in the windshield and side windows in addition to a quarter-inch of steel armor plating in the driver's compartment. The windows had a 3-inch hole one inch from the bottom to accommodate the occupants sticking their gun barrels out. A hole in the floorboard made it easy to drop roofing nails out onto the road to give pursuing police cars flat tires, and oil could be forced into the exhaust system to create smoke screens for thwarting ensuing chasers as well.

The Least You Need to Know

- Printed media and the Internet are excellent resources to use when searching for a collector vehicle.

- Word of mouth, car shows, and cruise nights are all effective ways of finding a car, too.

- Not all specialty car dealers are honest, so be wary when considering a vehicle purchase from them.

- Searching boneyards can often yield surprising results.

Part 2

Preliminary Considerations

So, what's it going to be for you: something domestic or some slick, imported collector car? How about buying your collector car at an auction, and how do you know if it's a rare find or a rust bucket? These are some of the many things you should know about as you hunt for a restoration project vehicle that will eventually be all you want it to be.

And don't forget that you have all sorts of options for restoration: You can make it bone stock so it is as good or better as the day it rolled off the assembly line, you can make it a wild custom vehicle, or anything in between. It's all okay in the collector car hobby.

Chapter 6

Cars Are Like Ham: They Can Be Domestic or Imported

In This Chapter

- ◆ Foreign cars dare to be different
- ◆ Scarcity usually means pricey
- ◆ The Marching Minis
- ◆ Canook cars, eh?
- ◆ Solving mechanical and parts problems

All too often we are myopic when considering a collector car restoration project and we only think about American iron. Some of the finest marques in the world were and are made overseas, however. Who could resist the allure of an Aston Martin, the understated elegance of a Bentley, the charm of a Karmann Ghia, the sultriness of a Citroën, or the fine lines of a Mercedes?

As you'll see in this chapter, restoring an imported collector car can be very rewarding and it has its own unique challenges as well. So put your seats in an upright position, fasten your seat belts, and stow your tray tables, 'cause we taking a trip overseas.

Cars Choices—Home Ground or Overseas?

Up to this point we've talked almost exclusively about American cars, but the collector car hobby is really an international affair. At any given car show or cruise night you are bound to see some foreign-made cars represented. The usual culprits are Volkswagen Beetles, MG and Triumph roadsters, an older Mercedes-Benz or two, Jaguars, and the occasional Rolls-Royce (usually complete with a jar of Grey Poupon in the rear passenger area). At larger, more grandiose sanctioned shows you are very likely to see high-end foreign marques like Minervas, Hispano-Suizas, Bentleys, Isotta-Fraschinis, Bugattis, and others.

Foreign cars are usually a lot of fun to restore but, by virtue of the fact that they were "born" on foreign soil, their restoration presents some unique challenges.

> **Brake It Down**
>
> **SAE** is an abbreviation for the Society of Automotive Engineers, a professional engineering organization that publishes research papers and defines various standards of measurement for the American automobile industry.

Foreign Cars Are Different

American cars, for the most part, have always been designed and built with great attention to driver and passenger comfort. Suspensions were intentionally made less stiff to yield a softer, cushier ride and automatic transmissions produced smooth shifts as the cars accelerated. Appearancewise, copious amounts of chrome were used to give the car more "eye candy," and huge, gas-guzzling engines helped to move these masses of metal along at a respectable clip. All of the nuts and bolts used to hold the car together conformed to *SAE* standards (inches, feet, pounds).

Conversely, the vast majority of foreign vehicles puts less emphasis on creature comforts and more attention on performance. Stiffer suspension made for better handling, which allowed these cars to negotiate narrow, winding roads more nimbly. Engines were smaller and more fuel efficient, with manual gear boxes much more prevalent than automatic transmissions. Luxury items such as air conditioning, power windows, and power steering were rarely the norm, except on the pricier luxury cars. The sizes and measurements for fasteners and other hardware used on them are based on the metric system (millimeters, centimeters, liters) or even more obscurely on old British cars, which used odd-sized wrenches called "Whitworth" sizes that you won't even find in the most copiously equipped Snap-On truck.

Scarcity Drives Up Prices

Because the American economy has traditionally always been robust, the American automobile industry has thrived throughout most of the twentieth century. Even in postwar years people wanted new cars, and that demand fueled production. Things were not so rosey in other parts of the world, however.

Much of Europe was war-torn in the late 1940s, and the rebuilding process took decades before national economies were back on track. Foreign automobile production, which was never anywhere near the level of America's, staggered as well. Bicycles, motorcycles, and motor scooters were the means of transport for many after WWII as countries collectively struggled to get back on their feet. Because there weren't many vehicles produced during these years, today they are inherently scarce. And that increases their value substantially. Even two-seat bubblecars, such as the BMW Isetta, command surprising amounts that exceed their original retail prices by 10 to 20 times on today's collector car market.

Foreign-made collector vehicles are currently enjoying unprecedented popularity that shows no signs of slowing down. This, in conjunction with the scarcity factor, also raises the demand for these cars and, subsequently, prices.

In the last few years there has been significant interest in restoring Japanese cars, particularly the Datsun "Z" series. Even the original "disposable" car, the Czechoslovakian-made Yugo, has enjoyed a popularity streak of late. Older BMWs, Hondas, Toyotas, Fiats and just about any other foreign marques you can name are being restored and showing up on the collector car scene today. And I've even seen an Australian 1973 Ford XB GT done up to resemble the Interceptor vehicle that was featured in the *Mad Max* movies, so literally anything foreign goes.

Foreign cars …

- ◆ Are usually smaller.

- ◆ Require less working and storage space.

- ◆ Mean a smaller car and fewer parts.

- ◆ Will frequently be economical to run.

Pit Stop

If you're considering a foreign vehicle for a restoration project, don't bring the local garage mechanic along with you to check the car out. Instead, search out a trained mechanic who has experience working on that particular marque to evaluate the car.

Brake It Down

A runabout is a small, light two-seat car. The term was mainly used to describe American cars that were small, very basic and inexpensive. The runabout was the predecessor to the roadster.

- Will attract attention at car shows or cruise nights.
- Will be lots of fun to drive.
- Will stand out in a crowd.

4-Wheel Jive

There's a magazine published by McMullen-Argus/PriMedia called *Mini Truckin* that caters exclusively to minitrucks and compact cars.

4-Wheel Jive

The DeLorean was manufactured in Ireland from 1981 to 1983 and had an unpainted stainless steel body, gullwing doors and a rear-mounted engine. Of the 8,583 total cars produced, about 6,000 are believed to still exist, with the majority of them here in the United States. They have become sought-after modern classics. The DeLorean is probably best known for its appearance in the *Back To The Future* movies.

Mini-Me?

I already mentioned that many foreign-made vehicles are smaller than their American counterparts, but I should also mention that there is another super-diminutive genre known as microcars and minicars. I call them mini/micros.

These mini/micros surfaced shortly after WWII in Germany and other European countries. Many of them were designed and built in aircraft factories that employed some of the countries' best aircraft engineers. As a condition of an end to hostilities, however, these countries were prohibited from building airplanes after the war.

These minimites included the Messerschmitt Kabinenroller ("kabinenroller" is German for "cabin scooter"), the Kleinschnittger, the Brütsch Mopetta, and the Italian Vespa 400, among others.

International Resources

While you can locate and purchase a foreign collector car through the same ways and means you'd use for an American marque, there are also some additional options open to you here. The websites of international classic auto brokers are a good place to start.

Usually these international classic auto brokers offer a complete package of services. They can locate, inspect, appraise, and even arrange to have a foreign automobile shipped over here. Many of them offer escrow services also.

> **Brake It Down**
>
> *Concours d'elegance* is traditionally a show of the most elegant, sporting, luxurious, and distinctive automobiles. The *concours d'elegance* in the United States has become a show of cars restored to beyond perfection, far better in fit, finish, and materials than they were when new. While *concours* generally feature the most exclusive marques—like Bugatti, Isotta-Fraschini, Ferrari, Rolls-Royce, Packard, and Duesenberg— they also frequently have classes for other more common but still distinctive automobiles. ·

Companies and brokers offering escrow services charge a percentage of the transaction because they act as the middleman between the buyer and seller to ensure that neither party gets burned. Sellers are typically not as willing to use escrow services as buyers are, and the problem that usually arises is which party will pay to transport the vehicle. Most sellers won't even do the deal unless the buyer agrees to pick up the tab.

If you're a buyer and you agree to this escrow arrangement, in a worst-case scenario you'll have to pay the cost of transportation both ways (to you and back to the seller in the event you don't want the car). This can be as much as $5,000 for the round trip, depending on the vehicle's point of origin and your destination.

Special Mechanical Requirements

Any foreign car manufactured for export to the United States must meet both federal safety and EPA requirements. This is not the case with vehicles that were not intended for export in the United States when new. Throughout Europe and the Far East there are few, if any, EPA requirements. This means that many of these cars, especially older vehicles, were designed to run on *leaded gas*. Because leaded gas is not readily available at the gas pump, these foreign engines may require special additives at every fill-up to run properly.

> **Brake It Down**
>
> **Leaded gasoline** refers to gasoline that has tetraethyl lead or other lead compounds added to it to increase its octane rating and reduce its knock or detonation tendencies. American cars manufactured since 1975 or foreign-made vehicles exported to the United States since 1975 require unleaded gas in order not to foul their catalytic converters that reduce exhaust emissions.

Brake It Down

GTO stands for Gran Turismo Omologato, which is Italian for Grand Touring Homologated. The name was originally applied to the famed 1962 Ferrari 250 GTO, and noted that enough of the vehicles had been built for FIA-sanctioned GT racing. The term was later used by Pontiac for the vehicle that launched the American muscle car phenomenon.

Because of the way they are constructed, many foreign vehicles require special tools such as special wrenches for servicing or overhauling their engines. And, as we touched upon earlier, a good set of metric sockets and wrenches will be required for removing and installing those metric nuts and bolts.

Many foreign cars have their steering wheels on the right side of the vehicle, which is the opposite of what we have here in the states. In come cases this can introduce some unexpected mechanical challenges, although they will probably be minimal. You will have to get used to driving from the opposite side of the car, however.

Parts Problems

Because today's foreign cars are commonplace and plentiful in our society, getting parts for current models is as easy as getting parts for domestic makes. This won't be the case if you need a distributor cap for a 1960 Ford Anglia, though. Getting a replacement passenger-side door latch for a 1980 Alfa Romeo might only involve taking a trip to the local boneyard in Palermo, Italy or the Italian equivalent of a NAPA store in Naples, but it's going to be a bigger ordeal finding such a part here in the states.

Pit Stop

Some British cars, particularly those that have Lucas electrical systems such as the Jaguars and MGs from the 1960s and 1970s, are particularly susceptible to malfunctions, especially in wet or damp weather. If you're contemplating the restoration of one of these cars, consider adding a complete new wiring harness to your parts list.

Once again, the Internet can be a wonderful solution for foreign parts hunting, too. Do some net surfing using key words in your searches that include the year, make, and model of the car and the part you need. Using our earlier example, the search key words would be "1980 Alfa Romeo passenger door latch," which will bring up several places to obtain this part as well as links to other sites related to Alfa Romeos.

There are also a number of magazines available at better booksellers that cater to specific marques like Porsche or all the marques of a particular country, such as England. Invariably, these publications have ads for parts from numerous suppliers, so they're another worthwhile resource for locating foreign parts, too.

Overdrive _____

When considering the purchase of a car that's too far away to check out in person, ask the seller to shoot a good videotape of the car showing it both inside and outside and running as well as standing still. Most reasonable sellers will be glad to comply, especially if you promise to return the tape if you decide not to take the car. It's also a good idea to offer to pay the postage or shipping on the tape for travel both ways as a gesture of good faith.

The Least You Need to Know

◆ Foreign collector cars have really come into their own and are now highly sought after.

◆ Frequently, the scarcer the foreign collector car is, the more in demand it will be and the higher its price.

◆ Micro/mini cars are unique and don't require much space to work on or store.

◆ Consider using an escrow service when purchasing a distant vehicle.

Chapter 7

Going, Going, Gone!

In This Chapter

- ◆ Going to a collector car auction
- ◆ Registering to buy a car at an auction
- ◆ Getting expert advice or using an agent
- ◆ Avoiding bidding wars
- ◆ Winning the bid

Buying a collector car at an auction is very popular. Collector car auctions offer a huge selection of cars—and they're all "For Sale." It's a fast-paced, exciting experience where it's easy to be swept away. Armed with even a little knowledge, buying at auction can be rewarding and fun. Approached without preparation, though, collector car auctions are an invitation to disappointment.

So grab a seat and let's attend class: Collector Car Auctions 101 is now in session—and here's the first lesson.

Do your research and know what you want to spend before you enter the auction gates.

The auctions are a cornucopia of unexpected, delightful, and intriguing cars. The atmosphere is deliberately created to generate enthusiasm and

Brake It Down

When a buyer has second thoughts about a successful bid because he didn't do the research and acted on impulse, he often experiences regret, or **buyer's remorse**.

urgency. It's easy for a novice to be captured by the spell of something weird, wonderful, and totally different from what they came to find. It is part of the auctions' fascination (they are the best car show in the world, where you're encouraged to kick tires and look in and under the car to get a closer look), but it's also a reason why so many inexperienced buyers suffer *buyer's remorse*. This is the single most important thing for a newbie buyer at an auction to know.

Collector Car Auctions

"Going once, going twice, fair warning—sold!" These are the words you hear just as the gavel drops, followed by: "Sold to bidder number (whatever your number is) for the high bid of (whatever the final amount is)." If you are the high bidder, you have an adrenaline rush as you realize that you won the auction. You became the proud owner of the car that was *your car* the minute you laid eyes upon it. However, you didn't just show up with a pocket full of money and join the bidding; several things led up to this happy ending.

There are on-site auctions and there are online auctions; both are substantially different from each other, as you will learn in the following sections.

The Cast of Characters and Auction Jargon

Before you go to an auction, you must know the terminology and the players. A collector car auction is a multiplayer drama, carefully orchestrated by the auctioneer to achieve and maintain enthusiastic participation.

The auction block at Barrett-Jackson's Scottsdale auction on Saturday "Prime Time" (when the best cars cross the block) has more energy than the playing field at the start of the Super Bowl. You can cut the energy with a knife. The auctioneer serves big helpings of adrenaline (basted in testosterone) to bidders in exchange for spending big money ... and anyone with a bidder number can be part of the action.

The Cast of Characters

Following is a list of the characters you can expect to find at the auction:

◆ The auctioneer is the only person who counts at the auction. Listen carefully and watch who the auctioneer is talking to.

♦ The *ringmen* spot bids for the auctioneer and work the buyers to keep them bidding. They're your new best friend—only as long as you're bidding.

Brake It Down _____

A **ringman** is the name for a male or female auction employee who calls out bids and points to the bidder so that the auctioneer knows from whom and where the bid came. It is the job of the ringman (there are usually several scattered throughout the buyers area) to keep the pace of the auction fast and to build the bidding frenzy, urging bidders to keep bidding higher. Though a ringman may act friendly, he is *not* your friend; his job is to drive the price up so the seller gets the most money for the vehicle and the auction gets the biggest commission, both at your expense.

♦ The grinder is the ringman on the block who "grinds" the consignor to get the reserve dropped and the lot sold.

♦ The describer sits on the block and introduces the cars. The words of the describer and auctioneer are the only verbal statements you can rely on.

The Jargon

You need to know some basic terminology to understand what is going on at the auction. Here's a list to get you started:

♦ *Reserve* is the seller's preset minimum price below which the lot will not be sold; the reserve may be the seller's realistic expectation of the car's value but more often it is an inflated figure established to give the seller room to negotiate on the block. The auctioneer can (and will) *bid against the reserve* even if there's only one live bidder. It's legal and it's explained in the auction's fine print when you accept a bidder number. A bidder can, and frequently does, find himself *bidding against the chandelier*, while the bids are below the reserve and there's only one live bidder. The seller can, however, *drop the reserve* at any time.

♦ A *no reserve* lot has no minimum bid and sells at the fall of the hammer to the last and highest bidder.

♦ A *shill* is a phony bidder who's usually acting on the seller's behalf to run up the bidding against a single real bidder. Shilling is illegal and reputable auctioneers will ignore shills, or if the shill is particularly obnoxious, drop the lot on them and force the shill/seller to pay the commissions.

♦ The *car card* contains the seller's representations and description of a particular car and is usually posted on the windshield of each lot.

♦ Auctions charge a *buyer's commission* on top of the successful hammer bid. Buyer's commissions range from 5 percent at Silver Auctions (rising to 6 percent in June 2004) through 6 percent at RM Auctions' consignment sales, 7 percent at Kruse, 8 percent at Barrett-Jackson to 10 percent at RM's catalog sales. Bonhams and Christie's charge split commissions that start at 15 percent and drop to 10 percent on amounts over a set bid. Dana Mecum has a unique commission structure with set dollar commissions at different bid levels. The buyer's commission is part of the cost of buying at auction. Consider it, along with your travel expenses, motel bills, food and car rental, when figuring up what the real cost is … and how much you are willing to bid.

On-Site Auctions

There are three kinds of on-site auctions:

♦ Catalog sales by RM Auctions, Bonhams, and Christie's—where the high-end cars are sold (the top sale in recent years: $6.5 million for a Le Mans-winning Ferrari Testa Rossa at RM Monterey 2002). However, plenty of low and medium-priced cars also can be bought; high buyer's fees (10 percent, 15 percent, and 17.5 percent respectively, stepped down to 10 percent for amounts over $100K at Bonhams and Christie's); better presale research, representations on history and condition in writing; posh venues (for example., Ritz Carlton, Quail Lodge, Pebble Beach); lush color catalogs; firm(er) reserves.

♦ Consignment sales by Barrett-Jackson, Kruse, Mecum, Silver, RM, etc.—The sale's content isn't set (except for high-profile early consignments) until the day of the auction; venues are all over the country and all year long; diverse choices with up to 1,000 cars across the block; plenty of opportunity to "dicker" both directly with the seller and through the auction company, including a formal "post-block" sales organization to manage cars that didn't sell on the block; some written basic description of the cars; ancillary services; experienced management of the sale and the consignments to resolve title issues; some sales (especially the two Kruse sales at Auburn) are like a country fair with car corrals, vendor vendors, elephant ears, and corn dogs; and lower buyer fees.

♦ "Country" and estate auctions that may have a few old cars—limited selection, no professional assistance, probably lower buyer fees.

The advantages of purchasing your collector car at an on-site auction are that you'll have a good opportunity to inspect the vehicle in person before it comes on the block, there will be a lengthy description of the vehicle and its features, and the auction company will have done some due diligence to make sure that the car's credentials are in order (the VIN number matches the title, and so on). In the event of some misrepresentation, the auction company might also intervene and solve misrepresentation problems if the buyer reports them within 24 hours of the sale.

Other advantages of on-site auctions are that they usually have services available that might be required by the buyer, including financing, insurance, and vehicle transport services. Some major auctions (Barrett-Jackson for example) have independent on-site inspectors with lifts and diagnostic equipment.

On-Site Auction Etiquette

Following are some etiquette rules for on-site auctions:

- ◆ It's okay to look and touch, but if the owner or a representative is there, it's best to ask first.

- ◆ *Curbstoning* is both illegal and unethical; the seller has a contract with the auction company, which gets compensated for putting on the show through the fees it earns. Curbstoning is considered stealing.

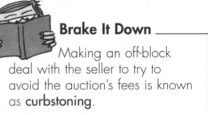

Brake It Down

Making an off-block deal with the seller to try to avoid the auction's fees is known as **curbstoning**.

- ◆ The hammer's fall concludes a contract to buy the *lot*; don't bid if you're not going to honor your commitment. The title transfers at the fall of the hammer. If the car burns to the ground on the way off the block, it's your cinder, at the full hammer bid plus commission. Jim Cox at Branson calls it the "50-50 Guarantee: If it breaks in half leaving the block, you own both halves."

Brake It Down

Lot is auction terminology for a single item or group of items sold in one transaction.

- ◆ Don't be cute and wait 'til the last second to bid. It slows down the action, annoys everyone, is an ineffective tactic, and you may see the car sold to another bidder just because the auctioneer wants to keep things moving.

- ◆ Each car gets about two minutes on the block; that's it, so be there when your car's number comes up.

Some auctions, however, do charge a buyer's premium, which means that you'll have to pay a percentage of the final bid price to the auction company (this is in addition to the actual final bid price). Because these companies also charge a seller's premium, they collect on both sides of the sale, and this is known as *double-ending*.

The downsides of on-site auctions are that they might be a long distance away from where you live, so travel and lodging expenses must be calculated in the cost of purchasing the vehicle. Also, if you are the winning bidder, you will have to get the vehicle from the auction site to your home. Driving it is out of the question, because you won't have plates for it, so plan on hiring a professional hauler or arriving with a trailer behind your car.

Online Auctions

Online collector car auctions have been developed, particularly by eBay Motors, to be very successful and reasonably safe. Cars worth over a million dollars have been successfully auctioned on the Internet, but it takes careful planning to make it work with confidence.

It goes without saying that you should ask for, and get, comprehensive information in writing from the seller.

In the end, though, you're going to put thousands of dollars on the table for a car that you've never seen or touched. A pile of photos is only as good as the photographer who took them (and that's the seller)—someone who wants the car to look as good as possible. The seller's photos probably aren't going to highlight the wavy sills that tell of sloppy rot repair.

So the online auctions offer independent inspections. They also offer escrow services that hold your money until the car arrives and you're satisfied that it meets the seller's material representations. What's "material"? Well, if the seller says "rust-free" and the car that arrives has rotten body supports, that's "material," but if it has some minor surface rust on the floorboards, inside the fenderwells, or in the spare tire compartment that's probably not material. If the seller says "1963 Thunderbird Roadster" and the car that arrives is VIN-coded "85" with an aftermarket tonneau ('63 Roadsters are VIN-coded "89") that's "material." Even if the transaction is unwound after inspection, you will still be responsible for the cost of shipping the car back to the seller … and that can be as much as $3,000 for a rapid-response haul in an enclosed transporter.

Ask the seller to e-mail you additional digital photos of the car showing multiple views (15–20 shots at the minimum) of all four sides, engine compartment, interior including the front and rear seats, door panels, dash, instruments, and the odometer showing the mileage (compare this number to the mileage shown on the title—the odometer figure should be somewhat higher).

If you are truly interested in the car, you might also ask the seller to shoot a videotape that shows all of the previous views and his commentary, assuring the seller that you will return the tape if you do not win the auction or decide against bidding on the car. These are not unreasonable requests if you are a serious candidate for buying the car and the seller is serious about making a deal.

Don't be unreasonable, though. If you're bidding on a $3,000 car, you really can't expect the seller to spend hours taking photos, shooting video, and overnight shipping the materials.

Okay, let's say the seller is very accommodating and has provided you with everything you requested. You like the car very much and you're ready to place a bid. As soon as you do, another person outbids you. You counter, and you're outbid again. You figure someone else is really interested in this car, too, but you might be dead wrong here. You might be bidding against a shill bidder, which is a common practice that sellers use to drive up the final price of the vehicle.

Although all of the major online auctions try to take active measures to prevent shill bidding, in reality, there's not too much they can really do about it. An unscrupulous seller will find a way to use shill bidders to rig his online auction.

There's very little recourse for the buyer and the seller if the online auction goes awry for some reason, or if either party fails to live up to their end of the bargain. The auction host gives a warning, which is really just a slap on the wrist, but that's about it.

Registering to Buy at On-Site Auctions

In comparison to online auctions, on-site auctions are really the only sensible way of purchasing a collector vehicle on a bidding basis. And, when you consider that many of the major auction companies conduct several auctions each year at many sites around the country, this is definitely a venue you will want to seriously consider.

Every on-site auction requires bidders to be registered. The registration process establishes that the bidder, should he be successful, is capable of financially completing the transaction and that he is, indeed, a real player. To register for an on-site automotive auction, you are usually required to provide all or most of the following items:

4-Wheel Jive

The first documented collector car to sell for $1 million in cash at a Kruse auction was a 1934 Duesenberg SJ La Grande long wheelbase dual-cowl phaeton. The car was sold to Tom Monnaghan, founder of Domino's Pizza and, at the time, the owner of the Detroit Tigers.

◆ A copy of your valid driver's license

◆ A photograph of yourself

◆ Contact information (bidder name, address, phone number, e-mail address, cell phone number)

◆ Social Security number

◆ Your signature on the bidding contract

Pit Stop

IRS regulations require that cash transactions of $10,000 or more be reported to the IRS.

4-Wheel Jive

Kruse International is one of the world's leading auction firms and, selling more vintage cars than all other firms combined, is the largest collector car auction company. It auctions more than 13,000 cars in more than 30 events each year.

If you wish to pay for the vehicle with a personal or business check (as opposed to cash or a cashier's check), the auction company also will require:

◆ Bank or investment company name

◆ Checking account number

◆ Desired bid limit

◆ Bank address, contact name, and phone number

◆ A bank letter of guarantee confirming that you are good for the money

The auction company also charges a bidder registration fee and has a minimum for the bid limit. Using Barrett-Jackson's Scottsdale auction as an example, the bidder registration fee is $300 and the minimum bid limit is $20,000. However, if you purchase a car as the winning bidder, the bidder registration fee is refundable.

The fees and minimum bid limits vary from auction to auction, but these are fair examples of what to expect. Upon submitting the fee and the requisite materials, you are issued a bidder's pass or bidder's credentials, which you can pick up in person when you arrive at the auction. After you have the pass or credentials, you are ready to place your bid(s) when the car comes up on the block.

Taking Along an Expert

When contemplating the prospects of acquiring a collector car at an on-site auction, it is a good idea to take along an expert who is well-versed in the particular marque you're interested in. The reasoning behind this is sound: You're probably going to be spending some major money bidding on this car, and you want to make sure that you're not overlooking any details during the inspection. Two passes are usually provided to registered buyers, so the extra expense of hiring an expert who can perform a thorough inspection and an accurate appraisal before you cast your bid is a very worthwhile investment. Experts are often available for hire at the auction site, or they can be contacted through referrals of the auction company itself.

Carfax researches a vehicle's history from insurance company and Motor Vehicle Department records and reports transactions (sometimes with mileages) and damage incidents. At $19.99 each or unlimited reports for $24.95 for a month, it's inexpensive. Carfax records are most valuable for late model cars from about 1980 on and are available online at www.carfax.com.

> **4-Wheel Jive**
>
> A dealer friend bought a 1986 Ferrari 328 GTSi one weekend at auction. It was represented as a 30,749 mile car. He checked Carfax and discovered that it changed hands in 1996 ... with a reported 106,000 miles on the odometer. Needless to say, he didn't complete the transaction.

Using an Agent

If you can't physically attend an on-site auction yourself, another option is to use an agent to represent you and place bids on your behalf. Most of the larger collector car auction companies can accommodate this kind of absentee bidding.

It works this way: You register as a buyer, but you stipulate that you will be doing proxy bidding. You can hire an independent agent to represent you, but in many instances the auction company assigns one of their staff to assist your proxy bidding. When the car you're interested in is in line to come onto the block, you establish contact with the agent over the phone. As the bidding progresses, the agent lets you know what the current bid is, and you can tell him to bid the next increment or to stop bidding when you've reached your ceiling. If you win the auction, you can make payment and delivery arrangements on the vehicle.

Do Not Get Caught in a Bidding Frenzy

The fast pace of a collector car auction, the excellent lighting to make the cars look the best they possibly can, and the excitement of being a "player" can easily blur common sense and good judgment. As soon as you cast your first bid, a *ringman* starts hovering around you and urges you to top the next bid. That is his job, and it is very easy to get caught up in the bidding as it grows to a fever pitch.

Based on your expert's advice, your own research, and an accurate appraisal of what this vehicle is worth, set a realistic ceiling bid in your mind. If you really like the car, it's okay to exceed the appraisal value, but only by 10 to 15 percent; if you exceed it by more than that, you're going to overpay. For example, let's say that the expert's appraisal figure is $20,000 for the car. You really like it, so you set your ceiling bid at $23,000, which is 15 percent over the appraisal. When the bidding goes to $23,500, it's time to bail out.

As much as you like the car, try not to get emotionally attached to it before the bidding starts. It is not like this car's the only existing model of this year, make, and model, and tomorrow is another day.

Remember: "Keep your cool and don't let your emotions rule."

A Winning Bid Is a Contract to Purchase

When you register as a buyer, you will receive an information packet that clearly details the auction company's terms and conditions. You should read this information carefully and ask questions before you bid. By participating in the auction as a bidder, you are legally bound to conform to these terms and conditions. The most important of these is that a winning bid is a contract to purchase, and you are legally responsible. For that reason, do not place a bid that you don't intend to honor. If you win the auction, you can't simply change your mind and walk away; there will most assuredly be unpleasant legal ramifications.

The Least You Need to Know

- Major auction companies hold on-site auctions several times each year at various locations throughout the country.

- Because you are physically separated from the seller and the car in an online auction, bidding online requires special care and precautions.

- You must preregister as a buyer to bid at an on-site auction.

- You are legally bound to honor your bid if you win an on-site auction.

Chapter 8

Is It a Rare Find or a Rust Bucket?

In This Chapter

- Knowing the eight condition categories
- Researching a car's history before purchasing
- Using an assessor to determine the car's value
- Not getting the wool pulled over your eyes and not fixing someone else's failure
- Assessing the car's value to you
- Not acting impulsively

You can't be too careful when considering a collector car for a restoration project. Depending on the quality of the raw material you have to work with, the restoration could proceed nicely with only a few minor snags along the way, or it could be the project from hell. Keep a sharp eye open. In this chapter we focus on evaluating and assessing what it takes to restore a vehicle.

Treasure or Trash?

This is the first question to ask yourself and the first answer you'll have to establish. Of all the restoration tasks, rust repair is the most time-consuming and costly. Even minor rust at the bottom of the quarter panels or doors requires skill and the right equipment to repair properly, and "properly" is the key word here. Taking shortcuts like filling in the rusted area with plastic body filler is not the correct way to do it; such makeshift repairs will simply rust out again in no time. The amount of repair work that has been done (or not done) plays a big part in establishing the overall condition of the vehicle.

> **Pit Stop**
>
> Don't get emotionally involved with a car or allow it to cloud your common sense and good judgment. A car that is badly rusted or has been damaged in a collision will cost you a lot more to restore than one that is in better shape. In addition to frustration and aggravation, you might end up hating the car.

Categories of Condition

There are eight important categories of condition for collector cars. These categories affect price and the amount of work and expense required to restore and maintain the car. These are condition categories only. They consider paint, interior, rust, and mechanical factors. Desirability—things like horsepower, appearance, and style—is not a factor in a car's "condition."

Most collector car value guides use the condition scale described here or a variation of it, which eliminates the lower conditions. In addition, publications such as *Old Cars Weekly, Car Collector, Hemmings,* and *Victory Lane* that report auction market transactions also use this scale. It is part of the lingo of car collecting.

The categories follow:

◆ **Condition 1— Concours:** A freshly restored, better-than-new car prepared to the most demanding standards; still sharp, crisp, and spotless with no more miles than were necessary to drive onto the car shows' fields since it rolled out of the restorer's shop. It is sometimes described as a "concours restoration" because it will be shown with pride in the finest *concours d'elegance*. The materials, finishes, and level of detailing of a condition 1 car are much better than it when came off the production line.

- **Condition 2—Excellent:** Like new and perfect, with factory-like finishes and details, clean and sharply detailed in all respects with no appreciable evidence of wear or use. A condition 2 car is the objective of most marque clubs and replicates the original appearance of a new car on the dealer's showroom floor. With even limited use on the street or highway, a condition 2 car quickly loses its edge, and "edge" is oh, so important. A "2" can be a restored car, or it can be an untouched time-capsule original and unused car (although it's usually not more than a few years before inevitable aging processes (due to sunlight, ozone, ultraviolet, oxidation, etc.) begin to deteriorate finishes and materials … causing it to loose its "2" status.)

- **Condition 3—Good:** Most cars are "3's." They have a few years on them, have been driven and used, and show the vicissitudes of daily existence, yet they have no major flaws or defects. The body and upholstery are sound; the engine, transmission, and driveline run well; the finishes are solid and everything (or at least everything important) works. On the other hand, the door edges will have parking lot chips, the seat coverings may be stretched from use, the chassis probably is covered with a light mist of oil and dust from being driven, the chrome might have some blemishes or rust spots, and the engine isn't clean enough to eat off of. As with "2s," condition 3 cars can be either older restorations or carefully maintained unrestored and original cars.

  The difference in collector value between an older restored condition 3 car and an unrestored original condition 3 car is immense, but remember we're talking about condition here, not desirability.

- **Condition 4—Fair:** A condition 4 car has important physical flaws. They may be cosmetic, mechanical, or both. A "4" needs a lot of work done to be even a reliable driver. These cars sometimes are referred to as "beaters" or "20-20s" because, from 20 feet away at 20 miles per hour, they look okay but as you approach it becomes evident from about 20 feet away that they need work. Usually all facets of the car need attention, but the car may be usable and functional as is.

- **Condition 5—Rough:** This is a complete vehicle that needs everything restored, including the body, running gear, chassis, and interior. It probably requires replacing, rebuilding, or overhauling major mechanical components such as the engine or transmission, which might or might not work in its current state. It may be incomplete in some major aspect, or a disassembled "basket case." Only the most experienced restorer starts out with a condition 5 car, and then only when it is particularly rare and desirable. To all intents and purposes, it is impossible to avoid going underwater (spending way more than the finished car is worth) when starting with a "5."

◆ **Condition 6—Parts Car:** A condition 6 car is usually buried up to its axles in 40 years accumulation of dirt, or has a tree growing where its engine used to be. It is valuable only for the parts that can be salvaged from it or as a frame and chassis number that can be used as the basis for a street rod or extreme custom.

Overdrive

When you find a car that has potential as a restoration project, there are a few things you can do to help determine the quality of the basic vehicle. Take along a refrigerator magnet and use it to check out the lower door panels and bottoms of the quarter panels; if the magnet sticks, a lot of metal is present, indicating little if any rust. If the magnet does not stick, a good amount of body filler is present. This means there was quite a bit of rust damage and a shortcut repair was made. That's not a good thing, because such shortcuts must be corrected during the restoration.

There also are cheap calibrated magnetic gauges that read in thousandths of an inch. "Spot Rot" costs under $13, is available from several vendors, and gives a reliable and repeatable reading.

◆ **Category 7—Basket Case:** A car that has been disassembled to a large extent, and whose parts are now in boxes, buckets, or other containers classifies it as a Category 7. None of the parts are labeled, and there is no documentation about the part of the vehicle from which these parts came. There is no way of knowing if all the parts are there or if some things are missing. Unless you like jigsaw puzzles and major headaches, walk away from a basket case.

◆ **Category 8—Rust Bucket:** Rust is so extensive and pervasive on a Category 8 vehicle that it has no potential for restoration. In addition to rusted-out door and quarter panels, frame rust is also quite advanced and may seriously affect the structural integrity of the chassis. While a basket case is bad enough, a rust bucket is even worse and belongs in the crusher at a metal-recycling facility.

Overdrive

Use a flashlight to inspect rust-prone areas like the spare tire well in the trunk, the lower portions of the doors that come into contact with the sills, the insides of the fenders, and the floor panels beneath the carpeting. Look under the car as well, using the flashlight to visually assess the condition of the frame and suspension.

Start on the right side. Why? Because that's the side of the road where puddles and piles of slush accumulate to keep replenishing the dirty, salty soup that eats away at unprotected steel.

The VIN (Vehicle Identification Number)

The VIN is the identification number assigned to each automobile by the manufacturer or by a state motor vehicle department. This number can usually tell you a lot about a car.

Federal law requires that every vehicle offered for sale by a dealer or at an auction (except charity auctions in some states) have what's called a Monroney Sticker (named after the senator who sponsored the bill in Congress) that carries its VIN number. If you go to an auction and the cars don't have their Monroney stickers, be very skeptical; in fact, you should probably say, "Thank you very much," and leave. If you speak with a dealer or an owner about a car and they decline to give you the VIN, you would be well advised to terminate the conversation.

An assigned VIN is a number assigned by a state to an automobile that has been assembled from parts (such as street rods and kit cars) or—and this is the important part—to an automobile that has been crashed or so severely damaged that it has been written off and the registration/title surrendered to an insurance company.

You can usually tell if a car has an assigned VIN in two ways. The number starts or ends with the abbreviation of a state (such as "CA" or "MONT") or the style of the number is not consistent with the nomenclature used by the manufacturer for that year and model. Some states will, however, assign the original VIN to a reconstructed or restored car on which the original chain of title has been lost.

> **CAUTION** **Pit Stop**
>
> Approach any vehicle with an assigned VIN very carefully. It may be the front half of one car welded to the back half of another. Also be aware that some states (Alabama is famous) will title just about anything, while others (Connecticut, for example) are rigid in their title requirements.

Following are examples of VIN numbers:

- **1961 Ferrari California Spyder Replica CA594954.** This is a California-assigned VIN.

- **1961 Ferrari 250 GT California Spyder 2903GT.** This car sold for $1,182,500 by RM at Amelia Island in 2000. 2903 equals the sequential production number for Ferrari (during this period road cars were assigned odd numbers and race cars had even numbers). GT equals the series.

Numbers-matching is the most misunderstood and frequently misrepresented term in car collecting. The loosest definition of numbers-matching is that the present configuration of the car is as it is described by its VIN number. In the case of a '57 Bel Air, this means only that it started its life as a Bel Air with the engine type now in the car (V8 or 6). In the case of a Mopar, such as the Challenger, it is more descriptive because there's more information in the VIN. This loose definition is all that a buyer can realistically rely on in the absence of more information.

Pit Stop

When it comes to numbers-matching, don't let rose-colored glasses tinge your buyer's vision and cause you to hear what you want to hear and not what is actually being represented.

The seller wants a prospective buyer to think that "numbers-matching" means its most extensive interpretation: that every component of the car is the original piece that came off the assembly line. This rarely happens, and the intermediate interpretation that the important parts are original off-the-line, and that other parts are correctly dated and the correct type of parts for the car, is not a bad thing.

Researching a Car's History *Before* Purchasing

The next order of business is to do some research, and the Internet is a terrific resource. You should find out as much about that particular year, make, and model as you can. You want to know how many were made, what the available engines were, what optional equipment was available, and what the original retail prices were for these cars. This information helps establish whether the car is a rare find or fairly common, a determination that affects such factors as the availability and prices of parts, the car's value in its current condition, and its worth after being restored.

Overdrive

Inspect the lines between the doors and the doorjambs, and the fit of the hood and trunk (the "shut lines"). The gaps between the panels should be equal front-to-back and should not taper in width from top to bottom. If they are not equal and do not taper, it could be an indication that the car was in a collision at some point in its life. At best, it indicates shoddy workmanship some time during its life. A more careful examination of the frame is warranted to check for crash damage.

Build Tags/Build Sheets

Like VIN numbers, many cars have build tags on them that describe the as-built car in greater detail. With some marques such as Corvettes, build sheets (computer-printed description sheets) are also used and list the options the car was equipped with on the assembly line. There also are books that decode these tags in detail. A serious buyer should know what he wants and is looking for and familiarize himself with the decoding details of a car's VIN and options tags. Memorize what you can (for a '57 Chevy there's not much to remember) and create a crib sheet to take with you for more difficult decoding tasks (such as 60's and 70's Mopars that have fender tags identifying every little detail of the car's build.)

Overdrive _____

Collector car value guides are excellent sources for basic production information as well as for guidelines on the values of cars in various categories of condition. However, value guides lag the market. They're low in a rising market and high in a declining one. They also tend to be conservative, so it's not "wrong" to pay more than a guide

Experts and Factory Resources

There also are authenticating authorities for some cars. Galen Govier (www.gvgovier.com) has made a very successful career out of authenticating high performance Mopars and no one in his right mind buys a Hemi without a Govier authentication. Marti Auto Works (www.martiauto.com) has access to Ford's 1967–1973 records and can provide backup data (including a reproduction of the original window sticker). Pontiac Historic Services (www.phs-online.com) is authorized by GM public relations to provide original configuration information for 1961–1999 Pontiacs (particularly important on early GTOs that were an options package, not a separate model).

Using an Assessor

You have another option available for getting a handle on the car's actual condition and value, and that is using a professional service to assess and appraise the vehicle. You can find them listed under "appraisers" or "services" in *Hemmings*, *Old Car Weekly*, and other collector car publications. While a professional appraisal might cost $100 or more, it is often well worth the fee to get an expert and accurate picture of the shape the vehicle is in and its true value as it stands. If you can't justify the expense or afford to have the car professionally appraised, find someone who is very knowledgeable about this particular type of vehicle to do the inspection and give you an assessment.

Another good resource is the body shop or mechanic to whom you'll turn to do work you won't undertake yourself. Get the car up on a lift and have a pro look underneath. Have your mechanic take it for a drive and perform basic diagnostic checks of the engine, brakes, transmission, and steering. Walk away from a seller who isn't willing to let you have simple checks like this done. The hundred or so dollars it will cost is cheap compared with what you'll spend on the car and its restoration, and can save you thousands.

There's also a national inspection service for collector vehicles that has more than 500 offices across the country. The company is Automobile Inspections LLC (www.automobileinspections.com), and they offer a comprehensive inspection and appraisal service that provides a six-page written report. Four different categories of reports are offered:

 ◆ The Silver Report is for street rods and custom cars.

 ◆ The Gold Report is for vehicles built in 1945 or earlier.

 ◆ The Blue Report is for vehicles built between 1946–1980.

 ◆ The Red Report is for vehicles built in 1981 and later.

> **CAUTION**
>
> **Pit Stop**
>
> Beware of cars that have new paint; it is easy to do a "quickie" rust repair using plastic body filler and to paint over it. Such repairs are often done to sell the car, and the problem reappears in a short amount of time. Look for a car that is not freshly painted.

Automobile Inspections LLC begins arranging the inspection immediately upon your request, and most reports are completed and delivered to you within 72 hours. The reports contain the answers to over 150 crucial questions that are specifically designed for collector vehicles. They also provide free professional consultation before and after you receive the completed report. Their fees start at about $269, but they offer a money-back guarantee, so it's something you might want to consider if you think you've found the right car but want to be doubly sure.

Don't Get Bamboozled: Fakery Is Afoot!

My friend Roy bought a 1972 Chevelle SS a few years ago. It looked like a Super Sport, but it was actually just your plain, garden-variety Chevelle. The fellow Roy bought it from was up front about it being a faux SS, however. He told Roy he thought the car needed a facelift, so when it was repainted he had the appropriate striping and emblems added to make it look like a real Super Sport. Roy was just looking for a nice cruiser, the price was right, and he didn't care that the car wasn't what it appeared to be. Later, Roy sold the Chevelle to my cousin Charlie, who also didn't care that it wasn't the real thing. There were happy endings for both Roy and Charlie, but that is not always the case.

Ted, on the other hand, wanted a 1957 Chevy convertible in the worst way, almost to the point of being obsessed. When he finally located one that rang his bell, he bought the car without doing his homework, taking the seller's word that it was an all-original "survivor" that just needed some freshening up to make it a head-turner. After Ted owned the car for a couple of weeks and started planning the restoration, he started to realize that this Shoebox Chevy wasn't all that it seemed at first blush. For starters, it should have had a 283 CID engine in it; instead, it had a 327 CID engine—a motor that Chevrolet didn't produce until 1961.

When he replaced the passenger side headlight, he discovered that the upper headlight housing was more body filler than metal due to severe rust damage; the same went for the driver's side headlight, too. Lifting the trunk mat revealed severe rust damage of the trunk floor, and the rocker panels were another visit to *Bondo*-land also. His dream car quickly turned into a nightmare. Some sellers pull the wool over your eyes and take advantage of the buyer. Beware: Don't get bamboozled.

> **Brake It Down**
>
> **Bondo** is the trade name for a line of body filler putty made by the Bondo Corporation, which has become generic in car enthusiasts' shorthand. Having your car described as a "Bondo-bucket" is most emphatically not a good thing.

Fixing Someone Else's Failure: Don't Go There

"Restoration is 75 percent complete, and all parts required to finish it are included. Must sell." I've seen ads like that many times. And in 99 percent of the cases, it can be interpreted as "current owner is in over his head, has lost interest, doesn't want to commit any more time or money" or some other real reason that he's not divulging.

Rarely, if ever, will this person have documented what's already been done to the car and, in most cases, can't produce receipts for parts or services purchased. So basically you don't know anything about the car, its history, or if the work already completed has been done correctly. Nor do you actually know if, indeed, everything needed to finish the car is included.

You can think of this car as a partially assembled basket case and, unless you're really up to a challenge and the price is ideal, you should pass this car by and look for a more promising restoration candidate.

What's It Worth to You?

The question of what it's worth to you is a subjective question that only *you* can answer. It depends on why and how badly you want a particular car, how much money you have to spend, and whether your plans include keeping this car for a long time to come.

Try to maintain some sense of relative value as you determine what this car is really worth to you. For example, if the price guides show that in Category 4 (good) condition this vehicle should be selling in the $4,500–$5,000 range, but this seller is asking $7,500 for it, is it really worth that extra money to you? Realistically, it is not. Or at least it shouldn't be, because there are probably a lot of other cars in comparable shape that are available at lower prices. Shop around.

Don't Act On Impulse

The seller *might* have the car you want, but you *definitely* have what he wants: money. The seller will try to close the deal on the spot, especially if you give any indication that you're keen on the car. Although it may be tempting, especially if he says something like "I have another party coming over to see it tonight, so it might not be here tomorrow," don't act on impulse. Tell him you want to discuss it with your spouse or that you just want to think about it, and you'll get back to him. That way you remain in the driver's seat in the negotiations, and you're in a better position to ask for price concessions when you do get back to him.

Chances are pretty good that the car will still be there the next day or even the next week, so the chips are stacked in your favor when you get back to him. And, if the car was sold to someone else in the meantime, remember that there are others out there, so keep looking.

The Least You Need to Know

♦ The condition of a collector car can vary from a bucket of rust to a museum-quality *concours* vehicle. Know what category it fits in and what category you are willing to buy in.

♦ Perform your research to learn as much as possible about the particular year, make, and model you're interested in.

♦ Check the vehicle to make sure it's the real deal so the seller does not take advantage of you.

♦ Avoid impulse buying. Take a day or two to think about the vehicle and check out others before you decide to buy.

Chapter 9

Don't Be Shy

In This Chapter

- ◆ Learning from the pros
- ◆ Talking to the people who have experience
- ◆ Comparing your notes with others
- ◆ Sharpening your communication skills
- ◆ Seeking out the information you need

Learning all you need to know about restoring a collector car is the first step to a successful restoration. The more folks you talk to who have done restorations, the broader your knowledge base will be. Some folks are really good at bodywork, while others are great mechanics, and still others are whizzes at upholstery and interiors. Talking to these folks is an education in itself. Collectors love to talk about their cars. They love to share information. They want to bring new acolytes to their altar, whether it's Bel Airs, Fairlanes, Challengers, MGs, or Pacers.

In the collector car hobby there are no strangers, only friends you have not yet met. Every new friendship should start with a smile, an introduction, and a handshake. Let's go make some new friends.

Don't Be Shy

Many newcomers into the world of collector cars feel a bit intimidated or even a little embarrassed about their lack of knowledge. This is perfectly normal. After all, this hobby has its own jargon, and there are so many facets that it seems overwhelming, at least at first. Just remember that everyone involved with collector cars was a novice at some time. Car collectors are generally a friendly bunch and are willing to help out beginners by answering questions, giving advice, sharing their experiences, and recommending good service and parts providers. There's a wealth of information and knowledge to be gained by talking to folks whose hobby is car collecting, so by all means, don't be shy!

Learning What the Pros Know

If you really want to know what the professionals know, you have to ask them. If you're contemplating taking the engine out of your collector car and rebuilding it, talk to a mechanic who does this for a living, and preferably one who owns his own shop. In most cases, this person will be happy to explain what's involved in removing the motor, dismantling it, checking the engine block for cracks or other serious problems, boring out the cylinders, ordering and installing the new components, torqueing the bolts to factory specifications, reinstalling it, and testing it.

This mechanic will also tell you what tools and equipment are required, about how many hours of labor it would take to do the job, and the cost of the parts. This person will gladly share this information with you because he knows that it's probably more than you can handle and that you're a potential customer for his services. He will also probably advise you that this is a huge undertaking if you've never done it before, and that they could do the entire job for a price in the neighborhood of what the cost of all the tools, equipment, and parts you'd need to do it yourself would be. Sure, he has a vested interest in trying to gain you as a customer, but by walking you through the process each step, he is showing good faith and sharing his knowledge, experience, and expertise with you. And the chances are pretty good that, if and when it's time to rebuild that engine, you'll give him the business.

The engine is the heart of any car and most owner-restorers want to be part of its assembly, but no matter how much you love assembly the really difficult technical parts of an engine rebuild have to be farmed out to a pro with machinery no enthusi-ast can—in his wildest dreams—justify buying. The basic choice for a restorer is: a) let the pro build the engine complete; or b) farm out the fussy machining and do the final assembly yourself. The first choice is simple, but more expensive. The second choice is more involved, but more emotionally satisfying. The thrill from first firing up an engine you've assembled yourself is pretty heady.

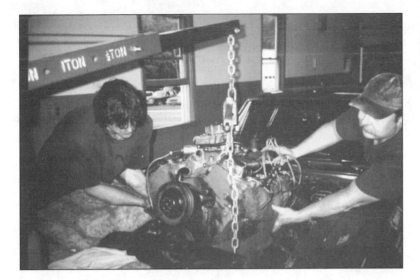

Rebuilding an engine requires skill, knowledge, and specialized equipment including an engine hoist and an engine stand, among other tools.

The same thing applies to bodywork, paint, upholstery, transmissions, suspension, and so forth. Ask professionals what is involved, including the tools and equipment required to do the job. Like the engine rebuilder, you are a potential customer, so a professional will be glad to share what he knows. And you'd be surprised how many people will offer their advice or pointers should you decide to do the job yourself and need some moral support along the way.

The Voice of Experience

Talk to folks who have finished vehicles like the one you want to restore. This is where you can really get the inside line on what is in store for you.

These people have already restored the same kind of car you're interested in restoring, so they know the little quirks and oddities of this particular model. From their first-hand experiences, they can offer a lot of advice and time- and effort-saving little tricks, and suggest tools or techniques to make the job go easier. More important, they can warn you of the problems you're likely to encounter and tell you how to work around them or bypass them completely. This is valuable information, so listen carefully and ask a lot of questions. The only really stupid question is the one you don't ask.

Compare Notes

Talk to many people and compare notes. Ask the same question to several folks who have restored a car that is similar to yours and see how their answers stack up against each other. If one person's answer is radically different from the rest, politely mention that you've heard something different from other people and ask him if there are exceptions or extenuating circumstances that made his experience unique.

You might want to ask questions such as these: Did you do all the mechanical work yourself? How about the bodywork and paint? The interior? How long did it take you? About how many hours would you say you have put into the restoration? These and other such questions will elicit a wealth of information.

Overdrive

Always have on your best people skills when speaking with people about their restoration experiences. Smile and make eye contact, compliment them on their cars, and have a pleasant demeanor. Remember, you're picking their brains, and they're sharing information and experience on a voluntary basis. Always be attentive while they're speaking, and don't interrupt them. Thank them verbally and with a sincere handshake. Another closing compliment about their cars never hurts, either.

Communication Is Everything—Talk it Out

Good communication will serve you enormously throughout your restoration project, so sharpening your communication skills is wise. Communicate effectively to your parts and service providers to tell them your exact needs and expectations to clear up any fuzzy or gray areas, and to help them help you more effectively.

Most professionals have vast experience. It's better to describe to them what you want in qualitative terms, describing how you want the car to appear, perform, and how you'll use it. Rely on their experience to interpret your qualitative goals in quantitative terms.

Don't run afoul of ordering up a "concours restoration" when you really mean "I want a car that I can show proudly at weekend shows within a 50-mile radius of my home." The restorer will see your checkbook as his kid's tuition at Harvard when all you really want is a thorough cleanup and body-on cosmetic restoration you'll be proud to drive to the Dairy Queen on Thursday evening. This is not the restorer's problem. He has a reputation to uphold. Delivering a Thursday DQ caliber car to someone who wants to be a contender at Pebble Beach won't do his reputation any favors, so he will err on the side of overdoing it. It's up to you to communicate clearly what you want.

Restoration Terminology

"Concours" restoration generally means taking every single piece of the car, right down to the hose clamps and cotter pins, and restoring or replacing each component to the highest possible condition using original parts, meticulously reproduced replacements, and the finest possible materials to build a car far better than it was when new. It can take half an hour to clean, debur, rethread, and refinish a single nut. At a good restoration shop's $50/hour rate, that makes it a $25 nut (plus its original cost.) The result of a concours restoration should be a condition 1 car that is above reproach, both cosmetically and mechanically.

A "Body off" restoration means that the car has been completely disassembled with all of the body and mechanical components taken off the chassis frame and rebuilt "nut and bolt" as it originally appeared when it came out of the original constructor's shop. A competent body-off restoration should give you a condition 2 car that will meet the highest standards of any marque judging.

A "Rotisserie" restoration is when the body and chassis frame are mounted on a frame that rotates like a barbeque grill's rotisserie so that all areas of the car can be accessed for cosmetic and mechanical attention without complete disassembly. A rotisserie-restored car will be a great drive, but you won't have the attention to detail that wins awards at the NCRS (National Corvette Restorers' Society) or JCNA (Jaguar Clubs of North America) judging.

Beware of the "complete restoration" description. It's dangerously vague because it depends on the speaker's concept of what "complete" means, or worse yet, what he wants you to interpret it to mean. I've seen cars described as "completely restored and finished last month" that barely rate a 3 on the condition scale.

Overdrive _____

A microcassette recorder and a digital camera are useful items to have on hand while "interviewing" people at car shows and cruise nights about their restoration experiences. Because some people really clam up if they see a tape recorder, you may want to keep it in your pocket while you're chatting with them. However, let them know you are recording the interview. Seek permission before recording someone. Also ask if you can take a picture or two of their car to use for your own reference, and ask to take a photo of them with their cars.

Seek and Ye Shall Find

If you don't know who to speak with, let that be the beginning of your search. Ask around at shows, cruise nights, or at car club meetings. Seek out marque clubs where the collectors of the car you want gather. Network with your friends to find a knowledgeable source. And when you find that source, continue to seek out references and other tangible evidence that this person is a good resource and is at the top of his game.

That's exactly what I did a few years ago when I needed to have my big block engine rebuilt. Because I have a matching-numbers car, I didn't want to go to a rebuilding chain like Jasper or Honest Engines for the work. I wanted *my own* engine rebuilt by hand, but I didn't know who to go to. I asked my friend Carl to bring it up at his next car club meeting, and he did. A couple of people recommended No Limit Performance in Morganville, New Jersey as a top-notch engine builder. I checked out No Limit's reputation and references, and the owner (Tom) gave me a tour of the shop and made recommendations on improving the overall performance of the motor. I agreed with him and therefore contracted No Limit to do the work. Because Tom's shop is about 50 miles away from me and he relies heavily on word-of-mouth referrals, I never would have found him if I didn't actively seek out a rebuilder who is known for quality work. I sought, I found, and I am happy with No Limit's excellent work. In fact, I've referred a few other people to Tom's shop.

You can also check out various Internet message boards and chat groups to find information on various service providers. These can be quite valuable in learning whether the shop does top-notch work or is a shoddy, rip-off house.

The Least You Need to Know

- Professionals are usually happy to answer your questions and tell you what's involved in their particular area of expertise.

- Due to their own experience with that vehicle, people who have done restorations on the same type of car you're interested in are a wealth of valuable information.

- Good people skills and communication skills are powerful assets for convincing people to share their valuable information and experiences with you.

- No matter what you need to know, the answers are out there. You just have to find them.

Chapter 10

Restoration Options

In This Chapter

◆ Is this correct?

◆ The quest for perfection

◆ Restoration levels

◆ Exceptions and compromises

◆ Leave it on or take it off

Depending on what your ultimate goal is, you can take several different restoration approaches, from a mild refreshing and the replacement of worn or broken parts to the complete disassembly of the entire vehicle. Herein we'll explore your various restoration options and the approaches you can take.

Restoration Options?

Of course you have options; this is your project, isn't it? You can decide how far you want to go in the restoration and the level at which you'll be satisfied and comfortable. To help you decide just what that level will be, we discuss everything from drivers to *concours* restorations, and everything in between.

How Correct Is Correct?

The term "correct" has different meanings for different people. Generally, it means that a part, component, or assembly matches the one that originally came on the vehicle. It can also mean that the vehicle is correct because it has all the right parts on it.

For example, let's say that you have a 1955 Chevrolet Bel Air that needs a motor. The correct motor would be either a 6-cylinder engine or a 265 CID V8 engine, provided that either of these engines had a 1955 date code. The date code is correct, so it is "a correct engine," even if it's not "the correct engine." Conversely, even though it looks identical, a 1956 engine would be incorrect. This example illustrates the strict definition of "correct" as it applies to restorations.

An example of a more relaxed definition of "correct" is a 265 CID 1956 engine in a 1955 being correct as long as it is still a Chevrolet motor. Incorrect, in this sense, would be putting a 1957 283 CID Chevy engine in the 1956 Chevy.

The strict definition of correct comes into play if you're going to be entering the vehicle in judged shows or you intend to sell the restored vehicle to a discriminating buyer. The relaxed definition works fine for local shows, cruise nights, and other such informal events or for the casual buyer who wants a cruising car.

Overdrive

Some of the best values in collector cars are meticulously restored cars that have just completed a year or two on the show/concours circuit. Many collectors enjoy showing their cars and to them a freshly restored car is a way to wangle an invitation to Pebble Beach, Amelia Island, Greenwich, or Meadow Brook. Once shown, a new project has to take its place and the old car is sold, usually at far less than the cost of its restoration alone. They aren't cheap, but they are a great value when they're sold—as they often are—for 50 or 75 cents on the restoration dollar. Best of all, the basic car is "free."

Do You Really Want Total Perfection?

You've probably heard the expression "be careful what you wish for—you may get it." Well, that's the case if you're going for a totally perfect restoration. When a collector car is restored to a full 100-point level, it ceases to be a functional vehicle and becomes a trophy to be displayed but never driven. It must be sheltered, protected, and pampered like a very expensive piece of art; it is transported in an enclosed trailer and will rarely, if ever, be started. In fact, some 100-point cars are rolled out of their trailers by hand and winched back in to prevent starting the motor. So, now the question is: Do you really want total perfection?

The trade-off to a restorer between absolute nut-and-bolt correctness and taking some liberties with correctness is very important. A '57 Chevy Bel Air convertible with its original from-the-factory fuel injected 283/283hp engine is today valued at well over $100,000, a rare and powerful early hint of the coming muscle car era. That same car but with a replacement engine block might be worth $100,000, while a spectacularly restored '57 Bel Air convertible with a correctly dated 283/283 Fuelie engine not originally delivered by Chevy in its chassis would be highly valued in the mid-seventies.

Collectors make allowances for cars that were raced, particularly dragged, when new. LS6 Chevelles, L88 Corvettes, Hemi Mopars, and 427 Fords were routinely blown up while questing for new low ETs (elapsed times) when new, and they are accepted with correctly date-coded replacement blocks as evidence of their history and competition.

Levels of Restoration

As previously mentioned, there are several levels of restoration, and there's bound to be one that will work for you. You'll see a correlation between the levels of restoration and the categories of condition we covered in Chapter 8.

- ◆ **Concours.** The *concours* level is the highest level of restoration, and a *concours* car is a 100-point vehicle. Everything down to the smallest detail is pristine and absolutely perfect in every respect.

- ◆ **Show.** A show level vehicle has undergone a professional restoration and has no major flaws.

- ◆ **Street Show.** Older street show vehicles may show some slight wear but still remain highly presentable. These can be older restorations or very clean, well-maintained original vehicles.

- ◆ **Driver.** Drivers are what you'll see most frequently. Doing a driver restoration is less expensive and time-consuming than restoring to any of the three previous categories. A driver restoration brings the vehicle back close to its original appearance, but it is still drivable.

> **Overdrive**
>
> Most collector car insurance companies' standard policies limit the miles you can drive your collector car to 3,000 to 4,000 miles a year. If you're going to be driving your collector vehicle a greater distance, you should consider an insurance policy that does not have mileage restrictions.

For Lack of a Nail the Kingdom Was Lost

If you intend to do a pristine and correct restoration with the goal of entering your car in judged shows or perhaps selling it for top dollar, you have a lot of homework to do to make sure that you do everything right. I'm still surprised at how some people spend small fortunes on restorations and miss first place because little details were not taken care of. Don't overlook things like hose clamps, screws, or bolts that may be incorrect and cost you points in shows or dollars if you want to sell the vehicle.

Overdrive

When estimating the costs for having an outside shop perform some services, remember to factor in the costs for time spent hunting parts and removing rust. These two items are the biggest expenses you'll encounter when using an outside source.

Parts frequently changed during production runs in a single model year. Elaborate books have been written about it, and specialist judges have searched factory records for the arcane minutiae of screws, clamps, joints, hoses, and wheels to refine the definition of "correct" to months and days. The best (and maybe the only) way to meet these esoteric criteria is to employ the best (and most expensive) specialist restoration shops that have expertise built from years of hard and costly experience.

Acceptable Exceptions and Logical Compromises

During your restoration you'll come to junctures where you may want to deviate from what was originally on the vehicle. I know of several folks who decided to upgrade their cars from manual to power steering and from manual to power brakes. Because these options were both available for their years and models, these were acceptable exceptions because they used the right factory components rather than aftermarket kits. I know of someone else who restored a 1969 vehicle that was equipped from the factory with a monaural AM/FM radio, even though a stereo radio was available as an option at additional cost. He located a 1969 stereo radio at a swap meet and bought it for $50 because it wasn't working. He sent it out to a house that restores and upgrades vintage radios, had them upgrade it using modern solid-state components, and installed it in his car. Because they used the original housing, it looks absolutely stock. The faceplate indicates that it is the optional FM stereo model; stereo it is, and big-time now, thanks to the modern electronics.

If you maintain a good degree of flexibility while doing your restoration, you'll be in a better position to make some logical compromises that can save time and money. For example, let's assume that you're restoring a 1965 Mustang with a 289 CID V8. The car runs, but sputters and dies frequently, and the diagnosis is a bad fuel pump. You have three choices: You can buy a kit for approximately $25 (plus shipping and handling) and rebuild the fuel pump yourself; you can order a "correct" replacement that will set you back about $90 from a Mustang restoration parts supplier; or you can go to the local NAPA store and get a fuel pump for about $28. If you're flexible, the logical compromise for saving time and money is to go with the NAPA unit. You'll come across many of these situations during your restoration project.

Another exception involves achieving cosmetic appearance while altering something internally. In this case, externally the car looks pretty much as it did on the showroom floor. If it's a pony car from the sixties, you might put a set of Cragar mag wheels on it because these were popular during that period, and you might also install a Hurst shifter for another custom "period" touch; other than that, the car basically looks stock.

Under the hood can be a totally different story, however. Instead of the anemic 6-cylinder the car was born with, you might decide to drop in a V-8 with some performance modifications to give it extra muscle, upgrade the suspension with air shocks, and replace the factory three-speed manual trans with a four-speed. These and many other modifications can be made while still maintaining cosmetic "correctness."

What to Do with the Frame

There are two trains of thought when it comes to collector car restorations. One is that to do a restoration the right way, the body should come off the frame; the other is to leave the body on the frame and work on it as a unit. There are pros and cons to both sides, so let's sort it all out here.

Leaving the Body on the Frame

Unless you intend to achieve *concours* or show level restorations, you'll want to leave the body on the frame while working on the project. This is certainly the most sensible and economical way to go for street stock and driver levels. You'll be able to do everything you need to restore the chassis with the body on by using a lift or tall jack stands. And because a body-on restoration takes less time and money, it's the way most folks choose to go.

Removing the Body from the Frame

A frame-off restoration entails total disassembly of the car, rebuilding or refurbishing every component, and totally reassembling the car. Removing the body requires special equipment including body slings, a hoist, and professional tools. It also requires a lot of space—usually three to four times the amount an intact vehicle requires. A frame-off restoration is not for the average enthusiast. It is very expensive, labor-intensive, time-consuming, and it requires a lot more skill and expertise than the average person has.

Don't Fix What Ain't Broke

Doing a restoration entails enough work repairing things that aren't functional or replacing incorrect parts or assemblies. You'll have your hands full, so don't go out of your way looking for extra projects that don't need attention. For example, if the windshield wiper motor in your project car works, leave well enough alone. Maybe give it a spritz of Spray Nine to clean the grease and gunk off, but why take it out of the car and disassemble it if it's working fine?

Total Disassembly

Although you may be tempted to do so, do not take the whole vehicle apart at once. If you do, you'll regret it. The total disassembly approach is the way many novices take and, more often than not, the ambitious project car quickly turns into a basket case. Taking everything off at once produces chaos and confusion. Although it is quite possible that by the time the restoration is finished the car may have been almost totally disassembled, ideally that will have been done in stages as individual systems and components were being worked on.

Restoring a Part at a Time

Restoring your vehicle one part at a time is the most sensible and orderly approach to restoration, and it's also the most time- and cost-effective way to go and you'll be able to use and enjoy your project car while it's being progressively restored. Let's use the engine as an example. Assuming it runs all right, rather than pulling the engine out of the car and disassembling the entire thing, concentrate on restoring individual components. Begin by removing the carburetor and rebuilding it. While the carburetor is off the motor, you might take the opportunity to repaint the intake manifold, tighten up the throttle linkage, and strip and repaint the air cleaner before your reinstall the rebuilt carb.

Restoring a collector car isn't one restoration; in reality, it's hundreds of smaller restorations that are all done to one vehicle. Think of it in those terms and the project will go much more smoothly.

The Least You Need to Know

- A 100-point car can't be driven and remain perfect.

- Restore your vehicle to the level that makes *you* happy.

- A restored vehicle is really a combination of many smaller restorations.

Party of the First Part

In This Chapter

- Using NOS and NOSR parts
- The skinny on OEM parts
- Getting reproduction, replacement, and used parts
- Interchangeable parts can cut costs
- Locating junkyard gems
- Finding parts sources for specific marques

Replacing worn, broken, or missing parts is a big portion of your restoration work. Parts come in several varieties and can be taken from a number of different sources.

This chapter will help you be more parts-savvy, which can save you time and money. Get ready to part-y!

Parts to the Left of Me, Parts to the Right …

There are different grades and classifications of parts, and some are more scarce and expensive than others. Knowing the differences between the grades and classifications is an asset because it allows you to make informed decisions about what part will be the correct or the most cost-effective choice for your particular restoration. This section explores what's out there in the way of parts.

NOS (New Old Stock) Parts

NOS parts are original parts in their original boxes that have been stored for several years. A NOS part is identical to the part used on the assembly line. These parts, produced by the automobile manufacturer while the cars themselves were on the assembly line, were made to supply the dealers' parts department with exact replacement parts for their customers. Because of their originality, NOS parts are usually scarce and command the highest prices of all the restoration parts choices. Very often, NOS parts have a natural patina caused by slight oxidation over the years; this gives them further credence as the real things that were made many years ago. For *concours*-quality restorations or if you wish to be as correct as possible, NOS parts are optimal if you can find them.

Overdrive

Going to car shows that feature swap meets as part of the agenda is an excellent way of finding the parts you need. Be sure to do some research to find out what the going rate is for the part so you don't overpay, and feel free to haggle over the price to get the best possible deal.

NORS (New Old Replacement Stock) Parts

NORS parts are original boxed parts that the original manufacturer or an aftermarket manufacturer made many years ago, usually to the same quality as the original part. These parts may not match assembly-line parts 100 percent, perhaps because of design changes during the production run. NORS parts were manufactured around the time the car was still new, so they also are scarce and command high prices. If you can't get an NOS part, an NORS part is usually the second-best choice for high-level restorations.

OEM (Original Equipment Manufacturer) Parts

OEM parts are replacement parts produced by and available from the original equipment manufacturers. For instance, say you need a distributor cap for a 1979 Mercury Cougar you're restoring. You can go with an aftermarket "generic" replacement part, or you can go to the parts department of your local Lincoln-Mercury dealer and purchase an OEM part. High-demand parts such as distributor caps, fuel pumps, and other items that eventually have to be replaced are usually kept in active production by OEMs as long as the demand for them maintains or exceeds a certain threshold. When sales drop below that threshold, the part is discontinued and becomes available from a reproduction source or an aftermarket producer. OEM parts are always more desirable than copies, and they are generally priced about the same.

Reproduction Parts

As the name implies, reproduction parts are reproductions of the original. They can vary significantly in quality from virtually identical to the original all the way down to a very phony-looking knockoff. Companies that are officially licensed by the original car manufacturer usually make the best reproduction parts. Very often, these parts are made using the original casting molds or machines the manufacturer used when the car was first built. Because licensing fees are hefty, officially licensed reproduction parts are more expensive than their nonlicensed counterparts.

Some reproduction parts have an identifier (like the letter "R" after the part number on a GM distributor cap) that indicates that it is a reproduction part; others won't have any identifier. Frequently, a licensed reproduction part is manufactured here in the United States, while a nonlicensed part may be produced in Korea, China, or other overseas location. As is usually the case, you get what you pay for, so purchasing officially licensed parts is your best shot at getting a reproduction part that looks, fits, and functions like the original.

> **4-Wheel Jive**
>
> If an automobile manufacturer still produces a replacement part for one of its vehicles and you can purchase it from a dealer's parts department, it is an OEM part. When the part is discontinued by the manufacturer, any remaining parts on the dealer's shelves automatically become NOS (New Old Stock) parts.

> **Pit Stop**
>
> When ordering electrical parts from a catalog or purchasing them over the counter, be absolutely sure the part you're getting is the exact item you need. Electrical parts are not returnable, so you won't be able to exchange it if it isn't right, nor will you get a refund.

Replacement Parts

Replacement parts are generic replacements that function like the original, even though they may differ in appearance. Examples of replacement parts are brake drums or rotors, brake shoes or pads, voltage regulators, horn relays, alternators, distributor caps, spark plug wires, and so forth. These parts are easy to get from the local NAPA or Pep Boys store and are significantly less expensive than the four previous categories of parts. In most cases they work just fine, and they are the most cost-effective and sensible way to go for driver restorations.

Used Parts

Used parts are exactly what the name says they are: parts that have been removed from vehicles that were used but are no longer in service. Frequently these parts are worn very little and are still quite serviceable and affordable. These parts can be had from salvage yards as well as parts dealers and individuals who are "parting out" a vehicle. Some clean up and refurbishment may be required to freshen-up used parts, but that's all part of the restoration process anyway.

Cutting Costs Using Interchangeable Parts

When it comes to parts, there's more than one way to skin a cat. Many parts from a given manufacturer's entire product line are used interchangeably on the various models and marques it produces. For instance:

- The alternator from a 1987 Ford pickup matches the alternator from a 1965 Mustang.

- The carrier assembly from a 1979 Ford LTD II interchanges with a 1968 Mustang.

- The torque converter in a 1981 Mercury interchanges with a 1969 Mustang.

- The fuel pump from a 1980 GMC van interchanges with a 1969 Camaro.

- The cylinder block from a 1978 Chevrolet Blazer interchanges with a 1971 Camaro.

- The transmission from a 1965 Chevrolet Corvette interchanges with a 1968 Camaro.

Knowing what interchanges with what can save you a lot of time, effort, and money. The ADP Hollander Company produces and publishes a line of interchangeable parts manuals as well as an overall interchangeable parts manual available on CD-ROM. Following are the marque-specific interchangeable parts manuals they produce in print, as of this writing:

- *The Hollander Camaro Manual—1967–1981*

- *The Hollander Chevelle Manual—1964–1972*

- *The Hollander Corvette Manual—1965–1982*

- *The Hollander Nova Manual—1968–1979*

- *The Hollander Mustang Manual—1965–1973*

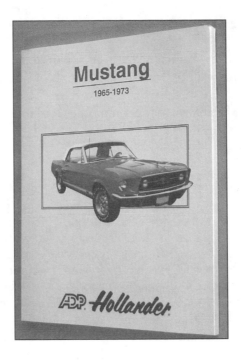

The Hollander Interchange parts manuals are a great way to save money and find out what alternative parts will fit on your project vehicle.

Hollander Interchange manuals help you identify interchangeable mechanical and body parts on most foreign and domestic vehicles—including light trucks—dating back to the 1920s. And if you're interested in restoration parts for a foreign marque, the *Hollander Interchange Classic Search Manual V* covers foreign vehicles from 1965 through 1975.

Whenever possible, I prefer to use electronic data rather than paper manuals, so the Hollander e-book CD-ROM suits my purposes ideally. Paper manuals inevitably get soiled by grease and oil when using them in the garage, whereas I can print out the data I need from the CD-ROM and use it in the garage. If it gets soiled, I can always print out another copy, because the CD-ROM is safe inside my den on a shelf. In addition to containing over 30 years of Hollander Interchange information, it also has a VIN decoder program, more than 3,700 images of wheels and wheel covers, dismantling worksheets, over 16,500 Hollander Interchange applications, updated coverage for all 134 active part types, and new coverage for Canadian models.

The print or CD-ROM version is entirely your choice. Without exaggerating, either is a must-have resource for knowing what parts are interchangeable with your restoration project. See Appendix A for Hollander's contact information.

Gems in the Junkyard

Once you've established what parts you need, a trip to the local salvage yard may be in order. You may also want to "visit" the hundreds of salvage yards available via the Internet as well as salvage yard databases. Scores of these yards offer rust-free parts from cars in Arizona, California, Texas and other low-moisture locales, and they will ship anywhere in the world.

Pit Stop

While salvage yards are excellent sources for getting the parts you need, be aware that some yard owners may seize the opportunity to capitalize on rarity, or at least perceived rarity. If the same air conditioning compressor that fits a 1979 Cougar is listed for $100, is listed as $75 for a Lincoln Town Car, and is listed as $50 for a Ford pickup, order the part for the Ford truck. You'll be getting the same compressor, but it will cost half as much as if you specified it for the 1979 Cougar. The reason is that it's a "vintage" part for the Cougar, for the Lincoln it is a "common car" part, but for the pickup it's just an "old truck part."

Parts Sources for Specific Marques

Numerous specialty houses cater to specific marques by selling their parts through catalogs and website stores. You can find them by performing web searches, but there is also another resource that makes finding the right parts source easy. Gardenof Speedin. com publishes parts locating guides in both print format and on CD-ROM. (See Appendix A for contact information.) The company guarantees that, using their guides, you'll find any part cheaper than through normal retail channels, and they back it with a 30-day money-back guarantee. As of this writing, they offer parts locating guides for the following vehicles:

- Ford Truck/Ranchero
- Mustang/Cougar
- Ford Lincoln/Mercury
- Full-Size Chevrolet
- Camaro
- Chevelle/El Camino
- Nova/Monte Carlo
- Chevy/GMC Truck

- Corvette

- Pontiac

- Buick

- Cadillac

- Oldsmobile

- Mopar

At $24.95 per copy, these parts locating guides are probably the best 25 dollars you can spend for your restoration. They also offer their guides on CD-ROM for $29.95 that include one make/model; access to an additional make/model on the CD-ROM is just an additional $9.95.

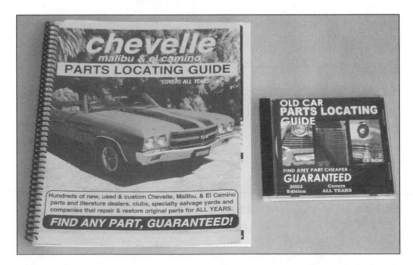

The parts locating guides are available in print or on CD-ROM from GardenofSpeedin. com. They make it easy to locate multiple vendors who have the parts you need.

You can also purchase the CD-ROM with full access to the 14 parts locating guides it contains for $99.95. As with the *Hollander Interchange Manuals*, these parts locating guides are essential restoration resources.

The Least You Need to Know

- Parts come in several varieties and from several sources.

- NOS and NORS parts are highly desirable, scarce, and expensive parts.

- Some parts have identifiers on them that indicate that they are reproductions.

- Using interchangeable parts can save a lot of time and money.

Part  3

Getting the Project Under Way

Okay, so you've decided on a car you'd like to restore—see how far you've come already since you first opened this book?

Now it's time to map out a game plan for the project. You're going to select your parts sources and service providers, decide on who will be performing the labor, and figure out how much time and money it's going to take to bring it all together.

Like a ship without a rudder, a restoration without a plan is bound to flounder—and it may even capsize!

Chapter 12

A Man with a Plan

In This Chapter

- ◆ Money management
- ◆ Haste makes waste
- ◆ Keep track of things
- ◆ Happiness is a good parts source
- ◆ Scavenging a parts car
- ◆ Scooping out service sources

We're almost ready to begin the project, but there are a few additional things we have to do so we can get off to a good start. We'll be getting all our ducks in a row, so to speak, as we firm up our plan of action.

Budgeting and Funding Your Restoration

Restoring a collector car is not just one project, it's a multitude of smaller projects. Having all these smaller projects completed makes the project's master plan come together more quickly and accurately. One of the biggest factors is working out the budget and financing, so that's the first project we'll work on.

Let's begin by formulating a budget. In addition to giving you a financial overview of the project expenses, it keeps you on track and helps prevent overspending. Overspending on some areas depletes necessary funds from other areas, and you may run out of money before the restoration is completed.

You can formulate your project budget using a pencil and ledger sheets, or by using your computer and spreadsheet software to work up your budget. The advantage of using the computer is that it allows you to add or subtract items and it will automatically adjust the totals for you.

There's also an inexpensive software program available called Vehicle Project Planner, which sells for approximately $10.00, that really speeds up budget creation and can generate several reports and keep track of your parts, part numbers, costs, vendors, their contact information, and much more. In my opinion, it is well worth the price.

The Vehicle Project Planner program makes keeping track of the project easy, and it can generate numerous reports.

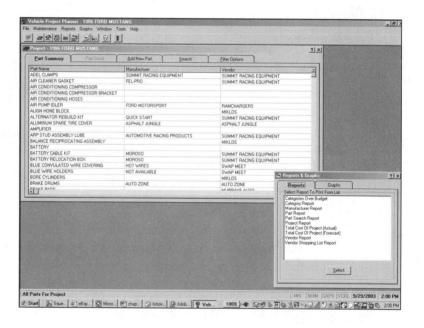

The nice thing about the Vehicle Project Planner program is that you can download it and use it for free for 30 days. The program also includes a sample restoration project of a 1986 Ford Mustang so you can get an idea of what the program can do to help you. If, at the end of 30 days you decide to keep it, you register the program and pay the $9.95 fee via your credit card or PayPal, and the company e-mails you a registration key number. You then enter this number in the registration box on the software screen and the program is unlocked for your full use. You can download your 30-day trial copy of Vehicle Project Planner by going to www.peedle.com/vpp/vpp.htm and clicking on the download button.

Whether you use a pencil and balance sheet or a computer spreadsheet, your budget should be divided into the following categories:

- Body
- Brakes
- Cooling System
- Electrical System
- Drive Shaft/Rear Axle
- Engine
- Suspension
- Exhaust System
- Gaskets
- Gauges
- Ignition System
- Fuel System
- Interior
- Weather Stripping
- Oil System
- Steering
- Transmission
- Valve Train
- Body Work
- Paint
- Plating and Bright Work
- Tools
- Labor

Each of these categories should list the parts that are required for that restoration segment and the amount you are budgeting for those parts. Use the parts prices on one supplier's catalog or website to get a base figure for the part, and add 15 percent to that price to cover the shipping and handling plus any applicable sales tax, and to cover any price increase over the life of the restoration. Add these prices together and make the total the amount you list in your budget. Remember, this is to get a budget in place so you have a realistic idea of what the entire restoration will cost. When you order the parts, you'll be shopping for the best price, so hopefully you can come in under the amount you're allocating in the budget.

Following is a short example of how your budget sheet should look:

Category: Brakes

Part	Total Cost	Budget Amount
Brake Pads (4 wheels)	$40	**$495**
Brake Rotors (4)	$300	
Front Brake Lines (stainless)	$30	
Rear Brake Lines (stainless)	$30	

continues

Part	Total Cost	Budget Amount
Front to Rear Line (stainless)	$70	
Fittings	$20	
Flaring tool	$10	
Flexible lines/chassis to wheels	$40	
Silicone Brake Fluid (quart)	$25	
Total Actual Cost:	**$565.00 (over budget by $70.00)**	

For outside services, such as rebuilding the engine or painting the car, obtain an estimate from a service provider and add an additional 20 percent to be on the safe side. Use this figure for your budget amount as well.

If you don't have a digital camera, consider adding the cost for one under the tools section. A digital camera is invaluable for taking pictures of parts before disassembly and for documenting the entire project, which is something you absolutely should do. Optionally, you can figure in the cost for throwaway cameras and processing, but digital is the preferred method because it allows you to immediately determine whether you have the shot or if you have to shoot it again.

Because things are bound to crop up in the restoration that can't be foreseen, it is a good idea to include a "miscellaneous" category as well. Enter an arbitrary amount that you feel comfortable with, say 1 percent to 2 percent, for the total budget amount. When you have figures in for everything, add all the budget amounts together and the resulting figure represents the total cost that you're forecasting for the project.

From this forecast, you can allocate the funds for each aspect of the restoration. You now have a plan with which you can proceed.

Also remember that this forecast budget isn't "cut in stone"; it is still flexible at this point, so adjustments can be made as required. Let's assume that, when you start working on the brakes, you discover that the rotors are good and they don't have to be replaced after all. Take that resulting $300 savings and drop it into the "miscellaneous" category for use toward something else you might need later. You might also want to make a notation on that entry like "brake rotors" so you know where the funds came from.

Rome Wasn't Built in a Day

Any restoration takes time, so you should also incorporate time into your budget to reflect how much time each segment should take to perform.

It's better to set up a separate ledger sheet or spreadsheet for the time forecast rather than adding it into the cost forecast, even though they are related.

Use the same format as for the cost forecast, but substitute time values instead of money values. Let's use the brake category for this example as well:

Category: Brakes

Part	Time Allocated	(Total Time = 6 hours)
Install brake pads	.5 for each pad	
Install brake rotors	2.0	
Install front lines	1.0	
Install rear lines	1.0	
Install front to rear line	1.0	
Fill and bleed system	0.5	

For outside services that you won't be performing yourself, include the time it will take to pack and ship the part or drive the assembly over to the service provider, as well as the time required to pick it up when it's finished. If, for example, getting the bumpers rechromed takes two weeks, but it only took one hour to wrap them and send them off to the plating company, enter one hour on the sheet rather than 2 weeks.

When you have time figures slotted in for all entries, add them up to get your total time allocation forecast. Arbitrarily, let's say the figure comes out to be 1,600 hours. Then figure how much time you're realistically willing to devote to working on the project each week. Most people do their restorations as a spare-time project, devoting a couple of hours one or two nights a week and a few hours over the weekend.

For purposes of illustration here, let's figure four hours during the week and six hours on Saturday, for a total of 10 hours per week. Divide that 10 hours per week into the total forecast of 1,600 hours to complete the project, and the result is 160 weeks. That equates to just over three years to complete in your spare time; however, this is a rough estimate because you have to consider things like Thanksgiving, New Years, and other holidays as well as when you're on vacation. Therefore, a more realistic time allocation forecast is 3.5 to 4 years for completion. Although it may seem like a long time period, any project worth doing is worth doing well, and restoring a collector car is no exception. Remember, Rome wasn't built in a day.

Document Everything!

You'll be amassing lots of information during the course of your restoration, so be prepared to keep lots of records. You can use whatever method of documentation you're comfortable with, from notebooks to index cards to computer database programs. The important thing is to have records of companies, contacts, phone numbers, addresses, websites, part numbers, manufacturers, magazines, and other resources that you've used for getting information so you'll have this information available if and when you need it as the project progresses. And don't forget to make notes about information you've gleaned from conversations with other people.

There's a computer database program available called CarRestore 2.5 that simplifies maintaining complete records of your restoration project and can handle four separate restoration projects. This program allows you to print, save, scroll, add, total, search, delete, and record all of your information. You can also add a new record at your convenience, or search for existing information. This program is easy to use while providing the means to keep a complete running record of your project. The downloadable trial version is limited to five records, but that is enough for you to decide whether this is a program you want to use for your project. The full version of the CarRestore 2.5 retails for $19.95, which I think is a good value. You can download the trial version at www.woodyg.com/carestore.html.

> **Overdrive**
>
> Even if you're using a throw-away camera, you can have a CD-ROM made when you have your film processed that contains digitized images. This is a good idea because you'll have digital photos that you can store on the computer or send via e-mail when you need parts or want to ask for advice about a particular aspect of the restoration.

CarRestore 2.5 is a Windows database program that tracks your time and money expenditures for the project. It's versatile and allows you to track the restoration of four separate vehicles simultaneously.

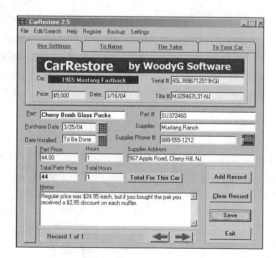

A Good Parts Source Is a Beautiful Thing

Every restoration project requires parts, and the search for parts is a very time-consuming element. This is why finding a good parts source is a beautiful thing, indeed. Resourcefulness in locating parts sources is something that shouldn't be underestimated, and there are many resources out there. Here are some you should consider.

Many parts supply houses have a "restorer's club" program that offers discounts to club members. These club arrangements differ from vendor to vendor, but following are some of the more common scenarios.

Some programs require a membership fee (usually approximately $25) to become a member. Once you're a member, you're entitled to a 10 percent discount on all parts purchases. Others don't give a discount, but they do provide free shipping to members. Either way, the membership fee is quickly amortized and the savings can be quite substantial over the course of the restoration.

Other vendors provide free membership and offer a discount when preset spending thresholds are met. For example, when your parts purchases total $750, you become eligible for a 10 percent discount on all purchases thereafter; when your total reaches $1,500, your discount may increase to 15 percent and then 20 percent when you reach the $2,500 mark.

Still other programs give you parts credits when you reach various spending levels. For instance, when you reach the $750 mark, you may get a bonus coupon or credit for $50 on your next parts purchase; similar to the discount scheme in the previous example, this credit can increase as your total expenditures reach higher levels.

These catalog suppliers offer these club memberships as incentives for you to purchase all your parts from the same source. Yet, while it's a good business idea for the vendors, it isn't always in your best interest to deal with one source exclusively, because you may be able to get a better deal on some parts elsewhere. Shop around by checking several different sources for the prices on the same items, and make a chart to establish whose price is the best. It doesn't have to be elaborate; something like this will do nicely:

Car: 1965 Mustang 289 CID V8

Part: Fuel Pump

'Stang Parts Source:	$39.95
Mustang World:	$39.95
Bill's Ford Supply:	$42.95

Ed's Blue Oval: $34.95

FoMoCo Joe: $37.95

Part: Running Horse Side Emblems (pair)

'Stang Parts Source: $19.95

Mustang World: $22.95

Bill's Ford Supply: $22.95

Ed's Blue Oval: $16.95

FoMoCo Joe: $20.95

Part: Tail Light Lenses (each)

'Stang Parts Source: $34.95

Mustang World: $34.95

Bill's Ford Supply: $34.95

Ed's Blue Oval: $32.95

FoMoCo Joe: $34.95

Part: Trunk Latch Emblem

'Stang Parts Source: $19.95

Mustang World: $19.95

Bill's Ford Supply: $19.95

Ed's Blue Oval: $19.95

FoMoCo Joe: $19.95

Part: Weather Stripping Kit

'Stang Parts Source: $89.95

Mustang World: $94.95

Bill's Ford Supply: $89.95

Ed's Blue Oval: $79.95

FoMoCo Joe: $94.95

In this example, Ed's Blue Oval has the best price on four of the five items, and the same price as the other vendors on the fifth item. So Ed's prices are the best bet when you add up all five items, even though he doesn't offer any discounts. A buyer's club might not be a bargain if another vendor has cheaper prices to start with, so shop around throughout the restoration process.

Even if you do become a member of one or more buyer's clubs, you don't have to purchase everything exclusively from them. Be a smart shopper and locate several sources for your parts so you can shop for the best price.

Considering a Donor Car for Parts

Depending on your particular restoration, acquiring a donor car as a major parts source might be a good way to go. There are pros and cons that you must consider, however.

On the plus side, major assemblies like front fenders, hoods, trunk lids, and other parts are expensive to purchase individually, and frequently you can purchase an entire donor car for what a couple of these parts alone would cost.

You'll have an intact vehicle to use as a reference for where everything goes while doing your restoration.

After you've taken everything you need off the donor car, you can sell the carcass to a scrap yard and recoup some of your original expenditure.

One downside is that you'll need additional space for the donor vehicle. If you intend to keep it in your driveway or next to your house, you must consider how your neighbors are going to feel about having what is likely to be an eyesore in the neighborhood, especially as you start dismantling it.

There's also a legal issue to consider. Some towns do not permit unlicensed or unregistered vehicles to be kept in a driveway or on the street, so check to make sure you won't be violating any ordinances.

Another downside might be the cost of the vehicle. If it's in fairly good shape, the price will be pretty high. If it's a rust bucket, it might be cheap—but for all practical purposes, it will be useless.

Before you shop for a donor car, do the following:

- Make a list of the parts you need.

- Ascertain the average prices for these parts from catalog sources if they're available new, or from salvage yards if you have to purchase them used.

- Add up the prices and figure in the shipping and handling or delivery charges to reach a total cost for the parts.

◆ Locate a donor vehicle that has all or most of the parts you need and whose parts are in better shape than those on your project car.

◆ Compare the price of the donor vehicle to that of the individual parts total, but be sure to factor in the time and material costs to refurbish the donor parts for a realistic comparison.

◆ Add on any towing costs or other expenses associated with getting the donor car to your location.

By completing these tasks, you'll be able to make an educated decision as to whether purchasing a donor vehicle is the most feasible and economical option for you.

At Your Service: Selecting Service Sources

There will undoubtedly be parts of the restoration that you'll purchase from various service sources. For example, refurbishing seat belts is a specialized task that may require derusting, plating, retractor spring replacement and new belting. This is certainly a task better left to a service company that does this as its main business.

As we did earlier with selecting a part source, make a list of the various automotive service providers for all the portions of the restoration you'll be contracting out. List the complete contact information for each source and the particular services they provide. Regardless of whether they're local or a distant service to which you'll ship parts for restoration, check out their references. Ask around at car shows and cruise nights to find out whether anyone has used their services and if it was a good experience.

Following are some of the services you'll probably need during your restoration:

◆ Chrome plating

◆ Upholstery

◆ Engine overhaul/rebuild

◆ Transmission overhaul/rebuild

◆ Rust repair

◆ Dent removal

◆ Painting

◆ Suspension bushing replacement

◆ Welding

While you may be up to doing some of these things yourself, many of these tasks require special equipment and some degree of skill. When you consider what the equipment may cost, it may be a more economical decision to procure that service rather than do it yourself. The time you save by having someone else tackle the task can be spent on other things that you *will* be doing yourself.

> **Pit Stop**
>
> When shopping for a chrome-plating service, beware of any service that is significantly lower than its competition. This is generally an indicator of a poorer-quality plating job. For example, if three plating houses quote a price of around $1,300 to plate the front bumper and a fourth house quotes $800 for the same job, that house is bound to take some shortcut. They may just buff the old chrome and re-dip the bumper, instead of giving it an acid bath and triple-plating it with nickel, copper, and chrome as it should be done.

Time Is On Your Side—Yes It Is

Our budget sheets have given us a pretty good idea how much the project will cost and how much time it will take. Keep in mind that you have time on your side. Remember, this is a hobby, and a hobbyist has all the time in the world.

If, for instance, you've had a hard week at work and you just want to kick back on the weekend, go ahead. You don't have to work on the restoration project if you don't feel like it. In fact, if you push yourself to work on it when you really aren't into it, you'll quickly look upon the restoration as drudgery instead of a pleasant pastime and you may start to resent or even hate the car.

When you're in the mood to work on the project, you'll be more productive. And remember that there are many tasks to be done, so if you don't feel like working on the brakes today, maybe you'll want to do something on the interior or find the electrical problem that is preventing the horn from working. Sooner or later, all these little jobs will have to be done, so make time work for you by using it wisely.

The Least You Need to Know

◆ Budgeting your time for the restoration is as important as budgeting your money.

◆ Documenting all your contacts, sources, and parts is a very important element of the restoration.

◆ Having several parts sources is generally better than restricting all your purchases to a single parts house.

◆ A donor car might be a cost-effective way to get the parts you need for your restoration project.

Who's Doing the Work Here?

In This Chapter

- Grabbing the brass ring
- How good are you?
- The experience equation
- Sweatin' on the oldies
- Getting and using tools
- Welcome to my garage

We're going to assess your skills, take inventory of the tools you'll need, set up our shop, and decide what jobs will be done by other people. We're also going to find out how you can save money—even on jobs you'll be contracting out.

The Work and the Worker

Who is doing the work? This a fundamental question that you're going to answer in this chapter. While it is entirely conceivable that you'll want to do the lion's share of the restoration yourself, there are bound to be some jobs that you should contract out. How many of these jobs get sent out depends on your skills, abilities, tools, equipment, working space, and know-how.

The Road to Hell Is Paved with Good Intentions

This old expression holds true to car restorations. I suspect everyone, myself included, to some degree falls victim to grandiose visions of how they're going to have a head-turning collector car when they're finished, and how they'll take pride in proclaiming, "I did it all myself." The reality is that, unless you're extraordinarily talented, you won't do it all yourself. There's no shame in contracting out jobs that are beyond your abilities or capabilities because of equipment or other extenuating circumstances. The important thing is to know when you're going to be in over your head and acknowledge it.

Be Realistic About Your Abilities

It's important not to kid yourself about your own abilities. For a realistic assessment of your abilities, answer these questions honestly:

- Have you ever done any bodywork (pulling out dents, using body filler, replacing panels, and so on) to a vehicle?

- Have you ever reupholstered a car seat or replaced an inner door panel or a headliner?

- Have you ever painted a car?

- Have you ever used a MIG welder?

- Have you ever used an oxyacetylene torch?

- Have you ever removed an engine or transmission?

- Have you ever rebuilt an engine or transmission?

- Have you ever taken apart a dashboard and removed gauges?

- Have you ever rebuilt a carburetor?

- Have you ever overhauled a car's front and rear suspension?

- Have you ever worked on a car's electrical system?

- Have you ever performed any brake work on a vehicle?

- Have you ever done any sandblasting?

Everyone has different aptitude and ability levels. Some things come naturally to certain people, while they are all but impossible for others. Some of the tasks on the list, such as rebuilding a carburetor or overhauling brakes, are fairly easy to do even if you've never done them before. Others, such as removing and rebuilding an engine, require more skill and special tools and equipment. In later chapters you'll see what's involved in all of these aspects and you can determine then whether it's a task you want to tackle yourself. I'm sure there are several jobs you'll want to do and others that you'll want to contract out.

Are You Experienced?

Experience is a wonderful thing because it teaches you while you're acquiring it. Even if you've never used an automotive tool in your entire life, restoring a collector car will give you a wealth of experience and you'll be amazed at how much you know about your vehicle when the project is completed. In fact, you'll be amazed at how much you've learned after working on your project for just a couple of weeks.

If you have any previous automotive experience working on cars, that's a definite asset you'll bring to the table when starting your restoration project. If you've rebuilt an engine in your youth, for example, it's a lot like riding a bicycle: It all comes back to you even if you haven't done it for several decades. From that experience you'll also be able to decide whether you want to do it again or let someone else do the heavy work while you concentrate on less demanding chores.

If it's something you've never done before, such as rebuilding an engine, and you think you might like to try it, there are several excellent books and videos available on the subject that show you how to do it step-by-step. Just peruse the "automotive how-to" shelves of your local bookseller and you're sure to find at least one helpful book.

Once again, you'll have to do some homework to decide what tasks you think you can do and want to try, and those for which you'll contract outside sources.

Sweat Equity

There are ways to save money even on the jobs that you'll contract out during the restoration. Doing some of the work yourself as a means of cutting down the cost of outside services is known as *sweat equity*.

An example of sweat equity is removing the transmission yourself and bringing it to the rebuilder rather than having the car towed to the shop for transmission removal. By removing the transmission from the car yourself, you're saving on a towing charge and an hour of labor for the rebuilder to remove it. Sweat equity is money in the bank—money that can be used for other things in the project.

Another example of sweat equity is prepping the car for paint. By removing chrome and other trim parts, stripping the paint, and masking the vehicle yourself instead of having the body shop do it, you can save a considerable amount of labor charges. Frequently, they'll let you do the masking right in their facility, too. And after the car is primed, you may also do the wet sanding yourself to save even more.

A further example of sweat equity is removing the vehicle's radio and bringing it to the repair shop rather than having them remove it. There are many things that you can do to lower your outside service costs by doing the removal and reinstallation yourself. Sweat equity can dramatically reduce your outside labor costs. You'll gain experience from doing this work, to boot.

While we're on the subject of sweat equity, you may have a particular skill that you can swap with another person who is also doing a restoration, in exchange for that person's labor in another area. Let's say that you're good at installing new seat covers and working on car interiors. Joe, a fellow you met at a cruise night and who is also doing a restoration, is quite good at replacing rusted panels, but interiors are his weak point. You need the quarter panels on your project car to be patched, and Joe needs an interior. You could strike a deal with him to do his interior if he'll do your panel repairs. This way both of you get the required work done, and the only out-of-pocket expenses are for the actual parts, rather than parts *and* labor. And when you also factor in that Joe owns a MIG welder, you save money because you don't have to purchase one for yourself.

To take it a step further, you may have tools that Joe needs and vice versa. By loaning each other tools you can both save money and have the tools you need to do the job properly.

Do You Have Tools and a Place to Use Them?

I admit to being a tool junkie. I love tools, and I have many that I've acquired over the years. I inherited some tools from my dad, but the vast majority of them were purchased over several decades.

There are some basic tools that you'll need regardless of the level of restoration you intend to do. There are other specialized tools and pieces of equipment that you won't need unless you're going to tackle some major jobs like engine removal and rebuilding yourself. Still other jobs, like replacing rusted panels and other bodywork, will require specific tools. Let's explore what you'll need for different aspects of the restoration.

I'm a big fan of American-made tools because, in my experience, they are the best tools you can get. I've used tools manufactured overseas, and they wear out or break; they also frequently don't fit the nuts and bolts properly, causing rounded edges.

While there are several excellent American tool manufacturers, including Stanley, SK, Snap-On, Mac and Matco among others, I prefer Craftsman for the following reasons:

♦ They're readily available from any Sears store nationwide.

♦ They're well made and affordable.

♦ They offer almost any kind of automotive tool imaginable.

♦ They carry a lifetime replacement guarantee: If any Craftsman tool ever breaks, wears out, or ceases to function, Sears will replace it on the spot, without any hassle. That's my kind of guarantee.

The Basic Tool Complement

Following is a list of what you'll need at the very minimum:

♦ **Screwdrivers.** As with everything tool-related, you get what you pay for. Purchase good screwdrivers with hardened tips and comfortable handles. Don't be tempted to buy cheap screwdrivers because they will wear out and have to be replaced soon. A rule of thumb with tools is "buy cheap and you'll buy often." Screwdrivers probably illustrate this point best. A minimum of three flat-blade and three Phillips heads is essential, but more of each type in various lengths is highly desirable. For the flat-blade screwdrivers, get one thin, one medium, and one wide blade for starters. For the Phillips heads, get a #1, a #2, and a #3 blade.

I'm also a big fan of the rechargeable pistol-grip electric screwdriver, which I use very often. It's a great timesaver and it's inexpensive—definitely a worthwhile investment to consider.

♦ **Pliers.** A good starting pliers assortment includes a pair each of straight slip-joint pliers, long needle-nosed pliers, offset slip-joint pliers (also sometimes called water-pump pliers), and a pair of side cutters. A pair or two of Vice-Grip pliers or other locking pliers in medium and large sizes is a good bet as well. I'd also add a couple of surgical hemostats (vein clamps), a pair of long tweezers and spring-loaded, plunger-activated mechanical "fingers." The tweezers and mechanical fingers are useful for retrieving small items like nuts or washers that were inadvertently dropped into inaccessible places during disassembly or reassembly.

You'll need a wide assortment of pliers for many tasks during your restoration project. Be sure to include a pair of spring-loaded "mechanical fingers" as well.

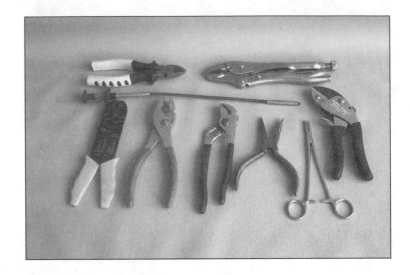

◆ **Wrenches.** A good set of combination wrenches is essential. These are wrenches that are open on one end and closed (or boxed) on the other end. The box end is great for breaking a nut loose or tightening it, while the open end is used for removing the nut completely when it is loose. I also recommend buying a set of gear wrenches. These are wrenches that have a ratchet built into the box end; they are great for reaching nuts in spots where a regular socket won't fit. A set of line wrenches is good to have for work on brake and fuel lines. These are specially reinforced box wrenches with openings cut into the boxes to allow the wrench to pass over the fuel or brake line to grasp the fitting. Normal open-end wrenches are prone to rounding the edges of the fitting, so line wrenches are the way to go for this kind of work.

High-quality combination wrenches and flat-blade and Phillips screwdrivers are essential tools. You'll also find that a set of gear wrenches, shown at the lower right, makes many jobs easier and faster.

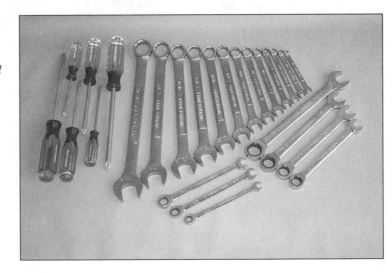

Be sure to get wrenches that are of the correct standard for your car. American cars used the SAE standard through the late 1970s, when a combination of SAE and metric came into use. British cars used the Whitworth standard through the 1960s, and cars of European and Asian manufacture use the metric standard.

Hammers. Having a small brass mallet, a medium ball-peen hammer, a soft-faced rubber, rawhide, or fiberglass mallet, and a 5-pound sledge hammer will cover you pretty well.

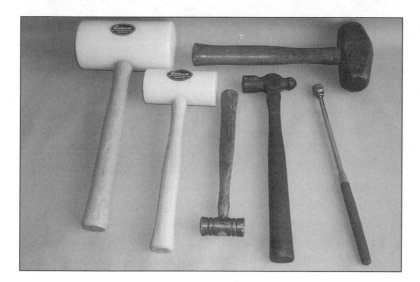

Assorted mallets and hammers make "persuading" tough parts easier. The fiberglass mallets are used for some light chores, while the heavier steel ones are primarily for chassis, suspension, and other jobs that require more oomph.

◆ **Sockets and Ratchet Drivers.** A good set of sockets and drivers is essential for a restoration. Sockets come in three sizes: ¼-inch drive, ⅜-inch drive and ½-inch drive; they also come in shallow and deep lengths, and in 6-point and 12-point versions.

You'll also need a couple of extensions (6 inches and 12 inches should do nicely). While you'll use the ⅜-inch sockets most of the time, there are many occasions when the ¼-inch set will be required for finer work and the ½-inch set will be used for heavy-duty work. As opposed to buying three individual sets, you can save money by purchasing a complete set that includes all three sizes.

Don't attempt to skimp by thinking a ⅜-inch drive adapter that accepts ½-inch sockets will work. The ⅜-inch drive handles aren't up to the demands of busting loose a big rusty suspension bolt. And, speaking of rusty bolts and nuts, which you'll encounter repeatedly, get a long and strong "breaker bar" handle for both the ⅜-inch and ½-inch sockets. It will become your best friend.

Don't skimp on quality because you'll use sockets and ratchets extensively throughout the project. The new laser-etched sockets from Craftsman (left) enable you to see the socket size easily, even at a distance. A ³/₈-inch drive shallow and deep set are shown at the left, while a ¹/₄-inch drive shallow and deep set are shown at the right. You'll also want to get a ¹/₂-inch drive set for heavier restoration chores.

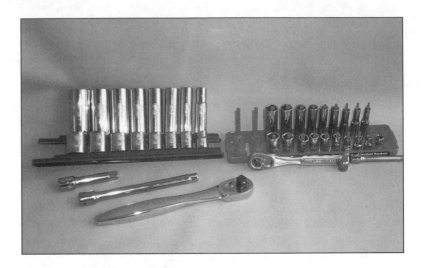

♦ **Electrical Tools.** A good multimeter is essential for testing and troubleshooting electrical problems. But rather than just buying a general-purpose multimeter, get one that has automotive functions, such as dwell tachometer measurements, built in. A soldering iron, rosin-core solder, and a pair of wire stripers should be standard equipment in your electrical tool box, along with a crimping tool for squeezing electrical connectors on wires. Electrical tape and a fuse puller are also must-haves, as well as a low-voltage circuit tester for checking "hot" wires. An automotive electrical faultfinder, though expensive, is a good tool to have if you can spend the extra money for one. Also, a portable battery jumper box is another good item to have on hand, and you can use it for your "normal" car as well as your collector vehicle.

A good automotive multimeter is a great tool to have, and this one (right) even comes with an inductive pickup attachment for checking tach and dwell settings. A low-voltage circuit tester (center) is also a handy tool to have, while wire strippers and a crimping tool, along with assorted electrical connectors, round out the picture.

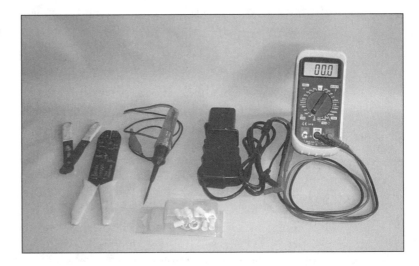

- **Pop Rivet Tool.** Every shop should have a good quality pop rivet tool and an assortment of pop for many fastening jobs. I prefer a pop rivet tool with a swivel head because it makes life easier when riveting in tight spaces.

- **Steering Wheel Puller.** This is an inexpensive tool that is indispensable for removing the steering wheel from the steering column. It is all but impossible to get the steering wheel off without one.

- **Hack Saw.** A hack saw and an assortment of blades will come in handy for numerous cutting jobs.

- **Dial Micrometer.** A dial micrometer is useful for determining the thickness of items such as brake drums and rotors.

- **Allen Wrenches.** These hexagonal "L" shaped wrenches are used for loosening and tightening set screws and socket-head bolts. They come in SAE and metric standards.

- **Pry Bars.** These are useful for persuading stubborn parts and assemblies.

- **Tap and Die Set.** It is inevitable that the threads of some assembly on the vehicle will be stripped, and that's where a tap and die set comes in handy. The taps are used to rethread the receiver holes in an assembly, while the dies are used to rethread bolts or threaded studs. These sets are available in SAE or metric.

- **Easy-Outs.** Sooner or later, you'll snap a bolt head off while attempting to remove it. When this happens, easy-outs are the solution. You drill a hole in the center of the remainder of the bolt, insert the easy-out in the hole, and give it a light tap to seat it; then, turn the easy-out with a wrench to remove the bolt.

- **Telescopic Wand Magnet.** Every shop should have a telescopic wand magnet. They are great for retrieving bolts, nuts, washers, or small parts that were inadvertently dropped and landed in hard-to-reach places.

- **Hand-Held Die Grinder.** A Dremel or other hand-held die grinder is a useful tool to have in your shop, and it is inexpensive. For small jobs like grinding out pop rivets to buffing small pieces, you'll be surprised at how often you will put it to work. You might also want to purchase a flexible-shaft attachment, which will add to its versatility and usefulness, especially in hard-to-reach places.

- **Torque Wrench.** You will need a good ½-inch drive torque wrench with a 30 to 150 foot-pound range if you rebuild the engine yourself. The torque wrench is used to make sure all of the critical nuts and bolts in the engine are tightened to the proper torque indicated by the manufacturer, as well as other nonengine fasteners including lug nuts. Torque wrenches come in three varieties: the older analog style has a needle mounted near the handle, the newer clicking style makes clicking noises when the desired torque setting has been reached, and the digital torque wrench has an LCD readout window indicating the torque. Of the three, the clicking style is the most accurate.

◆ **Assembly Manual.** The assembly manual is absolutely essential because it contains the actual assembly instructions and exploded views used by the assembly line workers when they built the vehicle in the first place. These manuals are fairly easy to obtain for cars built from the early 1950s and later, although they can also be found for many earlier vehicles with a bit of diligent searching.

◆ **Factory Shop Manual.** The factory shop manual, like the assembly manual, is the official book of procedures detailed by the manufacturer for disassembling, repairing, and reassembling the various components of the vehicle. In addition to procedures and sequential instructions for disassembly and reassembly, it contains essential listings for dimensions, tolerances, and fastener torque. This is another essential document you should have on hand for your particular model year, and you can usually get it from the same sources that sell assembly manuals.

◆ **Parts Book.** The parts listing for your car is absolutely essential. Not only is it the prime reference for the particular original part numbers, but its drawings and diagrams are an instruction book on how individual assemblies go together (Where does this little spring go? Oh, yeah, here it is in the parts book going between the cover and bracket.)

A factory shop manual for your project vehicle is not a luxury; it's an absolute necessity. Some shop manuals, like this one for mid-year Corvettes, are also available on CD-ROM and print versions.

The Advanced Tool Complement

If you're going to be doing more advanced aspects of the restoration yourself, you'll need these tools on hand as well:

- **Cylinder Hone.** A cylinder hone is a tool that has three honing stones attached to spring-loaded arms. It is used to hone the engine's cylinders to remove varnish and clean the metal walls. The hone is used with an electric drill and moved up and down the cylinder to give it a uniform surface.

- **Coil Spring Compressor.** If your project car has coil suspension springs, you need a coil spring compressor to compress and remove the springs so you can work on the suspension. The compressor has a pair of upper and lower hooks that grab the top and bottom of the spring coils. The hooks are attached to a threaded steel rod; when the rod is rotated clockwise, the hooks are pulled closer together, thus compressing the spring.

- **Hog Ring Pliers and Fabric Stretching Pliers.** These tools are used for doing interior upholstery work. The hog ring pliers are used to compress the upholstery clips, called hog rings; the fabric stretching pliers make pulling the seat cover fabric over the frame easier than using your bare hands.

- **Body Lift Sling.** A good body lift sling can make the removal of the nose of the vehicle and even the entire body of the car easy, especially when used in conjunction with a cherry picker or an overhead chain hoist.

- **Chain Hoist.** This is something you'll want to have if you're going to do heavy lifting for tasks like engine removal or removing the body from the frame. Because the hoist attaches to an overhead point, such as the beams of the garage, be sure the beams can sustain the weight you'll be lifting. Most wooden ceiling beams in a home garage can't handle the weight of an engine, although the complete nose assembly of a car usually isn't a problem.

- **Bodywork Tools.** Assorted hammers and dollies are useful for doing bodywork, as are files and a dent puller.

Setting Up Shop

Assuming you'll be doing the restoration in your garage, you'll have to outfit it with the equipment you'll need to do the job properly. Setting up shop isn't hard to do, but you should give it some thought because a sensible layout will make life easier and enhance your productivity. Following are the essential components of a well-equipped garage shop:

♦ **Hydraulic Floor Jack.** I recommend a 2-ton or, better yet, a 3-ton capacity unit. With tools such as jacks and jack stands, stronger than necessary is a definite benefit because it provides some added insurance. By all means, stay away from the "bargain" import models; common sense tells you that a jack selling for $49.99 can't be anywhere near as good or as sturdy as one that sells for $199.95.

♦ **Jack Stands.** Jack stands, which are used to support the car after it is jacked up off the ground, come in several varieties and large and small sizes. Be sure to buy a pair (they're not sold individually) with a minimum of 2-ton capacity; again, stronger is better, so spend a few dollars more and get a pair that is rated for 3 tons. The shorter ones are usually about 12 inches closed and 17 inches fully opened; the larger ones are usually 15 inches closed and 24 inches fully opened. The larger ones are the way to go for doing major work under the car if you don't have a lift. Because this work will be done while you're on your back, the extra elevation makes navigating under the car a bit easier.

Pit Stop

Never get under a vehicle that is not supported by jack stands. A hydraulic floor jack is designed and intended to get the car off the ground, but not to support it; jack stands are made for this purpose. Using a hydraulic jack to support the vehicle is foolish and dangerous.

Pit Stop

Don't use droplights with incandescent bulbs. In addition to the inordinate amount of heat they generate, the bulbs shatter easily, and therefore, have the potential for cuts from broken glass. Worse yet, if a solvent or gasoline drips onto the hot bulb, it will shatter and the resulting spark can ignite the liquid and start a fire.

♦ **Lighting.** You must to be able to see what you're working on, so good lighting is crucial. A small flashlight is a must, and I have personally disassembled several car dashboards with a mini-flashlight clenched between my teeth. Another essential is a good shop light. I prefer using a fluorescent shop light with a 25-foot cord, because it throws a lot of light and it remains cool to the touch. The older droplights with incandescent bulbs get much too hot, as do the quartz halogen shop lights. You can buy shop lights that use super-bright LEDs, and these are virtually indestructible, albeit expensive. They throw an amazing amount of light, however, and you can get them in AC (wall outlet) or DC (cigarette-lighter powered) configurations. You'll need plenty of light, so you might be able to justify the expense of an LED work light if you can save money elsewhere on the project.

♦ **Air Compressor.** You don't need a large, industrial air compressor, just one that can fill your tires and power some air tools. A compressor with a 30-gallon tank and 120 psi maximum pressure should be perfectly adequate for any restoration work you're likely to do yourself. I find that recoiling the air hose after use is a pain, so I invested in an automatic air hose reel. When I'm finished using the compressor, I give the hose a sharp tug and it automatically reels the hose back in—no muss, no fuss! If you don't think you'll be using your compressor very often, this is a luxury item. If you're going to use the compressor often, you will appreciate the convenience and will find an automatic hose reel to be a good investment.

♦ **Air Tools.** I like tools that make my life easier, give me a mechanical advantage rather than "armstrong" power, and make the job go faster. Air tools do all of these things. You don't have to spend a lot of money on them, because you probably won't need every air tool made. And remember that you don't have to go out and buy all your tools at once; add tools as they're needed for various jobs on the project. For a starting collection of air tools, I recommend getting a ⅜-inch drive air ratchet and a ½-inch drive impact wrench. You must use special impact sockets with an impact wrench—normal hand sockets are not strong enough and may shatter when subjected to the impact wrench's pounding. Later you might want to add a cut-off tool, a nibbler tool, an air chisel, an orbital sander, and a minisander for body and metal working.

♦ **Work Table or Bench.** A work table or work bench is also a necessary piece of shop equipment. To save space, you may want to get a collapsible unit that stows compactly when not in use. In addition to a work bench, I also have an old buffet from a dining room set that gives me additional bench surface for working. Its drawers and side compartments also provide tool and supply storage.

♦ **Oxyacetylene Torch.** A gas welding torch setup isn't an absolute necessity for most restorations, but it's nice to have for heating up frozen bolts, doing chassis repairs and other jobs where intense, concentrated heat is needed.

♦ **MIG Welder.** A MIG welder is required if you're going to be replacing rusted-out body panels or other jobs where you need precision welding. Unlike the oxyacetylene torch, a MIG welder uses an electrical arc and an inert, nonflammable gas (usually Argon) to isolate the metal from air, thus producing a hotter, stronger weld. The prices on MIG welders have come down considerably, so you can purchase a decent one for a few hundred dollars that includes all the requisite accessories (such as an eye-shield dimming mask).

♦ **Welding Gloves.** Whether you do gas or arc welding, a good pair of gauntlet-type leather welding gloves will protect you from burns.

♦ **Nitrile Gloves.** You don't have to have greasy, grimy hands while working on your restoration project. Nitrile gloves are available at many auto parts stores and mail-order automotive and restoration supply houses. Sold in boxes of 100, they're much more durable than latex gloves, which many people are allergic to. Nitrile gloves are thin and flexible and stand up well to contact with grease and solvents.

◆ **Plastic Bags.** Plastic bags of various sizes are useful for storing parts with their requisite hardware before and after they are restored. Zip-lock sandwich bags are especially useful because of their self-sealing feature. Larger garbage bags can be used for bigger parts and assemblies. Don't forget to label the bags to make part identification and inventory easier.

◆ **Shop Rags.** While you can purchase shop rags at the local auto parts store, why spend the money? Recycling those old towels and T-shirts is the more economical way to go. Because shop rags are usually used for cleaning up spills or wiping grease and grime from parts you've taken off your project car, almost any lint-free fabric can be used.

CAUTION

Pit Stop

Plastic or metal containers for hardware and other small shop items are preferable because they won't shatter and break like glass baby food jars or other glass containers.

◆ **Paper Towels.** Handy for so many wipe-up tasks, no shop should be without a roll or two of paper towels.

◆ **Spray Nine.** This is a very versatile spray cleaner that's great for wiping down the work bench and other areas that need to be cleaned of dirt and grime. It's also excellent for degreasing parts.

◆ **Parts and Hardware Containers.** Without a doubt you're going to need a lot of these and you can be very creative here. Almost anything can be used to hold small parts and hardware such as nuts and bolts, washers, and so forth. I use translucent 35 mm film canisters for the really small stuff, and old coffee cans and cookie tins for the larger stuff. Transparent plastic containers you can usually pick up at the local flea market work well, as do old Tupperware containers. And don't forget the snap-lid containers used for Chinese take-out. The rule of thumb here is that if it works, use it.

◆ **Magnetic Trays.** These are very handy items that are great for holding nuts, bolts, washers and other small iron or steel parts that are likely to get misplaced during disassembly or reassembly. They come in a variety of sizes as well.

◆ **Respirator.** You should always use a respirator when working with solvents or paints and when sandblasting outside of a blasting cabinet. The respirator keeps harmful minute particles from entering your air passages, and it should be used in conjunction with appropriate eye protection.

◆ **Extension Cords.** Have a couple of these in various lengths to get the power to the electrical equipment, lights, or tools you'll be using on your project.

◆ **Sandblaster.** Having a good sandblasting cabinet in your shop makes life a lot easier when restoring rusted parts. You put the part into the cabinet and blast it with abrasive media (sand, glass beads, silicon carbide, aluminum oxide, or other media) to clean it up and make it look like new. The advantage of the cabinet is that the media can be recaptured and used again. If money is tight, you can purchase a suction-feed or gravity-feed sandblast gun for under $50 and use an old shower curtain or tarp to catch the blasting media. When using this method, doing it outside is better than working indoors, although your neighbors may not be too crazy about sand or other media flying about. Eye protection and a respirator should always be worn when blasting outside of a cabinet.

◆ **Pad, Pens or Pencils, and Markers.** There will be many times when you'll have to jot down a measurement or make a note or reminder for yourself about a part number or date code, so keep these items on hand. Put the pad on a clipboard along with the pen on a string, hang it on the wall, and you'll always have it there when you need it.

◆ **Tape.** Masking tape and duct tape are both handy items to have in the shop for various tasks.

◆ **Denatured Alcohol.** It is a good idea to have this excellent solvent on hand. I buy it in half-gallon cans and refill a small jar as needed. It's great for removing gunk and grease as well as gummy sticker residue from parts.

◆ **Lubricants.** Lithium grease is useful for heavier lubricating jobs like packing bearings, while 3-in-1 Oil is more suited to lighter, more delicate lubricating jobs. An old-fashioned oilcan filled with clean motor oil is also useful for lubricating the moving parts of assemblies, such as vent control cables.

◆ **Rust Penetrant.** Soaking rusted nuts and bolts with a good rust penetrant often makes the difference between extracting the bolt intact or struggling with it and snapping it in the process.

◆ **Steel Wool and Sandpaper.** It's good to have various grits of sandpaper and some steel wool pads to remove the rust from parts.

Overdrive

Establish the good work habit of putting tools and other things back where they belong as soon as you're finished using them. Working in clutter causes unnecessary confusion, reduces productivity, and increases the chances for accidents. Work smart and work neat.

Pit Stop

Never smoke or have an exposed flame when working with flammable liquids like denatured alcohol or other solvents. This also goes for using a grinding wheel or other items that may produce sparks while the solvent is exposed. Fire is dangerous, so take the proper precautions at all times to prevent it.

- **Two-Wheel Bench Buffer/Grinder.** A good two-wheel bench buffer/grinder will come in handy for numerous restoration tasks. A wire wheel on one side and a buffing wheel on the other can be used to clean and polish parts, while a course grinding wheel on one side and a finer wheel on the other can be used for smoothing welds and other grinding chores.

- **WD-40.** WD-40 is a lubricant and moisture-eliminator that is great for many other uses, such as getting spray paint and grease off your hands. Always keep a can on hand.

- **Cotter Pins, Bailing Wire, Scissors, Ruler, Utility Knife, and so on.** You'll be surprised how handy these items are to have around once you start doing your restoration. And you'll also find it useful to have an ice pick or an awl and single-edge razor blades at your disposal.

Overdrive

Always keep a fully charged fire extinguisher in your garage. Get an extinguisher that is rated for A-B-C fires ("A" is for ordinary combustibles like paper, "B" is for combustible liquids like gasoline or solvents, and "C" is for electrical fires). A 15-pound extinguisher is the smallest one you should consider.

- **Bench Vise.** A large steel bench vise is a very useful tool. In addition to using it to clamp parts and hold them stationary, it can also be used as an anvil for many chores.

- **Shop Vacuum.** A good wet/dry shop vac on wheels is excellent for keeping the shop clean and tidy.

- **5-Minute Epoxy, Instant Glue, Automotive Spray Adhesive.** Good items to have on hand for those impromptu fastening and repair jobs that pop up totally unexpected.

- **First Aid Kit.** A first aid kit is a must-have item—or at the very least a box of band-aids and some disinfectant like peroxide or isopropyl alcohol. We're talking about your health and well-being here, so this is no area to skimp on. Accidents can happen to even the most careful restorer, so take a tip from the Boy Scouts and be prepared.

- **Safety Goggles.** These eye protectors are so important and inexpensive that you shouldn't do any kind of under-car or grinding or cutting work without them. You'll also be wise to wear them whenever you're working with fluids that can splash into your eyes.

- **Mechanic's Creeper.** A good mechanic's creeper with six wheels on it makes moving around under the car easy and comfortable. You might want to spend a few dollars more to get one with a head and neck cushion; this will add to your comfort while working under the vehicle.

- **Shelves and Cabinets.** You need storage space for tools, shop supplies, parts, and other items, so plan on acquiring some cabinets or putting up shelves.

- **Shop Stool.** A stool or chair will come in handy when working on smaller assemblies at the work bench, or simply to take a load off your feet when you want to take a break.

> **Overdrive**
>
> You can often give a worn-o
> tool a second chance at being
> useful. For example, if you have
> a screwdriver with a worn or
> broken tip, you can use a bench
> grinder to grind the tip to a point
> so it can be used as an awl or
> drift-pin for lining up bolt holes
> between two parts.

Finding a Good Wrench

You will probably decide to farm out some mechanical tasks rather than undertake them yourself because of equipment or skill requirements. For basic mechanical repair work, you don't necessarily have to go to a restoration specialist, depending on the job at hand.

For example, if the motor in your collector car runs but blows a lot of smoke, you might need a valve job. Any good, competent mechanic should be able to do this repair and you shouldn't have to pay a premium price for labor just because it is a collector vehicle. This is especially true if the parts are still readily available from local auto parts stores, and this is very often the case.

If you use a local garage for repairs to your everyday vehicle, inquire as to whether they would consider doing mechanical work on your collector vehicle as well. If they decline, ask them to suggest someone who might be willing to do such work. If you do go to the person they recommend, ask for some references and check them out to confirm the quality of the work and the fairness of pricing. And always ask for an estimate of how much the work will cost, including any required parts, before agreeing to let them do the job. Some certification as to the mechanic's qualifications, (such as an ASE Master Technician certificate) is reassuring.

Frequently, a local garage will agree to do the work if they don't have to hunt for a rebuild kit or other parts. You can obtain virtually any kind of rebuild kit for cars and trucks made between 1930 and 1986 from Kanter Auto Parts (see Appendix A) and other suppliers and even have them drop-shipped to the garage address in such cases.

If your local garage declines to do the repairs, one of the mechanics who works there might be willing to do the job as an after-hours project, so this is another option you may wish to consider.

A Bevy of Body Shops

As I mentioned earlier, most of the auto body shops earn their bread and butter working on insurance jobs and they shy away from custom work like restorations. The key word here is most shops, but not all of them.

Some shops do custom work on collector vehicles, racecars, motorcycles and even boats and other specialty vehicles exclusively. These shops don't do insurance claim work, but instead concentrate on providing their services to people like you. In my experience, a person who is actively involved in the collector car hobby often owns these specialty shops. That gives them an insider's perspective, not to mention puts them in an ideal position to advertise their business and show off their skills by using their own collector vehicles as examples of their work.

Body shops that take on restoration work also frequently mention in their advertising that they do custom work. Often they distribute flyers extolling the virtues of their custom work at car shows and cruise nights as well.

Don't be shy about asking for references and checking them out. Also ask to see pictures of completed work they've done. Inquire about their payment terms, guarantee of work quality and durability, how long the job will take, and a quote for the work in writing. In most states, auto body facilities are state licensed, so it's a good idea to check with the state licensing commission to find out if the shop has had any complaints registered against it.

As with every other aspect of dealing with vendors for your restoration needs, always try to get a good handle on who you're dealing with to have some assurance that you'll be satisfied with the work and the price.

The Least You Need to Know

- Be realistic when assessing your own abilities, and don't bite off more than you can chew.

- Sweat equity is an excellent way to save money, and you may be able to exchange services with another collector car hobbyist who is also doing a restoration.

- Tools can be purchased on an as-needed basis rather than blowing a bankroll on them all at once.

- A well-equipped and thoughtfully laid-out shop will make working on your restoration project faster and easier.

Chapter 14

Getting the Biggest Bang for Your Bucks

In This Chapter

- ◆ Cutting costs by doing your own work
- ◆ Time is money
- ◆ Restoring on the weekends
- ◆ Staying focused

This chapter focuses on the many ways of saving money during your restoration. It's foolish to spend more money than you have to, especially when that money could be put to better use elsewhere in the restoration project.

Making the Most of Your Money and Time

You've heard this expression before—get the biggest bang for the buck—but exactly what does it mean? Simply stated, it means getting the most value possible for your money, and there are several ways you can achieve this.

Unfortunately, money doesn't grow on trees, so saving money wherever you can on your restoration project doesn't only make sense; it is a practical necessity for most people. A little creative thinking can produce many ways of saving money. Following are a few ideas to help get you started on the road to frugality.

Cutting Costs, Not Quality

One of the best ways to save money and cut costs is to do as much of the work yourself as possible. Nobody works for free, so you can save a substantial amount of money on outside labor by doing your own work. And, because this is your own personal project, you have a vested interest in doing a good job, so the quality of your work is bound to be high. That's one way of cutting costs, not quality. But there are other ways as well.

Rebuilding Versus Replacing

You can save a lot of money by rebuilding some parts rather than replacing them. Rebuild kits are readily available for many parts such as disc brake calipers, fuel pumps, carburetors, master cylinders, and more. The cost of a rebuild kit is just a fraction of what a new or rebuilt part would cost you. Most rebuild kits include detailed instructions and do not usually require special tools, although there are a few exceptions, such as water pumps, that require the use of a bearing press for rebuilding. Some auto parts stores press the bearing into the pump for free if you purchase the rebuild kit from them.

Brake It Down _____

Early automotive distributors are equipped with a mechanical switch that has two contact points. When closed, these two **breaker points** supply current to the primary windings of the coil; when they open, the energy is transferred to the coil's secondary windings, which amplify it to supply the high energy needed to fire the spark plugs. Also simply called points, they eventually wear out and must be replaced as part of a routine tune-up. With the advent of electronic ignition, breaker point distributors became obsolete.

Some auto parts stores will loan you tools if you purchase parts from them. For example, you buy spark plugs and *breaker points* from the local auto parts store, but you need a timing light to do your tune-up. You can borrow one from the store, and a credit card is usually all that's needed as a deposit until the tools are returned. Other stores might require a cash deposit that is refunded to you upon return of the tool. Check with your local Auto Zone or other automotive parts stores to find out if they have a tool-lending program.

Refurbishing your existing parts is another way to save money over the cost of replacing them. For example, suspension parts like coil or leaf springs or anti-sway bars can be sandblasted to remove surface rust and then primed and painted to make them look like new. Just make sure they still have acceptable function (springs and torsion bars lose their springiness over time and use and need to be checked against factory standards to be sure they're still within the acceptable range.) If the parts are still good, why spend money on replacing them when they can be easily—and inexpensively—refurbished?

If you do have to get a replacement part, don't forget to consult your interchangeable parts manual and/or the parts locating guide to save some money.

> **Brake It Down**
>
> As the name implies, the distributor distributes the spark to each cylinder to initiate combustion. The distributor typically contains the breaker points and cam, centrifugal and vacuum advance mechanisms, and a shaft, usually driven by the camshaft. High voltage is generated by the coil and is passed to the distributor, which uses a rotor to supply this current to each spark plug through insulated wires.

Flea Markets and Swap Meets

Flea markets are often good places to find used tools and other items you may need for your shop or restoration at great prices. You can find things like disposable sponge paint brushes and sanding sponges for much less than you would pay at a retail store, so here's another opportunity to save money.

If you're buying tools, stay away from the imported tools (they will say "China" or wherever they were made) and inspect them closely to make sure that they're still serviceable. For example, check sockets, box wrenches, and the tips of Phillips screwdrivers for wear.

Automotive swap meets are often held in conjunction with car shows, and you can get some real bargains at these events if you're shrewd and are willing to haggle. Keep in mind that most items have an "asking price" that's not cut in stone, so make a counteroffer. Sometimes the seller will go for it, and sometimes he won't. It doesn't hurt to ask, however, and you might save some money by doing so. If there are several items you need, negotiate a "package deal" to save some additional cash.

> **4-Wheel Jive**
>
> Many auto parts stores accept used motor oil and batteries at no charge and recycle them.

> **4-Wheel Jive**
>
> The term "automobile" comes from the Greek "auto" (self) and the Latin "mobils" (moving). The term was actually coined in 1897 by *The New York Times*.

With flea markets and swap meets, the early bird catches the worm. Bring a list of what you need and arrive as early as you can because the really good bargains are snatched up fast.

Tool Rental Versus Purchase

There are some tools that you'll use during the restoration project that you may never use again. Good examples are a coil spring compressor, a crankshaft damper puller, and an air chisel. Tool rental stores have tools like these and many others that can be rented inexpensively by the day, week, or month, so consider that as another option for saving money.

> **4-Wheel Jive**
>
> The average price of a television set is half the price it was 20 years ago, while the average price for an automobile is four times higher

Lending Pools

"Neither a borrower nor a lender be" is generally good advice when it comes to tools, but there are exceptions. Some car clubs have lending pools where club members can borrow tools. The way this usually works is that a portion of the dues money and/or money raised from 50/50s or car shows is used to purchase tools like engine hoists, engine stands, spring compressors, and particularly assembly tools, jigs, and fixtures that are specific to the club's interest. When a club member needs to remove an engine, for instance, he can borrow the hoist and return it to the pool when he's finished. Check out the car clubs in your area to learn if they have lending pools.

> **4-Wheel Jive**
>
> The initials M.G. on the famous British-made automobile stand for "Morris Garages."

The Time Equals Money Equation

It is a fact of life that fast results cost more money. Think about it for a minute. Driving your car at 65mph will get you there faster, but it will burn more fuel than cruising at 55mph, so it will cost you more money. The same holds true for your restoration.

As an example, let's say you need to have the bushings on your project car's control arms replaced, and a press is required to do the job. The guy at the shop is very busy and says it will take a week to complete them. You tell him you'd like to get them back in a couple of days so you can install them over the weekend. He informs you that he can do it sooner, but he'll have to charge you more money for the rush service. Once again, time equals money.

You could save the extra charges by rescheduling your restoration activities. You could work on some other aspect of the restoration over this weekend and let the shop take a week to do the job. You can then install the control arms the following weekend and save some money in the process. Meanwhile, you didn't waste any time because you worked on something else that needed to be done. Time and money are inextricably related, so bear that in mind and do your best to waste neither of them.

Frequently, you may be able to make the equation work to your benefit. Often a garage or shop will take on a "no rush" project as fill-in work to keep the staff busy during slow periods. For instance, you might need a valve job done on your project car's engine or a camshaft and timing chain re-placed. If you tell the shop owner that there's no immediate rush to get the engine back, chances are good that you'll get a better price than if you want it back in a couple of days. While the engine is at the shop, you can proceed with other aspects of the restoration, so it's okay if it takes a month or so to get it back.

Brake It Down

The term shackle refers to a swinging support that attaches to the car's frame on one side and to the leaf spring on the other side. It is used to accommodate the change in the spring's length as it deforms in response to the wheels' up and down motions as they encounters bumps and other irregularities in the road.

Weekend Warriors

After putting in a full day at their jobs, many people just want to kick back and relax or spend quality time with their families in the evening, so they restrict their restoration activities to the weekend. If you're one of these weekend warriors, there are several ways you can maximize your productivity and save money.

The Sunday paper usually has flyers or inserts from local auto parts chains and home centers featuring items that are on sale for that week. Check these out for any shop supplies, tools, or parts that you need for your project and purchase them when they're on sale rather than at their everyday prices. Also check their business hours because some stores close early on the weekends, so you might have to do your shopping during the week.

Another way to maximize your time and save money is to register on leading automotive retailers' websites, such as Pep Boys, to receive e-mail alerts about special sales, promotions, rebate offers and other incentives. Frequently these specials are offered to registered users only and are not available to the general public. It doesn't cost anything to register, and you might be able to save some money by taking advantage of these specials for items you need.

Have a plan about what aspect of the restoration you intend to work on each weekend. For instance, let's say that this weekend your plan is to remove the front bumper and all of the chrome and stainless steel trim from the front of the car; next weekend's plan calls for removing the rear bumper and rear and side trim. Having a plan or schedule for

> **4-Wheel Jive**
>
> Automobiles use lead-acid batteries, each of which contains approximately 18 pounds of lead and a gallon of sulfuric acid, which are both hazardous materials.

> **4-Wheel Jive**
>
> *The Tonight Show* host Jay Leno owns more than 30 classic cars and more than 40 motorcycles. His first automobile was a 1934 Ford V8 truck, which he restored himself at the age of 14.

your restoration goals enables you to hit the ground running when you go into the garage on Saturday instead of standing there, scratching your head, while you try to figure out what you're going to do. You already know what your objective is for the day, so you can get right to it.

Another thing to think about is how you're going to spend your weekends. You may decide that you'll work on the restoration during the fall, winter, and spring weekends, but you will leave your summer weekends free so you can enjoy the outdoors and engage in other leisure pursuits. You might decide to work on the project only on weekends when there are not any football games on television, and so on. This is your free time, so budget it accordingly. If you feel that you're depriving yourself of watching the big game because you're working on the restoration project, you'll resent the car and start to hate it. Don't let that happen.

Keep Your Eye on the Prize

There will be many times during the restoration process that you'll feel frustrated. When this happens, step back and walk away from the project. Take a walk, get a beverage from the fridge, or do something completely unrelated to the project as a diversion.

The reason for taking a break is that when you're emotionally off-center, you won't be nearly as productive as you are when you're calm and focused. You're also more

> **Overdrive**
>
> Frequently, heating a rusted nut or bolt with a torch frees it up so it can be removed intact. While an oxyacetylene torch is hotter, you can also use a small, handheld propane torch. Although it will take a bit longer to heat the nut or bolt up until it glows, the propane torch usually gets the job done.

likely to be careless when you're emotions are keyed up, and this can lead to broken parts or, worse yet, injuring yourself. As an example, let's say that you're trying to remove a bolt that's frozen solid with rust. You struggle with it for several minutes as your frustration grows. Now you're really mad, you give it a powerful yank, and it snaps off. Well, that's just great—you've just compounded the problem because now there's a broken stud that must be removed and that's going to take even more work.

What you should have done at the first sign of a stubborn bolt was spray some penetrating oil on it and taken a little break. By the time you got back to it, you would have calmed down, the penetrating oil would have done its thing, and the bolt probably would have come out intact. This is supposed to be a recreational pastime, so don't let it become an exercise in aggravation.

There will also be times when, even though you have a plan, you won't feel like working on that particular aspect of the project that day. Fine; work on something else that needs to be done. If you work on something you're really not into at that time, you're not going to be productive, and the quality of your work probably won't be up to snuff, either. When this happens, the best strategy is to move on and do something else.

> ### 4-Wheel Jive
>
> The 1934 Ford street rod that was a featured player on the TV show *Home Improvement* was actually built by actor/comedian Tim Allen (under his character name Tim Taylor) from the frame rails up on the show. This street rod is still very dear to Tim, and it is one of several specialty and collector vehicles he owns, including a 1955 Chevrolet Nomad station wagon with a 327 CID Chevy motor. After the September 11 tragedy, Tim offered this Nomad to Ebay's Auction for America to benefit The Twin Towers Fund. This Nomad featured permanent signatures from Allen and Jay Leno.

The thing to remember is that all restorations take time, so get mentally geared up for the long haul. Work at a pace that's comfortable for you and remember to keep your eye on the prize—it will be worth it in the end, for sure.

> ### 4-Wheel Jive
>
> Prior to World War II, soybean oil was used to make enamel, glycerin, soft soaps, paint, linoleum, varnishes, waterproof goods, oilcloth, rubber substitutes, artificial petroleum, and ink. Soybean meal was used as a low-cost plywood adhesive. At Henry Ford's direction, the Ford Motor Company's laboratories discovered many industrial uses for the soybean. By 1935, a full bushel of soybeans went into the manufacturing of each Ford automobile.

The Least You Need to Know

- You can save a lot of money by rebuilding parts rather than replacing them.
- Time and money are inextricably related.
- Tools can be borrowed from some auto parts stores and car clubs if you are a member of the club.
- It is a good idea to take a break from the project when you're frustrated.

Part 4

Let's Get Down and Dirty

Well, we're at the point you've been waiting for—the actual hands-on part of the restoration. Time to put on the safety goggles and don the work gloves—we're talkin' nuts and bolts action here.

You're going to get very familiar with the architecture of your restoration vehicle and you'll form a bond with it as you work on its various major categories—the frame, running gear, power train, body, and interior. Auto Anatomy and Restoration Class 101 is in session now.

Takin' It Down

In This Chapter

- ◆ Documenting your car
- ◆ Disassembling one component at a time
- ◆ Cleaning and derusting parts
- ◆ Removing chrome and trim
- ◆ Assessing damage

Okay—by now you have all your tools, your shop is set up and you have all the manuals and catalogs you'll be needing, so we can actually get down to business. First, you're going to make a complete, detailed record of the car as it sits. You'll inventory it, check the fit of the doors, hood, deck lid, and more, as the first steps of the actual hands-on restoration process.

Takin' It Down

Now you're getting down to the real nitty-gritty. You'll be doing actual hands-on work to the vehicle and that's when you'll start getting intimately involved with it. By removing rust, muck, and grime you'll be taking it down to its bare metal in many instances, and removing trim and assessing damage that will have to be fixed. But before you do any of these things, it's imperative that you document the vehicle as it sits, before any work is performed.

A Picture Is Worth a Thousand Words

If you don't already have one, get a photo album and a camera, because you're going to be taking a lot of pictures—at least 100. The purpose of these photos is to document everything about the car before you start any actual work on it. A standard or disposable 35mm camera or a Polaroid camera will do an adequate job, but a digital camera is the most economical long-term solution because you won't have to purchase any film or pay for processing.

Another big advantage of a digital camera is that you can review the shot immediately after it's taken to see whether you got it. If it doesn't adequately show the detail, simply erase it and take another shot. You can also make color prints of your digital photos for the album and for keeping with the appropriate parts or assemblies.

If you have a camcorder, by all means use that in addition to the camera for further documentation. While shooting the video, be sure to narrate your comments about the part or section that you're shooting to provide additional information. You can't have enough information about the car, so don't think that you may be overdoing it.

Good lighting and crisp focus are critical when photographing your project vehicle. The entire purpose of taking these shots is to have a clear visual reference that shows all the details. For that reason, it is much more than a point-and-shoot exercise; concentrate on getting all the details of how the linkage is interconnected, how the fuel line is connected, or whatever your subject matter is. Having enough light to show these details is important, and a flash is often helpful. However, if the flash is too bright, it will wash out the details or make the entire assembly obscure due to an over-abundance of light. When shooting digitally, be sure to review each shot critically. If it doesn't show exactly what you need in crisp detail, erase it and shoot it again until you get a picture that will serve you nicely when it's time to put everything back together.

What to Photograph

Take your documentation shots in a logical order. For example, start with a full shot of the front of the car; then take detail shots of the various components that make up the front, such as the bumper, grille, headlights, hood, hood ornament, fenders, and so forth. Be sure to take detailed shots of the seam lines around the hood and doors to be used as reference for fitting these components on reassembly.

Little details, such as the corners of windshield and window moldings, are important to document. Although they don't seem to be of any special significance now, trying to remember how they go back together a year or two down the road would be a major chore without photos that show how they should look when installed. Don't rely on your memory. Trust me on this!

Work your way around the car, again taking a full shot of each side and then detailed shots of the doors, door handles, trim and other items, again working from front to back. A full shot of the rear, augmented by detail shots of the trunk lock and handle, bumper, taillights and other rear elements, as well as shots of all the glass, trim, and moldings will complete the exterior documentation.

Open the hood and take detailed shots of the engine compartment, including the firewall, inner fenders, and the underside of the hood. Take overall shots of the motor from the front and both sides, and then take detailed shots of subassemblies like the intake manifold and carburetor, generator or alternator, exhaust manifolds, fan/water pump, radiator, belts and pulleys, power steering pump, brake booster, air conditioning compressor, and other items. Don't forget to take shots of the horn(s), hood latching mechanism, hood hinges, and radiator and heater hoses showing the clamps used. In short, take pictures of literally everything under the hood.

Still working your way from the front to the rear of the car, open the doors and take shots of the door pillars, hinges, latches, sill plates, and weather stripping. Be sure to take full shots of the outside and inside of the doors as well.

Open the trunk and take detailed shots of the inside, making sure you get shots of the trunk floor and sides. Remove the spare tire, if present, and take shots of the tire well and pay particular attention to any rusted-out areas.

Also, take detailed shots so you can tell from the photograph whether the flat side or the curved side of the side trim, for example, faces upward.

With that finished, it's time to turn your attention to documenting the interior of the car. Once more, you should work from front to back. Start by sitting in the back seat and taking overall shots of the dashboard. Then move to the front seat and take more detailed shots of the dash, showing the gauges, steering wheel, pedals, front carpeting or floor covering, sun visors, and interior trim.

Be sure to kneel down and take shots of the underside of the dash as well. This is a great reference for where to put brackets and assemblies like the emergency brake, vent and heater control cables, steering column supports, and other such details.

Take shots of the doors showing handles and trim, and shoot the front seat(s) from both sides of the car with the doors open. Repeat these shots for the rear of the car and include shots of the front seat as viewed from the rear, the rear window with trim, package deck, and headliner as well as rear doors with trim if it's a four-door vehicle. Overall shots of the rear seat should also be taken from both sides of the car with the doors open, and shots of the carpeting, too.

Detailed shots like this one of a voltage regulator before its removal are invaluable when it is time to put things back together. This shot not only shows the correct orien-tation of the unit, but also the relationship of the other wires and components to it.

Taking Inventory and Ordering Parts

The next task is to inventory the vehicle. Take photos and make a list of everything that is missing, damaged, or deteriorated so you can start locating replacement parts even before you start the restoration. Using a pocket-sized notebook is a good way to inventory the needed items. By knowing in advance what you'll need, you'll have more time to locate the needed parts and shop for the best price.

Overdrive _____

Make sure you bring the parts list and prints of the photos to hunt for parts at flea markets or swap meets. This way you'll have a shopping list of what you need and photo references of what the part should look like or where it goes on the car.

When you have all the needed parts logged into your inventory notebook, refer to your assembly, parts, and shop manuals to get the exact part numbers for these items and enter these numbers next to the part description. Having the factory part numbers is very useful for establishing whether the part you locate is the correct one.

Don't forget to cross-reference the parts you need with other interchangeable parts by using the *Hollan-der Interchange Parts* manuals. When you do find interchangeable parts that you can substitute, note these part numbers in your inventory notebook. In so doing, you'll significantly increase the chances for successfully locating your parts.

Digital photos are also very helpful when trying to locate parts. For instance, if you need door trim molding, you can take a digital picture of the door and e-mail it to various parts suppliers with the description of what you need so they'll see exactly what you're missing.

Overdrive

Be sure to take your digital camera along to car shows and cruise nights. That way you'll be equipped to take a reference shot of a similar car that may have the parts you're missing so you'll know exactly what the part looks like.

Pit Stop

Injuries aren't fun, so don't get hurt while engaging in your hobby. And remember, because it's a hobby, you have all the time in the world, so there's no reason to play beat-the-clock. Always take proper safety precautions such as wearing eye protection, using gloves when handling sheet metal, having adequate lighting and ventilation, and keeping your work area free of clutter.

Disassembly

The biggest mistake first-time restorers make is to attempt to take everything apart all at once. This creates chaos, pandemonium and confusion. The same way we documented the car from the front to the rear is the correct order for disassembly—but not all at once!

Start at the front of the car and disassemble one component or assembly at a time. A component, for example, would be the hood of the car; conversely, an assembly would be the hood complete with its hinges, latch, and ornament still mounted on it.

Pit Stop

Some assemblies and components require assistance during removal. For example, if you were going to remove the hood from the vehicle, you would need another person to support it as you unbolt the hinges to keep it from crashing down on you. Don't attempt disassembling such items yourself; if it takes two people to do the job safely, then don't do it without help. Work on something else instead.

You'll make better progress during disassembly if you leave assemblies intact as much as possible rather than immediately reducing everything to its component parts. Again using the hood assembly as an example, it's easier to store the hood with its related elements still mounted, and it takes up less space. When you actually get to the stage where you'll be working on the hood, that's the time to disassemble individual components, refurbish, and remount them. At this point, reducing everything that comprises the hood assembly to individual components makes more work, requires individual storage space for each component, and there are many other things to do before you reach that stage.

Bag It and Tag It

Let's continue discussing the hood assembly to illustrate another point. Make sure that all of the nuts, bolts and washers that you take off to remove the hood assembly are put into zip-lock bags (one for each side) and attached to the hood assembly with baling (as in "hay bale," a "bail" is a bucket handle) wire or cable ties to keep them with the appropriate hardware. Label each bag with a marker that describes its contents; for example, "hood hinge bolts and washers, driver side." Even if these bolts and washers are rusted and you intend to replace them with new hardware, retain the old ones and identify them so that you can get exact replacements for them when you're ready.

Overdrive _____

Do it by the book! There will be many times when you'll encounter hidden bolts, clips, or other fasteners that aren't readily apparent or visible. In these instances you'll find the assembly manual and/or shop manual invaluable because the exploded views they contain show you exactly what's holding the part on and the procedures they outline will enable you to remove the part without damaging it. When it doubt, always do it by the book.

It's also a good idea to put a corresponding photo of the assembly with the parts, preferably in the ziplock bag, to prevent damage or soiling. You can go a step further and number the assemblies and parts bags to create an inventory log. This makes it easier to keep track of parts and the locations where they are stored. It doesn't have to be elaborate, and you can create the log in a notebook or on your computer, whichever you prefer. Here's an example of what it might look like:

1965 Mustang Restoration Project—Parts Inventory Log

I.D.#	Part Description	Where Stored
1	Alternator	Bag #1, Box #2, Shelf #3
2	Alternator bracket w/bolts	Bag #2, Box #2, Shelf #3
3	Air cleaner w/wing nut	Bag #3, Box #3, Shelf #2
4	Carburetor w/linkage & nuts	Bag #4, Box #4, Shelf #2
5	Hood release cable & latch	Bag #5, Box #1, Shelf #3
6	Hood release striker & spring	Bag #6, Box #1, Shelf #3
7	Left & right hood hinges	Cello Box #7, Shelf #3

This transparent, disposable plastic box originally held chocolate chip cookies; now it makes a fine container for holding the left and right hood hinges that were taken off a project car until it is time to work on them.

Keeping a log like this helps you to stay organized, which greatly enhances productivity. Let's say that you have some unexpected time on your hands, and you decide to rebuild your carburetor. Instead of searching through numerous boxes and wasting your time, you consult your log and you know exactly where it is: in bag 4 in box 4 on shelf 2. Locating it couldn't be easier, so you can work on it without any hassles.

You can use large plastic garbage bags for storing bigger parts or assemblies, and the plastic that is wrapped around your clothes when you get them from the dry cleaners also works well. You can also purchase a roll of translucent plastic overspray sheeting from the local body shop supply. Body shops use this thin plastic sheeting to protect undamaged sections of the car from overspray when painting repaired sections. One roll is enough to wrap the parts of several cars because it unfolds to be about twelve feet wide by any length you desire. It's handy for wrapping up large parts like hoods and fenders and, because it's translucent, you can see the part through it, which is an advantage over the large garbage bags. A roll of overspray sheeting will set you back about $25–$30, but it is well worth it.

Chrome and Trim Removal

Before you do any rust removal or other surface preparation, all chrome and trim should be removed from the vehicle. Attached with nuts and bolts, chrome items like the front and rear bumpers and grille are fairly easy and straightforward to remove. Other *bright work* such as hood ornaments, emblems and model insignias are usually made of chrome-plated pot metal and are attached with "speed nuts," which are thin, hollow self-tapping nuts that thread onto the stems of the bright work parts.

Speed nuts come in several sizes and are commonly used to secure trim pieces like the crossed-flag emblem shown here. The speed nut is threaded onto the studs on the backside of the emblem, and it cuts its own threads as it is tightened down.

Removing chrome trim strips and window moldings requires special trim tools. Attempting to remove these items with the wrong tools, such as screwdrivers, results in damaging the trim. Trim removal tools are very inexpensive (you can get the three major tools for under $20), whereas replacing a damaged piece of trim can easily be two or three times the price of the tools.

There may be times when trim removal from the doors or rear quarter panels requires removing the interior panels to gain access to the trim fasteners. In these cases, make sure you bag and tag all of the hardware that holds the inner panels in place, and document everything with your camera. Frequently, these clips and retainers will need to be replaced, and you'll make that determination as soon as they're removed. It's a good idea to start shopping for these clips as soon as you determine that they need replacement; sometimes they're quite difficult to get for older cars, and they might be on back order.

Trim and molding pieces are usually held in place with butterfly clips or snap clips. The butterfly clips get their name from the fact that they have spring "wings" that grab the sides of the trim and look like butterfly wings. With snap clips, the molding or trim snaps over the spring-metal clip.

Refer to your vehicle's assembly or shop manual to ascertain how many clips are used for each piece of trim and where they are located.

> **4-Wheel Jive**
>
> In its first year, only 330 Volkswagen Beetles were sold in the United States.

Cleaning and Derusting

By far, the biggest nemesis to older vehicles is *rust*. Of all the effort you'll put into your restoration, cleaning parts and removing rust, along with preventing future rust, command the lion's share of attention. While cleaning and derusting parts is a big job, there are different methods, products, and ways to make the job go easier and require less effort. First, let's talk about cleaning parts.

In order to truly assess the condition of a part or assembly, it must be clean so you can give it a thorough inspection. Many times the cleaning process amounts to simply knocking off road dirt, tar, and grime. Other times, cleaning requires grease removal, and sometimes it will also require the removal of old paint or plating material.

Dirt, Mud, Salt, and Road Grime

A wire brush and a few spritzes of an industrial-strength cleanser like Spray Nine will do the trick for most dirt and road grime on chassis and suspension parts. Even tar can usually be removed with vigorous brushing and a couple of applications of cleanser.

For cleaning individual parts, such as tie rods or spindles, a bench grinder/buffer with a wire wheel removes dirt and grime nicely, and it can also remove surface rust in the process. Purchasing a good grinder/buffer that has dual wheels will prove to be a very good investment because you'll use it for lots of tasks throughout your restoration.

Grease Removal

While some people use gasoline or carburetor cleaner to remove grease from parts, I absolutely caution you not to do this. Gasoline, carb cleaner and other solvents are highly flammable—not only the liquids, but also their vapors. When these liquids and fumes are present, any kind of spark can produce catastrophic results.

There are plenty of safer ways to degrease parts, so why take a chance of injury, property damage or even worse consequences when you don't have to? Burning down the house won't make you the most popular person with your family or neighbors.

Several excellent degreasing agents are available that pose no fire hazard. Among them are Spray Nine, Gunk Engine Degreaser and others, all of which are available on the shelves of your local Pep Boys or other automotive products retailer. Many of these products are available in spray bottles or aerosol cans, and they are a piece of cake to use. You simply apply the degreaser, let it set for a few minutes, then hose it off. Sometimes a little persuasion with a stiff-bristled brush gets the really tough, caked-on grease off a bit faster.

> **4-Wheel Jive**
>
> The city with the most Rolls-Royces per capita is Hong Kong.

Additionally, two other products for degreasing work really well. The first is Metal Wash from The Eastwood Company and the second is Marine Clean from POR-15. What I like best about both of these products is that they are water-soluble and nonflammable. And they both do a great job of degreasing parts with minimal effort.

Derusting

You have numerous ways to go about *derusting* your collector car's parts, components, and assemblies, and no one specific method will be the best for all of your derusting tasks. Rather, a combination of all of these methods will prove to be the best way to get the job done, so it makes sense to learn what these methods are.

Chemical Rust-Removal Agents

Oxisolv Rust Remover from The Eastwood Company is a specially formulated rust-fighting liquid that quickly dissolves iron oxide completely and leaves a zinc phosphate coating. This rust remover can be sprayed, brushed or used as a parts dip. If you use a wand sprayer to apply it, it's great for "killing" rust in hard-to-reach spots like the inside of fender wells. It is nontoxic, nonflammable and reusable.

Metal-Ready from POR-15 is another good product that also leaves a zinc phosphate coating when it is applied. Though Metal-Ready is touted as a metal prepping product that should be used before painting, it also does a good job of removing rust.

Mechanical Rust Removal

As the name implies, mechanical methods can be used to remove rust, and these methods involve using abrasive materials. Abrasive pads, sandpaper, and wire brushes all fall into this category of mechanical rust removal. These methods are fine for removing rust from parts or assemblies that are readily accessible, and mechanical rust removal is one of the fastest methods of getting down to the bare metal. Bench grinder/buffers fitted with various grit bristle brushes are also highly efficient at removing rust from parts, and bristle discs can also be used with handheld grinders. The vast majority of rust removal on restoration projects is performed using mechanical rust removal methods. Although labor-intensive, it is inexpensive, highly effective, and quick.

> **Brake It Down** _____
>
> **Rust** is any of various powdery or scaly reddish-brown or reddish-yellow hydrated oxides formed on iron and iron-containing materials (such as steel) by low-temperature oxidation in the presence of water. The chemical name for rust is ferric oxide (Fe_2O_3).

Media Blasting

Media blasting is one of the oldest, most popular, and efficient methods of removing rust. Sand was the original abrasive used, but today different media is used for different jobs and effects. Sand is still probably the most widely used media for rust removal, although some restorers prefer to use glass beads, silicon carbide, or aluminum oxide.

Media blasting can be done in an enclosed blasting cabinet or out in the open. The advantages of using a blasting cabinet are that the blast media is contained and can be reused. Blasting in the open disperses the media all over the place, although an old shower curtain or a tarpaulin can be used to contain it somewhat. Depending on your proximity to neighbors, they may become unhappy campers when airborne blasting media starts coming onto their property, so that's something to consider before you do your blasting out in the open. Whenever blasting in the open, it is important to use a blasting hood and protective gloves to prevent injury from the media, which is propelled at high speed.

A metal blasting cabinet that is big enough to accommodate wheels, intake manifolds, and other reasonably large items will set you back a few hundred dollars, but it is probably one of the most worthwhile and useful investments you'll make for your restoration project. You can also purchase gravity-fed handheld blasting guns for small jobs for well under $50,

> **4-Wheel Jive**
>
> The "cyclops" brake light in automobile rear windows was installed after Elizabeth Dole suggested it. It is known in automotive circles as a CHMSL (pronounced Chims'l), a Center High-Mounted Stop Light.

although their capacity is usually limited to about three to four pounds of blast media. That, plus the fact that they'll have to be used out in the open, make them a less desirable choice, albeit less expensive than a blasting cabinet.

Suction blasters are readily available for $30 or less, and as their name implies, they use suction to pull the blast media up into the air stream and shoot it out the blaster's nozzle. Typically, you stick the suction probe into a bucket of sand or other media and connect the air source to the blaster gun. When the trigger is pressed, the sand is blasted out of the nozzle onto the area to be derusted. These suction blasters are also out in the open units, so safety precautions like blasting hoods and gloves are the order of the day. They have the same media-containment drawbacks as the gravity-fed units.

> **Brake It Down**
>
> Bright work is a collective term for a vehicle's chrome, stainless steel, pot metal, or aluminum trim. The name stems from the fact that these pieces are bright (as opposed to painted).

Damage Assessment

With the car cleaned and the trim removed, you are now in a better position to assess any other damage that must be addressed and corrected as part of the restoration process. Keep a log of these areas that need attention and take clear, detailed photographs to document them.

It is usually fairly easy to decide what can be repaired and what must be replaced, but sometimes you can go either way. For example, let's say that there's a ding in a piece of stainless steel door trim. While the piece may be readily available from a catalog house, it will probably cost you a lot of money. Often, such little dings can be "bumped" out using a body hammer and a small anvil, and then buffed to make the surface uniformly shiny. If you're not sure whether repair or replacement is warranted, bring the photos of the damage with you to show other folks who have done restorations and ask their advice. Though you may not have the skill or experience to correct the damage, other people may have it and they'll frequently offer to help you out.

The Least You Need to Know

◆ Before any restoration work is started, detailed photos of the entire vehicle are an absolute necessity.

◆ Some tasks require a helper to be performed safely.

◆ All parts should be bagged and tagged for identification.

◆ Keeping a parts log makes it easier to locate the parts when it's time for restoration or reassembly.

Chapter 16

Automotive Elements

In This Chapter

- ◆ Car karma
- ◆ Framed!
- ◆ Running gear
- ◆ Feel the power
- ◆ Sheet metal
- ◆ Have a seat

Just as the human body is composed of the respiratory, digestive, circulatory, nervous, and waste systems, your collector vehicle is also a collection of interdependent systems that interact with each other. Understanding the components of these systems and their functions will give you additional knowledge about your vehicle that will be useful as your restoration progresses.

You'll be spending a lot of time working on your collector vehicle, so understanding it is the first step in what's going to be a long relationship with it.

The Seven Automotive Chakras

According to yoga philosophy, a *chakra* is one of the seven centers of spiritual energy in the human body. Your collector vehicle also has seven "chakras." These aren't spiritual energy centers; they're automotive energy centers. They are the frame, running gear, power parts, brakes, electrical energy, body parts, and interior. As you'll soon learn, each of these automotive chakras comprises many other smaller elements and assemblies.

Frame Factors

The frame forms the vehicle's basic building block. In addition to carrying the vehicle load, it furnishes support and maintains alignment for the body, power train, and other units. The engine, transmission, steering gear, front and rear suspension, the rear differential, and the body are all attached on the frame.

The chassis side rails and cross members are collectively called the frame when nothing else is attached. When all of the operating parts including the engine, drive train, steering, suspension, and brakes are attached to it (minus the body, accessories, and trim), it is called the *chassis*.

In addition to the aforementioned major components, there are several other items that attach to the frame that are crucial to the operation of the vehicle. Among them are the gas tank, fuel lines, brake lines, and motor mounts.

Virtually all pre-1970 vehicles used discrete frames on which the body was mounted. Gradually, *unibody* technology was introduced. The trend has continued to the point where almost all of today's production passenger cars use unibody construction. For all intents and purposes, unibody construction eliminates the frame; the bodies of these cars take on the function of the frame, with everything attaching to them. The exceptions are Corvettes, SUVs, trucks, and some other specialty vehicles.

> **Brake It Down**
>
> Also called unitized construction, *unibody* construction describes a car that is engineered so the body, floor pan, and chassis form a single structure. This results in a vehicle that is generally lighter and more rigid than one that uses traditional body-on-frame construction.

In a frame-off restoration, the body is lifted off the car and all of the chassis components are removed, thus leaving a bare frame. This is the most radical, costly, and time- and labor-intensive type of restoration, and a professional restoration house, rather than a hobbyist, usually performs it. However, it is still quite possible for you to do an excellent frame-on restoration yourself.

Running Gear

The vehicle's running gear ("rolling stock" is a railroading and trucking term for box cars, trailers, etc.) consists of the components that enable it to roll. These components include the suspension, brakes, axles, spindles, wheel hubs, tires, steering gear, tie rods, trailing arms, and other components. Virtually all of these components are, in reality, assemblies that utilize a number of parts working in unison. For example, the rear axles ride on bearings inside a housing; the axles connect to the differential gears on one end, and to the wheels on the other; the axles, housings, bearings, gears and other requisite components are collectively called the rear end.

Brake It Down

Rag joint is a colloquial term for the flexible steering coupler disc usually made of layers of canvas sewn together that connects the steering shaft to the steering box. The canvas helps prevent vibration and shocks caused by roadway irregularities from being transmitted to the steering wheel.

The rag joint, shown here, couples the steering shaft to the steering gear box.

The running gear also includes the steering gear, which consists of the steering wheel, steering column and shaft, *rag joint*, tie rods, idler arm, and the mechanism to convert the steering wheel's rotation to side-to-side movement, either a steering gear box and *pitman arm* or *pinion gear* and steering rack.

Brake It Down

The **pitman arm** is a lever connected to the steering box sector shaft that moves from side to side to steer the front wheels.

A typical steering component layout is shown here.

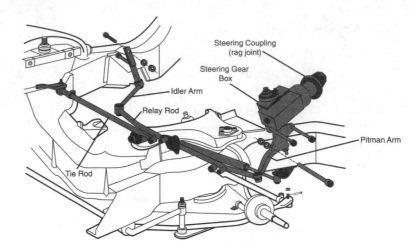

Brake It Down

Rack-and-pinion steering is a steering system with a **pinion gear** on the end of the steering shaft that mates with a rack (sort of like a geared wheel opened up and laid flat). When the steering wheel is turned, the pinion also turns, thus moving the rack to the left or the right. This movement is transmitted through the tie rods to the steering arms at the wheels.

The function of the vehicle's suspension is to absorb the harshness of bumps and jolts caused by road irregularities and to provide a stable environment that promotes safe cornering and handling of the vehicle over its entire speed range. The suspension consists of front and rear springs that can be coil or leaf springs or torsion bars, shock absorbers, upper and lower ball joints, upper and lower control arms, wheel spindles, wheel hubs, and spring shackles.

Power Parts

Here's where we get into the belly of the beast. The power parts consist of the power train and the electrical system because both provide power to the vehicle.

The Power Train

The power train consists of the engine, transmission, driveshaft, rear differential, and axles—the components necessary to deliver the power that propels the vehicle. As with other assemblies, the power train is composed of many components and subassemblies that are required for the vehicle to function. Let's take a quick look at them now.

The Engine

The engine could be described as the heart of the vehicle, because it is the main mechanical assembly that provides motive power. The engine itself contains several systems that it needs to operate. One system is the fuel system, which includes the gas tank, fuel lines, fuel pump, and carburetor or fuel injection unit, and the intake manifold. After the fuel is burned, the motor needs to expel the spent gas, so an exhaust system is required. The exhaust system consists of the exhaust manifold(s), exhaust pipe(s), muffler(s), and tail pipe(s). On 1976 and later cars, a catalytic converter is also part of the exhaust system.

The engine also requires a cooling system to prevent it from overheating. Except on Volkswagens, Corvairs, and other air-cooled cars the cooling system consists of a coolant liquid (water mixed with antifreeze) and the means to circulate it through the engine's cooling passages, including the radiator, a fan, radiator hoses, a thermostat, a fan belt, and a water pump. The engine drives the fan via a belt; the fan pulls air into the engine compartment through the fins on the radiator, and the cool air passing through the radiator cools the coolant liquid before it is circulated through the engine by the water pump. The thermostat prevents the coolant from circulating until the engine reaches its proper operating temperature.

The engine drives the generator or alternator via a belt. The generator or alternator produces electricity, which keeps the battery charged and provides electrical power for the ignition system, as directed by the voltage regulator. Electrical current is fed to the starter motor via a solenoid switch when the ignition key is turned to "start," and the starter motor is engaged to the engine's flywheel by "bendix gear." The starter motor spins the engine's flywheel. At the same time current is sent to the ignition coil through the breaker points. The coil amplifies the voltage several thousand times; this amplified voltage is then sent to the distributor, which passes it to each of the spark plugs in a predetermined sequence.

As the engine is "turned over" while starting, fuel is drawn into the combustion chambers along with air via the carburetor or fuel injection unit. This fuel/air mixture is highly volatile and becomes even more so when it is compressed. As the piston moves up in the cylinder, the fuel/air mixture is compressed. When the spark plug fires the mixture burns rapidly and the expanding gasses force the piston down. The sequence repeats itself in the other cylinders, and after the engine is running under its own power, the starter motor disengages from the flywheel as soon as the ignition key is allowed to return to the "on" position.

4-Wheel Jive
Buick introduced turn signals as standard equipment in 1939.

The transmission is responsible for delivering the power generated by the engine to the drive wheels. In a manual transmission, the rotational motion of the engine's flywheel is linked to the transmission's input shaft via mechanical friction using a clutch. In an automatic transmission, a torque converter that utilizes fluid flowing through turbinelike vanes provides this link. The transmission contains various gears that deliver sufficient torque to set the vehicle in motion from a standing stop, permit reverse motion, and allow high-speed driving depending on the gears selected. The output shaft of the transmission connects to the drive shaft, which, in turn, connects to the differential. Gears located inside the differential housing transmit power to the axles that drive the wheels.

4-Wheel Jive
Eugene Houdry invented the catalytic muffler (converter) and patented it in 1962.

Brakes

The brakes are another example of numerous components that form a functional assembly. The brakes slow the car down by converting its kinetic (moving) energy into heat. At each wheel, the brake consists of a drum or disc, a wheel cylinder or caliper, friction shoes or pads, brake lines, bleeder valves, springs, and other hardware that enable it to function. The brakes on all modern (post WWII) cars are actuated by hydraulic pressure. Hydraulic brakes have the advantage of applying equal pressure throughout the system and require little adjustment—in most cases almost none at all.

Hydraulic pressure is created in one or two master cylinders by pressing on the brake pedal, often aided by a power brake booster. The hydraulic fluid transfers pressure through lines to the front and rear brakes and moves pistons in small cylinders that press the friction material (shoes or pads) against the rotating brake drum or disc.

The parking brake is a separate system that is mechanically operated through rods, cables, and cams when you pull the parking brake handle. Most parking brakes work on the rear wheels, although some older designs used a separate drum on the driveshaft. Sometimes people will refer to the parking brake as the "emergency brake," which provides some mechanical braking if there is a failure in the hydraulic service brake system—a broken hose or pipe—for example.

Electrical Energy

The engine depends on electrical energy to fire its spark plugs, so the electrical system is also a major power part. The part of the electrical system that fires the plugs is called the ignition system. It consists of the storage battery, a generator or alternator, a voltage regulator, a wiring harness, the distributor, an ignition coil, spark plug wires, and spark plugs.

The electrical system also provides power for and controls many other important functions: starter, lights, accessories, and comfort and convenience features. It also powers the headlights, tail lights, and brake lights, horn, turn signals, interior lights, radio, cigarette lighter, and other electrical devices with which the vehicle may be equipped.

Body Parts

The bodies of most collector vehicles are made of sheet metal. This metal is usually sheet steel, although some European vehicles have bodies made of aluminum. Corvettes have bodies formed out of fiberglass, as did the Bricklin and Avanti (otherwise this sounds like the Avanti was made in Canada, not South Bend, Indiana), while the DeLorean's body was made of stainless steel.

Regardless of what material it's made of, the car's body attracts the most attention, both when it's standing still and when it is moving. In addition to discrete, removable body parts like doors, the hood, and trunk lid, a vehicle's body is made up of numerous sections that are welded together. The welds are ground smooth on the assembly line, so they're not readily visible.

Sections of the body that are usually welded are the roof, the rear quarter panels, the floor pans, and the inner trunk floor. The front fenders and grille are usually bolted in place rather than welded, as are the rear fenders of some older cars.

Chrome and stainless trim are used as decorative devices and styling cues to give the body some additional appeal. Emblems, insignias, and hood ornaments also have the same function.

There's more to the body than meets the eye. Closer inspection reveals that it contains inner fenders, supports for a number of functional items, and a firewall that separates the engine from the passenger compartment. The car's body also has insulation to keep engine heat from entering the passenger compartment and sound-deadening materials to quiet down the ride.

Rubber weather stripping is used around the doors, windows, and trunk to prevent water and outside air from getting into the car.

Seats and Such

Usually when you are spending quality time with your vehicle, you are occupying and (hopefully) enjoying the interior. In addition to the seats, the interior consists of seat adjustment mechanisms, sun visors, a headliner, door panels, the dashboard, gauges, carpeting, a clock, the radio, and speaker(s). It also has the steering wheel, gearshift, brake and accelerator pedals, a clutch pedal, parking brake, glove box, a heater/defroster, and vent or air conditioning outlets.

The rearview mirror, window cranks or switches, inner door handles, door locks, seat belts, console, arm rests, floor mats, ashtrays, cigarette lighters, and interior lights are also interior components, as are other optional items that may include a tissue dispenser, radar detector, or a GPS unit.

There's also bright work for interior trim that may include chrome knobs, cranks, handles and switches, a horn ring on the steering wheel, and emblems and insignias. It's the little things that most folks overlook when planning an interior restoration.

The Least You Need to Know

- The seven major automotive centers are the frame, running gear, power parts, brakes, electrical energy, body, and interior.

- Each automotive element is composed of several components and assemblies that work together.

- The body of the car is the thing we notice first, whether the car is standing still or moving.

- The car's interior is where we spend the most time, so make it comfy and make it look as good as you can afford.

Chapter 17

Chassis Restoration

In This Chapter

- Understanding the foundation
- Removing rust
- Scraping and shooting
- Fixing fissures
- Torch tricks

Because virtually the entire car sits on top of the chassis, this chapter is devoted to this very important automotive component. The basis for a quality restoration is a solid chassis, and you'll learn how to determine the current condition of your classic's chassis and take whatever remedial steps are necessary to make it all that it can and should be.

So get out your work gloves, work light, and creeper, 'cause we're gonna get down and work on that undercarriage.

The Car's Foundation

It may help you to think of the chassis as the foundation of the car because the rest of the car sits on it like your house sits on its cement foundation. Still using that analogy, you can easily understand why the chassis must be strong. But your house is stationary—it doesn't move. By virtue of the fact that your car does move, the chassis is subject to lots of additional stress from acceleration, braking, and cornering—stress your house doesn't have to contend with.

Brake It Down

A **transverse** beam is situated or lying across, crosswise, at a 90-degree angle to the perpendicular. Cross members are transverse beams.

The rails of the chassis are made of thick steel that forms a hollow rectangular frame running from the front to the rear of the car. Along the way, there are many bends and angles in the rails, and the left and right rails are held together with *transverse* steel pieces called cross members that are welded to each rail.

Top and side views of a typical box girder frame.

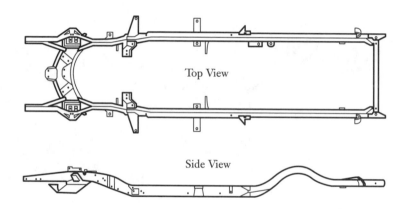

Top View

Side View

Brake It Down

A **box girder frame** is a chassis frame that uses side rails connected by cross members only at the front and back. The "box girder frame" name comes from the rectangular box which the side rails and front and rear cross members form.

There are two basic types of frames: the *box girder frame* and the *ladder frame*. The box girder frame, as its name suggests, is a rectangular frame made of steel girders that are welded and riveted together. The ladder frame uses cross members along its length to hold the side rails together and add rigidity to the frame. The type of frame your vehicle has depends on its age, make, and model, but the two types are easily distinguishable.

Although there are other types of chassis configurations, the vast majority of classic restorations are performed on box girder frames or ladder frames.

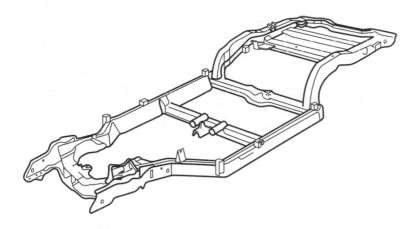

A typical ladder frame showing the cross members.

Let's take a few minutes to understand what the chassis is responsible for:

◆ All of the suspension components attach to it.

◆ The engine is supported by it.

◆ The transmission is supported by it.

◆ The brake and fuel lines are attached to it.

◆ All four wheels are connected to it (via the suspension).

◆ The body is attached to it.

◆ The steering gear is attached to it.

◆ The fuel tank sits under or on it.

◆ The exhaust system is attached to it.

◆ The bumpers are attached to it.

> **Brake It Down**
>
> A chassis frame that uses side rails connected by cross members throughout its length is called a **ladder frame** because the cross members form the "rungs" that are attached to the side rails, thus resembling a ladder.

Quite a bill of goods, wouldn't you say? But that's not all. The chassis has to be flexible enough to cope with the stress of bumps, cornering, acceleration, and braking without cracking or breaking, and yet it must be rigid enough to deliver a safe ride with handling that the driver can easily control. And that's another tall order.

In addition to road salt from decades of winters, wear, tear, age, and the elements can all take their toll on a collector car's chassis. For the most part, however, your old car's chassis is probably in remarkably good condition, all factors considered. At least, it may look that way on the surface.

Remember what I said about the frame rails being hollow? This is where problems can be hiding—on the inside of the rails. This happens when moisture (for example, rain water, or condensation) gets inside the frame rails and sits there, usually nestling within a coating of dirt and crud, causing the steel to oxidize or, in plain English, rust. You won't see this from the outside of the frame rail until it has gotten to the critical stage where it is actually rusting through the steel of the frame. When this happens, you have a major problem that requires serious damage control; this usually means a lot of welding and replacement steel panels.

> **4-Wheel Jive**
>
> Years ago, spermaceti oil—from the sperm whale—was used as transmission oil in Rolls-Royce automobiles.

Let's assess the shape of your chassis. Begin by getting the necessary tools together. You need a work light, an ice pick or awl, a hydraulic floor jack, and jack stands. If you have two pairs of jack stands, you can have the entire car elevated; if you only have one pair, you must inspect the front and the back separately. There's an advantage to having the entire car elevated at the same time because you can work on both ends of the car without interruption. You also need a mechanic's creeper (or a *Tom's Cheaper Creeper*) to facilitate moving around under the car while you conduct your evaluation. And don't forget to wear protective glasses or goggles so you don't get dirt or rust in your eyes. It is also wise to wear a dust mask or a respirator to keep debris out of your respiratory tract.

Overdrive

What is a Tom's Cheaper Creeper? Go to your local home building/remodeling depot and purchase a 4-by-8-foot sheet of ¾-inch thick Owens-Corning Energy Shield Outside Insulation (less than $10). I describe it as an expanded-foam board with foil facing on both sides. The material is light, cuts easily with a utility knife, and is very comfortable for use as a shield between you and the garage floor when working underneath your classic. And, because the surface of both sides is reflective, it even shines some additional light on your work area. Another advantage is that you'll have about 2½ inches of additional working room between you and the underside of the vehicle compared to what you'd have with a wheeled mechanic's creeper. You can cut four 4-by-2-foot cheaper-creepers from a single sheet and reuse the same piece several times. When it has finally reached the end of its useful life, simply dispose of it (responsibly, of course). Even though I have a professional mechanic's creeper, I use the lighter, (not to mention more comfortable) cheaper-creeper for most of my projects.

Up, Up, and Away

It's time to jack up the vehicle. If the car has an automatic transmission, make sure that it is in park; if it has a manual transmission, put it in gear. Next, chock the rear wheels with blocks of wood (a ½-foot length of two-by-four for each rear wheel works fine). The idea is to keep the car from rolling when you jack up the front, which is the next item on the agenda. Position the cradle of your hydraulic floor jack underneath the center of the front cross member; this is usually just ahead of or directly underneath the radiator. Once positioned, continue jacking up the front end until you reach the jack's maximum elevation. Now position your jack stands underneath the side frame rails directly across from each other, on both sides of the car. Make sure the stands are both extended to the same height and are both locked in position and squarely seated on the garage floor. Now slowly release the jack to gently lower the car onto the jack stands. It is absolutely imperative that the jack stands be solidly seated on the floor with the weight of the car on them. If they are not, rejack the car and reposition the stands so they are absolutely stable, and then relower the car onto them.

If you only have a single pair of jack stands, you can start your inspection and evaluation now. Skip down to the section, "Gettin' Down and Checkin' It Out." When you're done with the front end, jack it up again, remove the jack stands, and gently lower the car back down. Remove the chocks from the rear wheels and put them in front of the front tires, again to prevent the car from rolling. Position the jack under the rear end, jack it up and position the jack stands under the rear of the frame rails across from each other, just ahead of the rear tires. When you're satisfied that they're solidly positioned, slowly lower the car onto the jack stands and proceed with your inspection and evaluation of the rear half of the chassis.

For those of you who *do* have a second pair of jack stands, position the cradle of the floor jack under the rear differential and jack the car up to its maximum elevation. Position the jack stands slightly forward of the rear tires under the frame rails, directly opposite from each other, and slowly lower the car down onto the jack stands. I can't overemphasize how important it is that all four jack stands are solidly positioned on the floor, and that the chassis rails are firmly seated on all four jack stands; be sure that you're careful when doing this. When you're satisfied that the car is solidly and safely elevated, you can proceed.

4-Wheel Jive
In the early 1900s, the first cars were essentially motorized carriages and shared many characteristics with horse-drawn vehicles of the day, including wooden chassis! In 1919 Dodge brought out the first enclosed vehicle with steel frame members.

Gettin' Down and Checkin' It Out

Put on your safety glasses and work gloves, turn on your work light, and position yourself under the car. Using your ice pick or awl, tap the point against the bottom and sides of the chassis rails and listen. As you tap along, you should hear fairly consistent sounds of metal hitting metal; that's an indication that the steel of the rails is solid and sturdy. Pay particular attention to all of the welded joints because these are more susceptible to weakening from rust. If you come upon any section that feels or sounds less than solid, mark it with chalk or a grease pencil for a more in-depth inspection later.

> **4-Wheel Jive**
>
> The world's most solitary tree is located at an oasis in the Tenere Desert in Central Africa. No other standing tree lies within 31 miles. In 1960, a Frenchman ran into it with his truck.

If you've opted to do a frame-off restoration, this inspection is considerably easier because you're not encumbered by the body, and you have uninhibited access to the top of the chassis, its sides, and bottom. If the body is still attached, you won't be able to get to the top of the frame rails, but you should still be able to conduct a thorough inspection and evaluation based on the sides and bottom of the chassis rails.

Work your way down the full length of the side rail, tapping approximately every six inches and paying extra attention to any welds or joints. Repeat the process on the opposite rail as well, marking any suspicious areas as you go. When both side rails are done, tap across each cross member, again paying special attention to the welds that connect the cross members with the side rails.

If you didn't come across any suspect areas during the inspection, chances are very good that you have a solid chassis and that you've made a good purchase. Congratulations!

If you do have a couple of areas that you suspect may be less than healthy, make a rough drawing of the chassis and note on the drawing the areas you marked on the frame. The next section pays special attention to these areas as we start removing rust and refurbishing the chassis.

Rust Never Sleeps

That may sound like a cutesy, trite statement, but it's true. As long as there is moisture in the air, oxidation continues relentlessly to turn iron and steel into rust. The only way to prevent rust from forming is to put a barrier between the metal and the atmosphere, and there are a couple of ways to do this.

The first way is to remove loose surface rust with a wire brush or wire wheel mounted in a drill, and then to paint the cleaned surface. For best adhesion, use a self-etching primer, followed by a couple of coats of satin black chassis paint. The purpose of the primer is to provide a "first line of defense" barrier that both coats the metal and provides a better "grip" to which the chassis paint can adhere.

Although this is a good way to get rust under control and probably the least expensive way to go, the same airborne moisture that causes rust will also eventually soften the paint. When it softens, it becomes more porous; moisture can then penetrate the paint and primer and work its way down to the metal, where oxidation will once again occur.

4-Wheel Jive
In 1896, only four cars were registered in all of the United States. Two of them collided with each other in St. Louis!

Powder-coating the chassis is an excellent way to put a permanent barrier between the atmosphere and the metal, although it is very difficult to apply to a chassis with the body still attached because powder-coating requires heat to cure. This curing is usually done in curing ovens, although high-temperature lamps can also be used to cure. The problem with the high-temperature lamps is that, while they're curing the powder-coating, they can cause heat damage to the other components of the car by warping the body and door panels.

However, for frame-off restorations, powder-coating is a great way to protect the chassis from rusting for the long term.

There are also products available that neutralize rust and prevent it from spreading further. These products are applied directly over the rust, so derusting is not required.

The best known and most widely used of these products is POR-15 Rust Preventive Paint. POR-15 chemically bonds to rusted metal and forms a rock-hard, non-porous, ceramic-like coating that doesn't crack, chip, or peel. Unlike ordinary paints that are softened by exposure to moisture, POR-15 is actually strengthened by it. While this paint can be brushed or sprayed on, I prefer to use a disposable brush with it. POR-15 comes in black, silver, gray, and clear colors. It is important to wear gloves while using it and to take other safety precautions because it is all but impossible to remove from skin or clothing after it has dried; it's a good idea to have a can of POR-15 thinner on hand when using this product. Always use it in a well-ventilated environment because the fumes are hazardous to your health. POR-15 is an excellent product that produces a durable protection from further rusting.

The Eastwood Company's Rust Encapsulator paint also stabilizes rust and prevents further rusting. It is especially good for use on areas where the rust can't be removed.

It can be brushed on or sprayed, and because it is somewhat thinner than the POR-15 product, it lends itself to spraying nicely. It is available in pint, quart, and gallon cans as well as in 16-ounce aerosol cans. The available colors are black, silver, and red. It is also flammable and the vapors are harmful, so the proper safety precautions should be observed, such as wearing a respirator and eye protection. Rust Encapsulator is easy to apply, does a very good job of stopping rust, and is very economical.

When using either POR-15 or Rust Encapsulator, be sure to mask off adjacent areas of the vehicle that you don't want these coatings to touch. These areas include the rocker panels, fender edges, brake calipers and discs, brake cables, and other such parts. Masking is particularly important when spraying on either of these coatings because overspray is always present whether using aerosol cans or a spray gun. Be sure to use a respirator and eye protection when using these products, and have an adequate flow of fresh air.

Sanding and Blasting

Without a doubt, you'll be doing a lot of sanding during your restoration. Although you can simply use your fingers and palm to push the sandpaper across the surface of the chassis, using a sanding block makes the job easier on your hands and faster as well.

You can purchase a sanding block from the local NAPA store, Home Depot, Lowe's, or even the neighborhood hardware store for under $10. While these commercial sanding blocks make changing the sandpaper fast and easy, you can save some money by using a 5-inch piece of two-by-four as a sanding block by stapling the sandpaper to it. When you need to change the sandpaper, rip it off and staple on a new piece.

Sandpaper comes in various grits, which are designated by numbers. The lower the number, the coarser the sandpaper, and the more aggressively it will remove rust. For most of your chassis rust removal work, 60 or 80 grit sandpaper works best.

> **4-Wheel Jive**
>
> The Jeep got its name from saying aloud the Army's name "G.P.," an abbreviation for "general purpose" vehicle.

You can also use an electric sander, which really lessens the required manual effort and considerably speeds up the job. If you don't already have one in your household tool collection, you can get one from the local home improvement center for under $30. It's well worth the price, especially if you have a lot of rust on your chassis.

An air-powered orbital sander is another great tool for removing rust. These sanders use adhesive-backed sanding discs that come in various grits. While these sanders remove rust very aggressively, the downside to using them is that they are inherently noisy because the air compressor supplies the power. The exhaust air from the sander also stirs up the sanding dust. Because I personally hate the noise of the compressor, I prefer to use the electric sander in most instances.

You will inevitably encounter rounded or irregularly shaped areas while derusting your chassis. For the areas where a sanding block won't get the job done, you can wrap a piece of sandpaper around an old piece of automotive heater hose. This gives you a flexible sanding block that you can use to follow contours or to get to hard-to-reach areas.

I've also used sanding sponges on occasion, and they yield good results. Compared to the price of sandpaper, however, they are expensive. They're good for small areas, but I wouldn't recommend trying to sand your entire chassis with them because of their cost and the fact that we have discussed faster and more efficient methods of removing rust.

Sandblasting Guns

Sandblasting is one of the oldest and most efficient ways of removing rust and taking the chassis down to bare metal. There are three different types of sandblasting guns: the siphon gun, the gravity-feed gun, and the pressure-blasting gun.

The siphon-blasting gun is the cheapest and most basic of the three. It works by siphoning the sand or other blast media out of a bucket or other container using a rubber siphon hose. Compressed air flowing through the gun creates a vacuum in its path that sucks the abrasive media up through the hose and propels it out the nozzle. A siphon-blasting gun can be purchased for $30 or less.

As the name implies, the gravity-feed blasting gun relies on gravity to put the abrasive media particles into the air stream. These guns usually have top-loading hoppers that hold 2 to 4 pounds of abrasive media. While they are convenient for small jobs, the weight of the media in the hopper makes them tiring to use for long periods. Also, they require frequent reloading of media, which slows down your productivity. Gravity-feed blasting guns generally sell for $50–$75.

Pressure-blasting guns use abrasive media that is dispensed from a pressurized hopper and mixed with the compressed air stream to propel the media out of the nozzle at a very high speed. On the average, pressure-blasting is five times faster and uses less air and media than siphon or gravity-fed blasting. Although

> **CAUTION**
>
> **Pit Stop**
>
> Whenever you use any type of sandblasting equipment, be sure to wear a blast hood and use a respiratory mask. Minute particles of abrasive media can wreak havoc on your eyes and respiratory tract, so be sure to take the appropriate precautions before blasting.

they offer excellent speed and high-capacity hoppers, the downside of pressure blasters is their cost; an entry-level hobbyist unit costs approximately $350, while a professional model is in the $900 neighborhood.

Coping with Cracks

Frame cracks can be caused by a variety of things, the most common of which are vibrations, harsh jolts, and collision damage. Cracks are frequently hidden by rust, which is another reason for cleaning up the frame as much as possible.

Cracks at weld junctions are by far the most common. These junctions can be where the cross members attach to the frame rails or where reinforcing gusset plates are welded to the frame and cross member. Vibration from untold miles of wear and tear, as well as potholes and other major roadway irregularities, all take their toll on a vehicle's chassis, and a crack or two is not uncommon on older, high-mileage vehicles. Severe rust damage to the chassis also increases the chances for cracks to develop.

> **4-Wheel Jive**
>
> The Beverly Hillbillies' truck was, in actuality, a cut-down Oldsmobile car.

Brake It Down

Also called a wire welder, MIG stands for metal inert gas. A **MIG welder** uses electric current to create a high-energy electric arc. Welding wire is fed through the tip of the welding gun, and an inert gas (usually argon) flows out of the tip of the gun to displace the air around the area being welded. Because there is no air, the weld is fast and smooth, with little or no slag produced. In body shops, MIG welders are a favorite tool for doing sheet metal repairs, and heavy-duty MIG units can be used for welding thicker metal such as chassis rails.

Small, hairline cracks can usually be fixed by welding them shut, although I've seen effective repairs done using steel mending plates bolted in place. Of these two methods, welding is the better method. An oxyacetylene welding outfit is usually required for welding chassis components, because the steel is too heavy to weld with a standard MIG unit. However, heavy-duty *MIG welding* units can also be used successfully for these kinds of repairs.

Larger, more severe cracks require welding backing plates over the damaged area, most often on two or three sides to provide additional strength. Again, gas or arc welding is usually the way to go for such heavy-duty repairs.

Welding Wizardry

Before welding, the area should be scrupulously derusted and cleaned for the best welding results. It is highly desirable to take the area to be repaired right down to bare metal for the strongest welds.

Regardless of which welding method you use, eye protection is of the utmost importance. Irreparable retinal damage can occur literally in an instant if your eyes are exposed to the light waves emitted by welding arcs and flames. For this reason, the proper goggles or face shield should always be worn when welding.

If you're using a MIG welder, a high-quality auto-darkening welding helmet is a must. These helmets permit normal viewing through a transparent shield, but as soon as the arc from a MIG welder is sensed, the viewing shield instantly darkens to protect the eyes from retinal damage. The best of these helmets have an auto-darkening response time of a millisecond or less. The human eye cannot perceive a millisecond in response time.

It's important to understand what arc flash is in order to select the right helmet. Arc flash is the unexpected exposure of the eyes to the welding arc. The welding arc emits several forms of light including ultraviolet (UV), infrared (IR) radiation, and high-intensity visible light. Both IR and UV radiation can cause permanent damage to the eyes, including retinal burns. The high-intensity visible light emitted from the arc usually won't do any permanent damage, but it will certainly cause temporary discomfort like being exposed to the flash of a camera's strobe or flash bulb.

All welding helmets that comply with the ANSI Z87.1 standard (when in the proper down position) always protect the wearer from the harmful UV and IR damaging elements of the arc. (ANSI standard Z87.1 is a standard set for the minimum level of eye protection with which welding helmets must comply). When shopping for a helmet, the first thing to look for is a label on the auto-darkening cartridge that certifies its compliance with ANSI standard Z87.1.

Auto-darkening welding helmets are available in two types: battery-powered and solar-powered. The battery-powered helmets usually have an auto-off switch to conserve battery life, whereas the solar-powered helmets are instantly activated when a welding arc is struck. The type you choose is a matter of personal taste because both work equally well. The important thing is to verify that the helmet is ANSI Z87.1 certified.

The process of welding involves heating the metal until it is in a molten state so that it can be fused together. Obviously, to get metal hot enough to liquefy, a lot of heat is required. Protect yourself from burns by wearing welding gloves and an apron or other protective clothing. It's also a good idea to use a welding blanket to protect adjacent areas from stray molten particles or slag.

CAUTION

Pit Stop

Whenever you are welding, make sure that other family members and pets do not enter your work area while you're working. Even though you are wearing eye protection, another person can suffer eye damage if he unexpectedly walks in while you're welding. Small children and household pets are particularly fascinated with the brilliant light emitted during welding, and staring at this light even for an instant can cause retinal burning.

The Least You Need to Know

◆ The only way to prevent rusting is to put a barrier between the metal and the atmosphere.

◆ Rust removal and repairing rust damage are major chores in the overall restoration process.

◆ Rust can be removed by both chemical and mechanical means.

◆ The light generated by welding is harmful to the eyes and can cause irreparable damage.

◆ Proper precautions should be taken while welding to prevent other family members or pets from exposure to welding light.

Chapter 18

Where the Rubber Meets the Road

In This Chapter

- ◆ Springy thingies
- ◆ Taking stock of shocks
- ◆ Give me a brake
- ◆ Time to re-tire
- ◆ What's on your hub, bub?

A safe vehicle must be able to maneuver and stop over a wide range of road conditions. In order to maneuver and stop quickly and safely, there must always be good contact between the tires and the road. The suspension is responsible for keeping the tires firmly planted on the road, and it also provides a comfort buffer between the rough road and the passenger cabin.

This chapter focuses on springs, shocks, brakes, wheels, and tires. So let's put the pedal to the metal.

The Suspension System

The vehicle's suspension system includes springs, shock absorbers/struts and the linkage used to suspend and locate a vehicle's frame, body, engine, and drive train above the wheels. There are many different types of suspensions. Each is a compromise among comfort, cost, and road-holding. To meet these compromises for each vehicle, many types of suspensions have been developed. Each design shares two essential components: springs and shock absorbers.

Speaking of Springs

Springs isolate the driver and passengers from road imperfections by allowing the tire to move over a bump without drastically disturbing the chassis. If the chassis remains fairly steady, the tires are better able to follow road contours. The two types of springs that are used most often in passenger vehicle suspension are the *coil spring* and the *leaf spring*. Other varieties of springs used on vehicles are *air springs* and *torsion bars*. Despite the differences in design, these variations all perform the same job and react with the suspension in the same manner.

> **Brake It Down**
>
> A **coil spring** is a spiral of elastic steel wire that is used in many sizes for different purposes throughout a vehicle, most notably as the springing medium in the suspension system.

> **Brake It Down**
>
> A **leaf spring** is composed of one or more long, slightly curved flexible steel or fiberglass plates. Several plates of diminishing lengths are mounted on top of one another and clamped together. Leaf springs are attached to the vehicle's frame by shackles.

Springs are durable items; however, over time, they can become "tired," which affects the vehicle's ride quality and ride height. Springs are easy to inspect visually. If the ride height of your vehicle appears lower than it should be or if you find a broken leaf or coil in a spring, it must be replaced. There is no acceptable way to repair a broken or sagging spring.

Some people intentionally change springs to alter their vehicle's ride and handling characteristics. This is commonly done when restoring muscle cars or other high-performance vehicles. In these instances, stiffer springs are usually substituted for the stock units to give the vehicle better handling under hard acceleration and cornering.

A mounted spring contains a large amount of potential energy. This energy is stored while the spring is compressed and released when it is decompressed. It is this storing and releasing of energy that enables the spring to do its work.

> **Brake It Down** _____
>
> An **air spring** uses air compressed inside a flexible rubber container instead of a metal spring. Air springs, also known as air suspension, can deliver excellent driving comfort over a wide range of vehicle loading because they can be made very soft for a lightly loaded condition, and their pressure automatically increased to match any increase in the load.

Because of this stored energy, working with springs can be very dangerous if the proper precautions are not taken. Before removing a leaf spring shackle, the spring end should be compressed slightly and supported with a hydraulic jack to take the pressure off the shackle bolt, which can then be removed safely. After the shackle bolt is removed, the jack can be lowered slowly so that the spring decompresses fully and safely.

Like leaf springs, coil springs also store a lot of potential energy when they are mounted on the vehicle. It is necessary to use a coil spring compression tool to remove these springs safely.

> **Brake It Down** _____
>
> A **torsion bar** is a long, straight bar fastened to the frame at one end and to a suspension part at the other. It is, in effect, an unwound coil spring that twists to absorb the energy produced by road irregularities. In a front suspension, the primary advantage of the torsion bar over the coil spring is that it provides an easy means of adjusting suspension height.

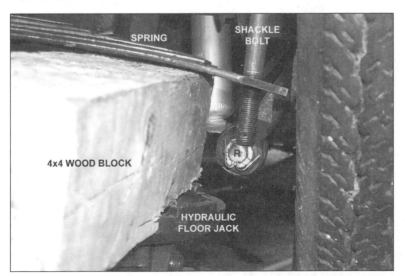

SPRING

SHACKLE BOLT

4x4 WOOD BLOCK

R

HYDRAULIC FLOOR JACK

This rear transverse leaf spring is being compressed and supported by a 4-by-4 wood block on a hydraulic floor jack. The nut and grommet has already been removed from the shackle bolt, and the jack is then slowly lowered so the spring can decompress and slide off the shackle bolt.

This coil spring compressor is a required safety tool during the installation and removal of coil springs. This internal type does not interfere with coil spring towers, suspension, or frame components.

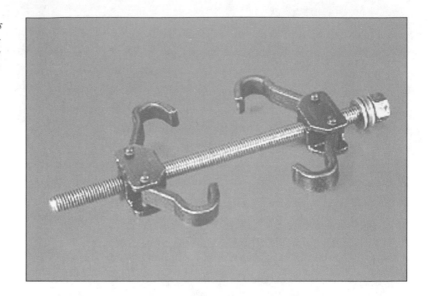

The coil spring compression tool is a threaded rod with two threaded yokes. Each of these yokes has two hooks. The tool is inserted inside the coil spring, and the hooks of the upper yoke are positioned on one of the upper coils; the hooks of the lower yoke are positioned on one of the lower coils. When the threaded rod is turned clockwise using a wrench, the yokes move toward each other, thus compressing the spring in the process. When the spring is compressed sufficiently, it can be lifted out of the chassis along with the compression tool.

Brake It Down

A monoleaf spring is a leaf spring with a single, long, slightly curved flexible plate that is usually made of fiberglass.

Reinstalling the spring or installing a new spring is the exact opposite of the removal operation; the compressed spring is inserted into its mount, and the threaded shaft is turned counter-clockwise to allow the spring to expand. When it is completely expanded, the hooks are removed from the coils, and the tool can then be removed by withdrawing it from the inside of the coil spring.

Restoring your vehicle's springs, whether they are coil or leaf springs or a combination of the two, generally involves removing them from the vehicle. After they are removed from the vehicle, they can be derusted using abrasive or chemical means, painted with a rust-preventive paint (usually satin black), and reinstalled in the vehicle. Of course, their mounts and mounting hardware should also be derusted and painted while the springs are off the vehicle as well.

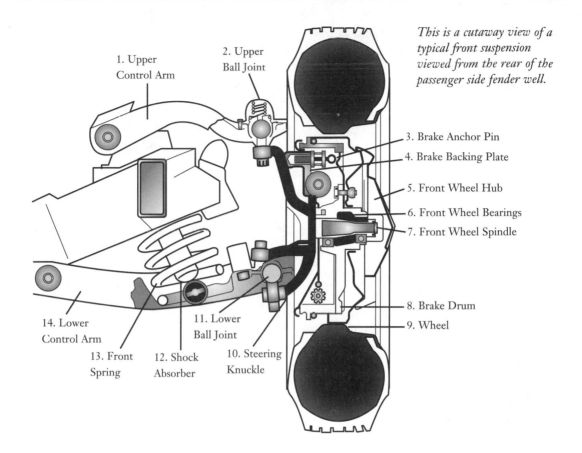

1. Upper Control Arm
2. Upper Ball Joint
This is a cutaway view of a typical front suspension viewed from the rear of the passenger side fender well.
3. Brake Anchor Pin
4. Brake Backing Plate
5. Front Wheel Hub
6. Front Wheel Bearings
7. Front Wheel Spindle
8. Brake Drum
9. Wheel
14. Lower Control Arm
13. Front Spring
12. Shock Absorber
11. Lower Ball Joint
10. Steering Knuckle

How Shocking

While springs do an excellent job of smoothing over bumps, they continue to oscillate once they've started to bounce. In other words, the chassis continues swaying and the tires keep hopping long after the vehicle strikes a bump. Left uncontrolled, springs give an uncomfortable ride with very poor tire-to-road contact. A shock absorber is used to control this undesirable behavior. As the name implies, the shock absorber absorbs road shocks and keeps the spring from overreacting to every bump or dip, thus preventing excess movement of the tire and chassis.

Some vehicles, especially those made from the 1980s to the present, have struts instead of shocks. In reality, a strut is just a shock absorber built into a suspension link. The strut is generally replaceable as one unit. For our purposes, all references to shock absorbers also apply to struts.

The shock absorber controls spring motion by damping (absorbing) energy from the spring. A shock absorbs energy by forcing oil through valves whenever it is moved. It takes a lot of energy to push oil through the valves so that when the spring is done pumping, it doesn't have much energy left to keep bouncing. Hence, the shock of the bouncing has been absorbed.

To illustrate what the shock absorber does to the spring's oscillation, imagine running 300 feet on bare ground—you could probably do it and have plenty of energy to run back again. Now imagine running the same 300 feet through 6 inches of mud. How much energy would you have left for a return pass? The oil in the shock absorber is the "mud" that saps the springs bouncing energy.

Shocks also control the car body's reaction to road undulations. A stiffer shock tends to transmit more road irregularities to the driver, but also does not pitch and roll as much as a vehicle with softer shocks. Shocks, like springs, can therefore be changed to obtain a personalized ride, and this is frequently done while performing a restoration.

Like tires, shocks wear out and need to be replaced occasionally. Although there are exterior signs of a damaged shock that indicate a need for replacement, frequently a shock absorber will have stopped working without any visible indicators.

It isn't possible to tell if a shock is functioning simply by examining it. Putting new shock absorbers on your vehicle during restoration is the best bet all around. Although it is possible to rebuild your own shocks, this is not practical for the average hobbyist because of the required time, labor, and special equipment.

If you need "correct" shocks for an older vehicle, it's worthwhile to check out specialty restoration parts houses such as Kanter Auto Products that stock obsolete auto parts for American cars from 1930 through 1990, including a huge inventory of shock absorbers for 1933–1985 vehicles.

Virtually all shock absorbers use oil to absorb energy. As the shock compresses and extends, oil must be forced through valves in the shock piston. These valves provide resistance to the flow of fluid, which absorbs energy from the suspension. The valves let a different amount of fluid through at different shock piston speeds. This means that the shocks absorb different amounts of energy depending on how fast the suspension is moving. So the valves allow the suspension to provide a comfortable ride by controlling chassis movement (low piston speed) and, at the same time, provide firm contact with the road surface by controlling suspension movement (high piston speed). There are two basic types: the two-tube shock absorber and the monotube design. All shocks are designed to provide comfort and safety, but, like all products, some are better than others. Some shock absorber designs are better suited to handle rough road conditions without losing effectiveness. Other differences in shock design center around the quality of components and how that affects the shock's life expectancy.

Gas Shocks

There is also a variation on the monotube design, in which a "gas" shock intentionally mixes the pressurized gas with oil. Because the gas is under very high pressure, the oil does not foam. The gas just travels around with the oil in little bubbles. The valving on this type of shock is located on the piston and is specially designed to handle the air/oil mix. A rule of thumb for all types of shocks and struts is that "gas" shocks are better for almost all circumstances because the oil in them remains cooler. In addition, the larger the tubes used to construct the shock, usually the higher quality it is. Larger tubes hold more oil, which then does not get as hot. Cool oil retains its molecular properties longer than hot oil.

When purchasing replacement shocks for your collector vehicle, it's a good idea to consider using gas shocks rather than the stock units for improved ride and handling characteristics.

Aftermarket shocks that have softer damping rates at normal travel but get firmer at extreme positions are becoming popular. These designs give a comfortable ride under most conditions but become firm when aggressive vehicle maneuvers are required. There are also very high performance shocks available that have multiple to infinite damping adjustments, allowing you to precisely tune suspension performance. This is another shock absorber option you might want to consider.

Better Binders

Good brakes are absolutely crucial to the safe operation of your vehicle, and you should not skimp or take shortcuts on the brakes during your restoration.

CAUTION **Pit Stop**

Whenever you are working on your vehicle's suspension—whether it's springs, brakes, shocks, etc.—always wear eye protection and make sure that your work area is well lit and uncluttered. Many suspension components are under pressure and stray particles of dirt, rust, or other debris can be propelled at considerable speed when these parts are freed from their mounts, thus presenting a very real and present danger to the eyes.

Pre-1967 domestic vehicles invariably have drum brakes, while disc brakes came on the scene in the latter part of the decade. When first introduced, many cars of the late 1960s and early to mid-1970s featured disc brakes on the front wheels and drum brakes on the rear because most of the vehicle's stopping power comes from the front wheels. However, as the Department of Transportation and federal law mandated more stringent safety regulations, four-wheel disc brakes soon became the norm.

With drum brakes, brake shoes expand to make contact with the inside of the brake drum, generating friction that slows and stops the vehicle. Conversely, with disc brakes, pads mounted on calipers are pressed against the metal brake disc, which generates the friction for slowing and stopping. Disc brakes stay cooler because the pads and the disc are not encased like the shoes in a drum brake. Because of this, they are less prone to *brake fade* due to heat buildup.

One of the simplest and best ways to improve the efficiency of drum brakes is to use high-performance brake shoes rather than stock shoes. High-performance brake shoes come in several different grades, each of which is specifically designed to outperform stock shoes by providing superior wear characteristics and resistance to brake fade under varying degrees of usage. They also provide shorter stopping distances than stock shoes.

Brake It Down

When brakes get extremely hot they lose their effectiveness at stopping. Two reasons for this **brake fade** are that the brake shoe or pad material loses its ability to grip as it gets hot, or that the brake fluid actually boils, creating air bubbles that reduce the pressure at the wheel; lower brake pressure results in less stopping power.

You can also use high-performance brake drums rather than stock drums. Aftermarket manufacturers like Raybestos offer premium drums that, when combined with their shoes, deliver significant improvements in braking performance.

By using a micrometer, you can ascertain whether or not your brake drums need to be replaced. You'll find a minimum-thickness number stamped onto the outside of the drum, and if the measured thickness is less than this number, the drum can't be cut and must be replaced. As a rule of thumb, when half or less than half of the brake shoe lining remains, the shoes should also be replaced.

Another way to improve braking performance is to use DOT4 silicone brake fluid rather than standard fluid. The silicone fluid is extremely resistant to high temperatures, and, as noted earlier, cooler brakes (and brake fluid) provide better stopping power.

Conventional brake fluid is hygroscopic: It likes water and tries to mate with it. Water boils at a lower temperature than brake fluid. It also rusts the calipers, cylinders, and pistons. Silicone brake fluid is not hygroscopic.

In addition to the shoes, drums, and fluid, there are other components in your collector vehicle's braking system that will require rebuilding, overhauling, or replacement as part of the overall restoration program. You would do well to consider purchasing a brake overhaul kit from a supplier like Kanter Auto Products. Kanter has complete brake overhaul kits starting from about $120 that contain the master cylinder, wheel cylinders, cables, and individual components such as lines, springs, shoes, and so forth. These kits are very convenient because they contain everything you need to restore your vehicle's braking system, they use quality components, and they're a great value—purchasing a kit is much more economical than purchasing the components individually. As an added bonus, Kanter offers a lifetime limited warranty with their brake overhaul kits.

Even if your collector vehicle has disc brakes on all four wheels, you can still improve the car's stopping power. There are bolt-on modifications you can make that will definitely improve your braking performance.

Using heavy-duty disc brake pads is the first step toward improving your binders. As with drum brake shoes, disc brake pads are available in several different formulations for different driving situations from improved street use to all-out competition. Those restoring GM-based performance cars such as Camaros, Firebirds, and Corvettes can check out aftermarket suppliers of performance braking products like Vette Brakes & Products; for the Mustang, Cougar, and Cobra restoration aficionados, vendors such as www.cobraautomotive.com offer several high-performance brake components and complete packages. And there are other retail houses that cater to Thunderbirds, Mopars, Porsches and virtually every other marque under the sun.

As with brake drums, disc brake rotors have a minimum thickness measurement stamped into them. The rotor's thickness can be measured using a caliper, and if it falls below the stamped thickness measurement, it can't be cut and must be replaced.

If you're replacing your rotors, you have the opportunity to improve braking performance here as well. Rather than using stock replacement rotors, consider using slotted and/or drilled rotors. These high-performance rotors dissipate heat much better than stock units, and the slots and/or holes also improve braking performance in wet weather by providing channels for water to run out of.

And, again, DOT4 silicone fluid improves heat resistance and dissipation throughout the braking system with disc brakes just as it will with drum brakes.

Often forgotten and thus neglected is the parking brake. Be sure to inspect and replace the actuating cables if they appear to show even the slightest bit of wear. I recommend replacing the cables, tensioners, and pulley(s) with stainless steel units because they won't rust or corrode.

You may also want to consider stainless steel brake lines while doing your restoration for a couple of reasons. First, stainless steel doesn't rust, so these lines should last indefinitely. The second reason is purely cosmetic: Stainless steel lines look very handsome, especially when they're mounted on a pristinely detailed chassis.

Tire Tales

This is really where the rubber meets the road. The scant few square inches of rubber that contact the pavement make all the difference in the world between cool cruising and catastrophe.

Why is it so important to have good tire contact? All of the actions a vehicle performs—acceleration, cornering, and braking—are transmitted through the tires. The tires perform these actions through a phenomenon called friction. The most important rule of friction is that the more two objects are pressing together, the higher the frictional forces between them.

Therefore, it is necessary for the tire to press firmly on the road at all times if the vehicle is going to brake and turn optimally.

In an emergency situation, you need as much contact between the tire and road as possible. Without maximum contact, the vehicle might not be able to perform the emergency maneuver that is necessary to prevent injury and property damage.

Bias-Ply Tires

Bias-ply tires were once the conventional automobile tires, but they were replaced first by bias-belted tires and then by radial tires. They are no longer used on passenger cars, but are still found on some collector vehicles. Bias-ply tires gave a very stiff ride, and cornering was not their strong point, to say the least. They also tended to squeal like a stuck pig when making a sharp turn.

Brake It Down

Bias-ply tires were once the conventional and predominant automobile tires. They have cords in their plies of structural fabric that are at an angle (the bias angle) to the circumferential centerline. The carcass is constructed of adjacent layers of fabric that run continuously from bead to bead. The "bead" is the strong inner circumference of the tire which mates up with the wheel rim. A typical bias-ply passenger-car tire has two plies of fabric with cords running at an angle of 30–40 degrees to the circumferential centerline.

Companies like Coker Tires still produce bias-ply tires for car restorers, and they make their tires from the original molds using the same materials the original manufacturers used. Coker even has licensed the tire manufacturer's name for the sidewall. For purists, these tires are the only way to go.

Others may want to take advantage of the tire technology improvements that have developed since their vehicles left the assembly line, and there are several options here. You can purchase "faux" bias plies that look like the real thing but, in reality, are radial tires. For the muscle cars of the late '60s and early '70s, these present a particularly attractive alternative. Rather than putting a hot Ram Charger or Barracuda on a set of anemic bias-ply redlines, the restored Mopar can cruise in style on a set of radials with red lines that appear to be correct.

Still others just want modern tires such as Goodyear GT-IIs with the raised white lettering on their sides, and they'll forego the vintage-look route. While these tires are not completely correct, they do deliver improved comfort, handling, and a snappy appearance.

Tire Size

While you can deviate from the correct tire size to some extent, such deviations in tire size can adversely affect steering and handling geometry. To illustrate this point a bit more vividly, let's say that you wear a size 9 shoe but suddenly you're forced to wear a size 11. Obviously, the shoes are too big, so they are going to affect your stride. The same happens when you put tires on that are too big or too small for the vehicle.

Another thing to consider is the way a larger tire size affects the accuracy of your speedometer and odometer. With older vehicles, the gearing of the speedometer largely depended on the size of the rear tires. For example, let's say the car originally came with 6.75-by-14 tires. If you mount 7.50-by-15 tires on the car, the speedometer calibration will be off, as will the odometer, because the diameter of the replacement tire is one inch larger than the stock rubber. The result is a 3.1416-inch larger circumference of the tire. The original calibration of the speedometer and odometer were based on 43.98 inches for each rotation of the rear wheel; with the increased diameter of the larger wheel, the distance for each rotation is increased to 47.12 inches. Over the course of a mile, three-plus inches of additional distance covered per rotation amounts to a considerable difference. The stock setup would have performed 15,151.43 revolutions to complete the mile, while the 15-inch wheel setup would do it in 14,141.766 revolutions—that's a difference of 1,009.666 revolutions, a 6.7 percent reduction both in the speedometer reading and the mileage shown on the odometer. That's enough to earn you a ticket!

Tire Appearance

Some collectors seem to think the only attractive tire is one that's drenched in some gunk to make it shiny. This accomplishes only two things. It makes the car look tacky and it sucks the preservatives out of the tire, causing it to age prematurely and crack. Tires are not naturally black. Rubber is white or tan colored (like a gum eraser); natural rubber is aged by the sun's ultraviolet rays. Early tire makers learned that adding carbon black to rubber retarded this process. Today's tires have additives not only to retard ultraviolet degradation but also the attacks of environmental agents like ozone. Drenching a tire in a silicone goop accelerates its aging. Just wash them with water and a mild detergent. Unless, of course, you really want the "wet look."

Spiffy Wheels

Many collector cars are equipped with full wheel covers, so not much attention is usually paid to the wheels themselves. In most cases, the stock wheels are lackluster steel units that don't offer any particularly exciting visual cues. But even the most mundane wheels deserve to be included in the overall restoration process.

While masks are available for repainting the wheel with the tire still on it, I don't recommend this method. The right way to restore a wheel is to have the tire taken off so you have complete access to the entire wheel, both inside and out. After removing the tire, pry off any balancing weights and remove the tire valve stem as well.

Next, thoroughly derust the wheel. Although you can use chemical agents to do this, I highly recommend sand- or media-blasting the wheel to take it down to the bare metal. Be sure to get thoroughly into the crack between the wheel center and the rim, and then carefully remove any blasting media that's caught in there. A few coats of high-quality self-etching primer should then be applied to the entire wheel, and then allow the wheel to dry thoroughly. After priming, a few coats of the desired color wheel paint should be applied, and when thoroughly dried, a new tire valve stem can be installed. The old tire (or, preferably, a new one) can then be mounted and the tire/wheel combination balanced.

Specialty wheels, like the optional factory styled-steel wheels available on the 1965 Mustang GT Fastback, require different restoration techniques. The Mustang wheels cited here were chrome plated, so restoring them requires using a special solution like Busch's Chrome Wash to clean them up and remove light surface rust. If the wheels are badly rusted, they must be rechromed, which can be a pricey proposition.

Styled "honeycomb" aluminum wheels like those found on the 1971 GTO and other muscle cars of that era don't have rusting problems, although pitting and brake dirt are their nemeses. Busch's Aluminum Wash does wonders at spiffying-up these wheels.

Some folks like to go with "period" wheel treatments, such as Baby Moon hubcaps or spun aluminum "dry lake" wheel disks. Other popular treatments include using chromed "acorn" lug nuts and spinner or bullet hubs in lieu of conventional wheel covers.

Another period wheel treatment was the use of chromed reverse wheels. These were conventional steel wheels that had their rivets ground out and the hub of the wheel reversed, then reriveted or welded back together. Performing this modification gave the wheel additional offset so that more of the tire faced the outside of the fenders than when the wheel was unmodified. The effect was to give the car a wider stance without going to a larger tire size. The modified wheel was then chrome-plated and usually outfitted with a Baby Moon hubcap to finish off the look. This was the hot setup to go with in the late 1950s and early 1960s, but with the advent of *mag wheels*, the chrome reverse wheels faded from popularity.

Anything that widens the front wheels' track dimension (the distance between the tire centerlines is called "track") will affect the car's steering and the geometry of its independent front suspension. When turning a corner, the outside front wheel has to follow a larger diameter circle than the inner front wheel. This is designed into the steering, but it becomes greater when the track is increased and the outside wheel tends to grab, chewing up the outside edge of its tread.

Chrome wire wheels always attract attention, as do the tried-and-true Cragar mag wheels and American Racing mags. Another recent trend is the use of custom polished aluminum billet wheels on collector cars from the 1950s, 1960s, and 1970s. Another trend that seems to be on the rise is to use ultra low-profile tires with huge (17-, 18-, or even 19-inch diameter) custom wheels. This trend, originally the vogue setup for small, fast imports like the Toyotas and Hondas, is now showing up with more frequency on such unlikely vehicles as the 1955 Chevy Bel Air!

> **Brake It Down**
>
> The term **mag wheel** originates from lightweight magnesium alloy wheels used on racing cars that appeared in the '50s and '60s. Although the style of these wheels was adapted to aluminum alloy wheels, the name stuck. Most likely a "mag wheel" isn't really magnesium. It's aluminum.

Wheels Vintique has an enormous assortment of reproduction wheels available for restoration, and the company has everything from vintage wire wheels for Model A Fords through slotted rally wheels for Camaros and just about everything in between. The company also makes custom combinations (for example, classic chrome Cadillac wire wheels mated to a chromed Ford hub), and they also offer lug nuts, wheel locks, spinners, and other custom hubcaps.

The way your wheels look can make or break the appearance of your collector vehicle, so they deserve some thought and consideration while you're doing your restoration. Even a slight wheel change, say from a stock wheel to a slotted rally wheel, can have a profound visual effect on the appearance of your ride. However, this also means it's no longer "original."

Overdrive

Want to see how your collector vehicle would look with a different wheel treatment? Take a side-view photo of your ride and measure the distance from the camera to the vehicle. The next time you go to a car show or cruise night and see wheels that you think would work on your car, take a side-view picture of that vehicle from the same distance you used for photos of your own car. When you get the prints back, simply cut out the wheels from the show or cruise night car and put them on the picture of your vehicle to see how it would look. If you're using a digital camera, it's even easier to do using cut-and-paste with your favorite painting or drawing software.

The Least You Need to Know

◆ Leaf and coil springs are the predominant kinds of springs on collector vehicles, although there are other types including torsion bars and air springs.

◆ Shock absorbers absorb road shocks and keep the springs from overreacting to every bump or dip in the roadway.

◆ Braking performance can be improved by upgrading the shoes or pads, drums or rotors, and brake fluid.

◆ Heat causes brake fade, which diminishes braking performance and increases the vehicle's required stopping distance.

◆ Bias-ply tires were once the conventional automobile tire, but they gave a harsh ride; they were replaced by bias-belted tires and then by radials.

◆ When restoring a stock steel wheel, it's advisable to remove the tire, valve, and balancing weights to get the best results.

Putting the Muscle Back into Your Mill

In This Chapter

♦ Tuning and timing your engine

♦ Cleaning your carburetor

♦ Cleaning and degreasing your engine

♦ Painting different parts

♦ Cleaning and detailing the engine compartment

Without a doubt, the engine is the heart of any vehicle. More than just a power plant, a spiffy motor (it is particularly offensive and confusing to use "motor" and "engine compartment" in the same sentence) and a well-detailed engine compartment can be a joy to behold. You don't necessarily have to be a mechanical marvel to coax some extra horsepower out of your vehicle's old and tired motor, and you might even have some fun doing it.

So pop the hood, roll up your sleeves, and let's get to work on that motor.

Putting the Muscle Back into Your Mill

Before you go the drastic route of removing and overhauling your engine—whether or not you're planning on doing the work yourself—first determine whether it actually needs to be overhauled. More often than not, engine problems can be corrected without removing the motor.

Having a motor that already runs is a really good start (so is breathing). Minor smoking can sometimes be corrected or substantially lessened by using any number of commercial additives such as Stop Smoke available on the shelf of your local Pep Boys, Auto Zone, or other automotive retailer. Likewise, valve and lifter taps can often be quieted using off-the-shelf additives. Recognize, however, that the use of additives other than cleaning agents is only masking a more severe underlying problem that eventually will have to be dealt with.

If the engine isn't currently running, you'll want to establish whether it is seized. The easiest way to do this is to remove all of the spark plugs from the motor, squirt some engine oil through the spark plug holes and put the car (if it's an automatic transmission) in neutral. Then use a socket mounted on a breaker bar to rotate the nut on the *harmonic balancer*. Rotate the nut at least one full turn in a clockwise direction. As you rotate the nut, you'll hear the pistons moving up and down within the motor; this indicates that the motor is not seized, which is a good thing. It's even easier with a manual transmission. Put it in high gear and push it. If it moves and the engine turns over (watch the cooling fan), it's not seized. After you have established that there is no seizure, it's simply a matter of diagnosing the problems that are preventing the engine from being started.

Brake It Down

Also sometimes called a vibration damper, a **harmonic balancer** is a cylindrical weight attached to the front of the crankshaft to reduce the torsion or twisting vibration, which occurs along the length of the crankshaft in automotive engines.

If you can't rotate the engine, that's generally a bad sign; however, it might not necessarily indicate seizure. Frequently, a motor that has sat for a long time may have developed rust on the cylinder walls, or hardened gasoline varnish (the gummy residue left when gasoline evaporates) may be preventing the pistons from moving up and down freely. Spray a liberal amount of WD-40 or penetrating oil into each cylinder via the spark plug holes and let it sit for a day; then, try to turn it over again. Hopefully, you'll be pleasantly surprised to find that the motor really wasn't seized at all, but merely stuck.

Removing an engine from a vehicle and rebuilding it yourself is an ambitious undertaking, to say the least. It's a lot of work, and it requires special equipment, tools, and skill. There's no question that some folks prefer to do their own engine rebuilding, while others gladly farm this work out.

Depending on the level of your restoration, you may even elect to replace the engine entirely with a remanufactured motor from Jasper, Honest Engines, or another engine remanufacturing source.

You might also decide to purchase a used engine as a replacement. If you go this route, it's best to see and hear the engine running before you buy it. If you don't verify that it is in good working order, you might buy a motor that's in worse shape than the one that's already in the car. This is a good time to understand the distinctions between remanufactured, rebuilt, and used engines.

- **Remanufactured:** A remanufactured engine is one that has been completely reconditioned, and all internal parts are replaced using only new or remanufactured parts. The castings are remachined and the engine is assembled with all tolerances meeting or exceeding the original manufacturer's specifications.

- **Rebuilt:** A rebuilt engine is one in which only the severely worn or broken parts have been replaced.

- **Used:** A used engine is one that was taken out of one vehicle and installed in another with no parts replaced or remanufactured.

Here are the components in a typical engine rebuild kit. If you don't have the skill and the right tools, you may want to farm the engine rebuilding out to a professional.

(Photograph courtesy of Kanter Auto Products)

If you're really stuck on the idea of redoing your engine yourself, here's a list of what you're going to need to do the job:

- An engine hoist (also called a cherry picker)

- Engine lift chains and brackets

- An engine stand

- A full set of shallow and deep sockets

- A full set of combination wrenches

- Assorted shop tools including a vise
- A gasket set
- A torque wrench (30–150 feet/pound range)
- A piston ring tool

- A rebuilding manual
- A cylinder hone
- An engine rebuild kit
- New motor mounts
- Plenty of time and patience

The engine hoist, also known as a "cherry picker," can be rented for a few dollars. Because you only need it the day you take the motor out of the car and the day you put it back in, renting the hoist for these two days makes more sense that buying a cherry picker for several hundred dollars, because this is probably the only engine you'll remove and re-install.

The engine stand, on the other hand, is something that you'll want to purchase because you'll have the motor on it the entire time you're working on it; this can be several months. These stands are readily available at better auto parts stores for under $100. You may be able to pick one up at a flea market or through the local classified ads for a fraction of what it costs to buy a new one.

The smartest way to overhaul your engine is to purchase an engine overhaul kit. This way you'll get everything you need to do the job right. Typically, an overhaul kit consists of a new camshaft, valves, springs, lifters, retainers, push rods pistons, rings, timing gears, timing chain, and other items required to do a complete engine overhaul. Kanter Auto Products offers engine overhaul kits starting at $350, which is a significant savings over the cost of purchasing these items individually. But before you buy a kit, you'll need to evaluate the engine's condition after disassembly to see what size pistons and bearings you'll need.

Tuning and Timing

It's amazing how a full tune-up puts some pep back into a tired engine. But go the whole nine yards—don't just replace the points and plugs. Do it right.

Start with an oil and filter change. Who knows how long that old oil has been in the motor, probably accumulating moisture from condensation? Drain it out and dispose of it responsibly (most auto parts outlets accept used motor oil for recycling without charge). In addition to installing a new oil filter, you might also want to invest $5 for a magnetic drain plug. These are great for trapping minute metal particles suspended in the oil that can cause internal engine damage.

The stock oil drain plug is shown at the left, while a magnetic drain plug is on the right. The magnet pulls and holds minute metal particles suspended in the oil and, for about $5, a magnetic plug gives you some added insurance against engine damage.

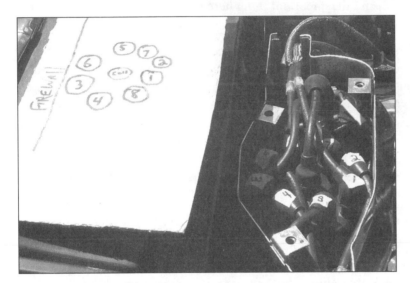

Making a diagram of the position of the plug wires on the distributor cap and labeling the wires make it simple to replace them and lessens the chance for confusion.

Next on the agenda is installing a new distributor cap and spark plug wires. Be sure to note the position of the wires on the distributor cap before you pull the old ones off—you can draw yourself a little diagram and use pieces of tape to label the wires. Replacing the wires one-by-one is a good way to avoid any confusion as to which wire goes to which cylinder.

New breaker points and a condenser are also on the order of parts to be replaced at this time. It's a good idea also to replace the distributor cap and rotor. Their contacts arc each time a plug fires and eventually become burned. Be sure to adjust the gap of the points to the car manufacturer's specifications using a feeler gauge.

Get yourself a full set of quality spark plugs and new plug wires. Don't try to clean up the existing plugs and reuse them; you can't be sure that these plugs are in good shape internally (remember what I said earlier about skimping). Faulty plug wires can cause all sorts of hard-to-identify problems. The carbon conductors used in the plug wires to suppress radio interference break down over time. Also replace the wire from the coil to the distributor cap. Use a feeler gauge to gap the plugs' electrodes to the car manufacturer's specifications.

You should also replace the air cleaner element at this time. Even a new cheap after-market air cleaner element is better than an old, dirty one. Your engine needs to be able to breathe for proper combustion, so help it to breathe easier.

Replacing the fuel filter is also something that shouldn't be overlooked. I prefer to use the transparent glass filters with replaceable elements so I can see what kind of debris the filter is catching, but that's a matter of personal preference. The plastic and metal filters also do a good job, and the important thing here is to install a new filter, regardless of the type.

Fresh gasoline is the order of the day. If the car has been sitting for any length of time, chances are pretty good that the gas is stale and it may even have water mixed with it from moisture condensation. The best bet here is to disconnect the fuel line and drain the tank completely. Again, I must stress that gasoline and its vapors are extremely flammable, so do not smoke or have any electrical equipment around that may cause sparks when you're draining the tank. As an alternative to disconnecting the fuel line, you can also use a siphon to drain the tank. Regardless of how you empty the gas tank, be sure to dispose of the drained fuel in an ecologically responsible manner.

The battery gets the attention now. Make sure the cells are filled up to their upper levels, replenishing them with distilled water as required. In a pinch you can use tap water, but distilled water is better.

While we're working with the battery, inspect the terminals for corrosion and make sure that the cable clamps are tight and making good contact.

Pit Stop

Do not use bottled spring water in your battery! It usually contains more minerals than tap water, and these minerals damage the car battery's cells. It is best to use distilled water because it does not contain any minerals or chemicals.

You are now ready to crank it up. Connect your timing light and start the car. While it is idling, check the timing and adjust it as necessary to bring it right on the designated mark according to the car manufacturer's specifications.

If you don't know what the correct specs are for your particular vehicle, you can purchase a Chilton or Haynes manual that covers your year, make, and model. These books are great for specifications, routine service, and repair procedures, and they're well worth the few dollars that they cost.

Carburetor Capers

A dirty carburetor can have seriously detrimental effects on your motor's performance, and it may even prevent the engine from starting altogether. Dirt and built-up gum can clog the venturi tubes in the carburetor and cause the floats that regulate fuel flow into the carburetor to stick.

One of the simplest remedial steps you can take with your carburetor is to clean it thoroughly. You don't necessarily have to remove the carburetor from the manifold to do so, either. Purchase an aerosol can of carburetor and choke cleaner from your local auto parts store. First, remove the air cleaner. Then spray the carburetor and choke cleaner liberally on the exterior of the carburetor to remove the caked-on grease and fuel varnish. Because this cleaner is highly flammable, take the same precautions you take when you are working with gasoline, and make sure that you have good ventilation because the vapors are harmful to your respiratory system.

After the carburetor's exterior has dried completely, start the engine with the air cleaner still removed from the car. Spray a squirt of the carburetor cleaner into the mouth of the carburetor with the engine idling. The motor will bog down a little, but it will return to a normal idle after a minute or two. If you spray too much carburetor cleaner, the engine will stall completely. After a normal idle has been established again, spray a little more cleaner into the carburetor.

A common malady of engines that have not been started for a long time is a stuck fuel *float* in the carburetor. When the fuel level in the carburetor's float bowl falls below a predetermined level, the float drops and opens a valve that allows more fuel to enter the float bowl from the fuel pump. As the fuel level in the float bowl rises, so does the float until it closes the valve (like the float in a toilet tank.) This opening and closing of the valve continues as long as the motor is running.

If the float is stuck in the up position, no fuel can enter the carburetor, and the car won't start. If you suspect that this might be the problem, try pouring a little gas directly into the mouth of the carburetor and attempting to start the car. If the car turns over and starts, but dies within a few seconds, you have established that the motor will start and run if it receives the fuel it needs. The next step is to determine why it isn't receiving that fuel.

Brake It Down

The **float** is a part of the carburetor that meters the fuel coming into the carburetor from the fuel pump and ensures that there is a steady supply of gasoline available for the engine even while making sharp turns or going up steep hills.

Disconnect the fuel line where it enters the carburetor and have someone turn the engine over. If gasoline spurts out of the fuel line while the motor is cranking, you know your fuel pump is okay. In this case, the carburetor is the culprit.

Sometimes you can get lucky and free a stuck float by rapping on the float bowl with the handle of a screwdriver. If that works, you're on a lucky streak, and you might want to go to the 7-11 and buy a lottery ticket. Realistically, tapping the float bowl is worth a try, but don't be surprised if this doesn't do the trick.

The majority of the time you encounter a stuck float, the carburetor must be removed from the manifold and disassembled to free up the float. Because the carburetor is already off the car and you're partially taking it apart to access the float bowl, you should completely rebuild the carburetor at this time.

This carburetor needs a rebuild, and here are the contents of the rebuild kit. Although the kit came with instructions, the book goes into much more detail and is well worth the extra expense.

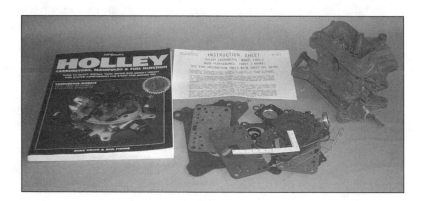

Rebuilding a carburetor isn't rocket science, although even a single-barrel carburetor contains an amazing number of parts. Carburetor rebuild kits are readily available, and they're inexpensive. While most of these kits come with instructions, I recommend purchasing a book on carburetor rebuilding for your carburetor's particular make and model. The books take you through the process step-by-step and assume that you know nothing about carburetors. Frequently they explain in great detail the principles and function of the carburetor, things that will make you a much more facile troubleshooter. The instructions that come with the kits, however, are usually written with the professional mechanic in mind, so they cut to the chase and leave out all of the background.

Make sure you have a clean work surface and plenty of light. I also like to have my digital camera handy to take pictures frequently while disassembling a carburetor. Pictures serve as handy references when it comes time to do the reassembly.

I also recommend that you have some containers available for storing the screws, springs, and other parts as the disassembly progresses. Small Tupperware containers serve this purpose well.

I generally use some 3-in-1 Oil to lubricate the float's hinging mechanism, and I find that it's also good for removing any accumulated corrosion and crud on the float. You can use a cotton swab and a soft cotton cloth to clean the float and the float bowl.

When you have the carburetor completely disassembled, you should take this opportunity to thoroughly clean the carburetor body and all of its components; small, stiff-bristled brushes come in handy for cleaning these parts. The Eastwood Company has aerosol Carburetor Renew paints that are specially formulated to look like the original factory silver or bronze colors the carburetor had when it was new.

Reassemble the carburetor in the reverse order of disassembly. Be sure to follow the instructions in the rebuilding manual and refer to your own photographs for reference. When the carburetor is completely reassembled, reinstall it on the intake manifold using a new gasket.

This is also a good time to check the throttle linkage for loose bearings, frayed cables, and worn connectors. Replace them now so the linkage is tight and free from slop. Reconnect the linkage and the fuel line coming from the fuel pump, as well as any choke connections. You'll probably have to crank the engine for several seconds while the float bowl fills before the car will start; however, if you did the rebuild as prescribed, the car should indeed start.

Cleaning and Degreasing

I'm a big fan of nonflammable cleaning and degreasing agents. There are plenty of excellent products for these chores that are nonflammable, so why take the chance of working with materials that pose a fire hazard?

Spray Nine is my favorite product for cleaning up a dirty, greasy engine. Spray Nine comes in a one-quart trigger-spray bottle that makes it very handy to clean and degrease even remote parts of the motor that aren't readily accessible by hand. I simply adjust the nozzle to give me a tight, narrow spray and shoot the Spray Nine onto the part until the part is thoroughly soaked. After letting it sit for a few minutes, I hose it down. If it still isn't cleaned to my satisfaction, I repeat the process a second or even a third time until all the grease and dirt are gone.

When you get the gunk off your engine, you'll have a much better idea of what else you'll need to do to make it look spiffy and operate sharply. And, regardless of other work you'll have to perform on the motor, having it nice and clean makes it all go smoother and without as much mess.

Painting Your Parts

Contrary to popular belief, you don't have to remove your engine to give it a new coat of paint. While some partial disassembly may be required (for example, unbolting the exhaust manifolds) to get at some portions of the motor, you can do a very respectable job on it while it's in the car.

It's better to take some parts off the car to work on them. For instance, removing the valve covers gives you the opportunity to strip them or sandblast them before priming and painting. The water pump is another part that is better to repaint off the motor. However, unless there is a mechanical need to take a part off, items such as the intake manifold and cylinder heads should be left on the car; taking them off creates a lot of unnecessary work.

Because of the inevitable overspray, using aerosol paints on the engine while it is in the car is not advisable. Aerosols are fine for parts that you're refinishing off the engine, such as the valve covers and water pump. Using a brush is the best way to paint the engine when it is in the car. Be sure that you buy engine paint because it's formulated to withstand high temperatures. Regular paint blisters and peels when the engine gets hot.

While almost every auto parts store carries aerosol engine paints, you may have a hard time finding the correct engine color in a pint or quart can. If this is the case, you can still use the aerosol paint, but do not spray it on the engine—brush it on. Here's how.

I've frequently used an empty baby food jar as a "paint pot." Let's say, for example, I want to paint the engine of my Mustang Ford blue. I go to the local NAPA store and pick up a couple of aerosol cans of blue, shake them vigorously to make sure the paint is uniformly mixed, and then hold the spray nozzle very close to the mouth of the baby food jar. I spray the paint into the jar until I have about an inch of paint in the bottom of the jar, and I use a one-inch brush to paint the motor, dipping it into the jar as required. When the jar is empty, I shake the can again and refill the jar from the spray can. Remember what I said about the inevitable overspray? That is also a problem when filling the jar with spray, and to get around that problem I wear nitrile gloves so I don't wind up with blue paint all over my hands.

For hard-to-reach areas of the engine and those that are beyond the reach of my arms, the brush can be attached to an extension that is made from an old mop or broom handle. For the extremely low portions of the motor, such as the flywheel cover and the oil pan, I elevate the car on jack stands and do the painting from beneath the vehicle.

One last bit of advice on engine painting: Be sure to have some rags and paint thinner available to clean up any inadvertent drips or sloppy work. A little time and effort will reward you with an engine you can be proud of.

Detailing the Engine Compartment

As with painting the engine, detailing the engine compartment is easier if the motor is out of the car, but that's not to say you can't do it with the motor present.

The first step is to clean up the engine compartment, and Spray Nine does a wonderful job here as well. The idea is to get all of the grease, dirt, and road grime off everything so you have nice, clean surfaces to work with. Don't forget the little details, such as grease on wiring, the windshield washer bottle and hoses, the battery tray, and so forth.

After everything is clean, assess the engine compartment's overall condition. Are there scratches or other marks on the inner fenders? The inner fenders are usually painted satin black, and, again because of overspray, you'll have to use a brush to retouch or re-paint these areas. I've found Rust-Oleum Satin Black to be excellent for painting these areas, and it comes in a very convenient half-pint can that contains enough paint to detail an entire engine compartment. I also prefer to use disposable sponge brushes for this type of painting.

Pay attention to your under-hood wiring. You might want to use some cable ties to tidy things up and retape bundles of wiring from the harness. You can also use the plastic wiring sleeves that are available at most auto parts stores, but you have to make a choice between original appearance when most cars had tape-wrapped wiring bundles and a neater but not "correct" modern appearance using plastic sleeves.

Braided steel hose covers also give things a smoother look, as well as flexible chrome hoses. You can also use anodized bolt-head covers for some additional eye-candy.

High-temperature manifold dressing gives your exhaust manifolds a like-new appearance. Although this paste-like dressing can be applied with the manifolds still mounted to the engine, removing the manifolds and then applying it will yield a better finish and an easier application.

Cadmium-plated parts such as master cylinder caps and brake boosters can be revitalized using the Golden Cad Paint System from Eastwood. The system is easy to use and, if you have several cadmium-plated components that need refreshing, it's very economical.

Don't neglect the underside of the hood itself. You may need to replace any torn insulation or weather stripping. Spray Nine also works well for removing soot and grime that accumulates here.

Some fine steel wool and a couple of old toothbrushes are very useful for detailing under the hood. Finally, use a good quality metal polish to clean up any chrome or stainless parts. You never thought this old clunker could look so good, right?

This before (left) and after (right) shot of this master cylinder cover shows how well the Golden Cad Paint System works.

The Least You Need to Know

- ◆ Removing and overhauling an engine is a major undertaking that requires special equipment, tools, and skill.

- ◆ Some superficial motor problems can be remedied using off-the-shelf additives.

- ◆ A thorough tune-up yields excellent results when revitalizing old, tired motors.

- ◆ A stuck carburetor float can prevent the motor from starting, and rebuilding a carburetor is not rocket science if you have a rebuild kit and a manual that explain how to do it step-by-step.

- ◆ Nonflammable degreasing agents are the safest to use.

- ◆ You can clean up your engine and detail the engine compartment with the engine in the car.

Chapter 20

The Body Beautiful

In This Chapter

- Repairing dents and dings—body repair materials
- Weather-stripping your vehicle
- Stripping to save money
- Installing a new convertible top
- Pot metal, plating, brightwork, and lenses
- Being ecologically responsible

The body of a collector vehicle is the first thing that catches your eye and attracts the most attention. Few man-made objects are more beautiful to behold than a tastefully restored collector vehicle with a smooth body and pristine paint.

The Body Beautiful

The body of the vehicle is its skin. And like your own skin, it is most pleasing to look at when it is devoid of scars and pocks or, in automotive terms, dents and dings. Good bodywork, like plastic surgery, can correct these flaws so perfectly that you would never even know they had existed previously. Bodywork techniques are the primary focus of this chapter.

A basic complement of body hammers and dollies is required for removing dents. This set costs only about $20 with the plastic storage case and is an excellent value.

Dealing with Dents and Dings

Dents and dings are a fact of life, period. Dents can occur from collisions, and dings can be the result of hail, falling acorns, or careless drivers letting their doors swing open and hitting yours in the process.

Taking a dent out cold (without using any body filler) can sometimes be done if you have access to the inside of the dented panel. Frequently, if the dent isn't too deep, it can be "popped" out by pushing on it from the inside of the panel. Other times, it may require tapping with a body hammer from the inside with a dolly on the outside to absorb the shock and prevent denting in the opposite direction.

Inflatable air bladders can sometimes remove a dent without damaging the paint. The bladders use a hand-operated bulb for inflation; this gives you nice control as the dent starts to pop. They are most effective when they can be inflated against a strong surface, such as a door brace.

Traditional slide-hammer dent pullers are also frequently used for fixing dents. While they have been used for decades, they fix the dent damage but inflict other damage in the process. These slide-hammer dent pullers require that a series of small holes be drilled in the dented area. These holes accommodate the threaded tip of the puller. With the puller threaded into the hole, the sliding weight is slammed back against the handle, and the metal of the dented area is pulled out. The process is repeated several times using the other holes until the dent is out. The screw holes are then ground flat and body filler is used to fill them in.

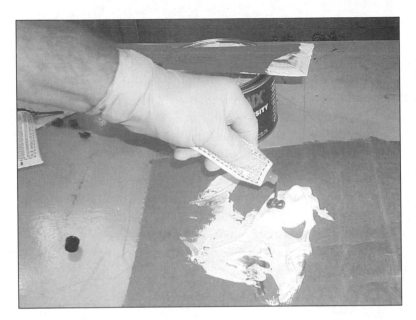

Body fillers like Duramix #4056 High Density Filler, shown here, or Bondo are perennial favorites for filling in dents and dings because the material sets up quickly and it is easy to work with. The creme hardener being squeezed onto the dollop of filler starts a chemical reaction when mixed, causing the filler to harden into a solid within minutes.

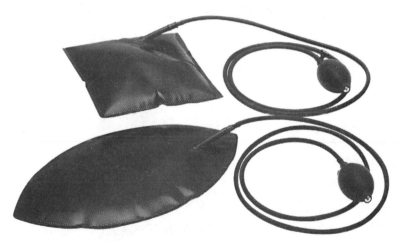

Air power can also be used to remove dents successfully from areas like the sides of doors. The deflated bladder can be slid down a window channel and hand-pumped at the dent location until the dent pops out. The bladder can then be deflated for easy removal from the channel.

Slide-hammer dent pullers have been around for decades. They pull out the dent, but leave a series of small holes in their wake that have to be filled in to complete the repair.

Suction-cup dent pullers have also been around for quite a while, and they can sometimes be used to successfully pop out a slight dent. As the name implies, these pullers are suction cups with handles on them. The cup is moistened and positioned on the dent, then pushed in to expel any trapped air in the cup and establish suction. The handle is then pulled and, in the process, it pulls the dent out. The edge of the cup is then lifted to break the suction so it can be removed from the panel. Other types of suction-cup dent pullers have release tabs or levers that engage the suction cup to the dent when moved up and release it when moved down.

Other dent removal tools include the newer stud welders. With these units, pins are spot-welded to the dented area and a slide-hammer puller is used to pull the dent out. The slide-hammer pullers used with these systems attach to the welded pins, so holes don't have to be drilled into the panel. After the dent has been pulled out, the pins are snipped off and the remainders of the pin hubs are ground smooth.

Pit Stop

To minimize the chances of injuries to your hands, be sure to wear mechanics gloves when using body shop tools like hammers, dollies, and slide-hammer dent pullers. Eye protection should also be worn to protect your eyes from debris produced by dent removal.

The latest dent removal tool is the paintless dent repair system. With this system, a hot-melt glue gun attaches the crossbar puller right over the dent. The puller's shaft is then tightened with a handle to pull the dent out. Once the dent is out, a release agent disengages the puller from the vehicle, all without damaging the paint. This system works very well for small dents and dings, provided that they are dimple-shaped and don't have any creases.

Body Solder, Bondo, Sheet Metal, or Fiberglass

You've undoubtedly heard the expression, "different strokes for different folks," and it is also true for body repairs. Different materials are required for different types of repairs. Let's examine each material in depth to understand its applications, benefits, and drawbacks.

Body Solder

Body solder is the oldest form of body filler that is used for automotive body repairs. It is a lead bar that is melted onto the surface to be filled. Before applying the solder, the work area must be free of paint, and tinning butter (flux) is painted onto the area so the solder will adhere. An oxyacetylene torch or a propane torch is then used to melt the solder. Wooden paddles made of hard rock maple are coated with tallow to prevent sticking and are then used to flow and shape the molten lead. When a sufficient amount of solder has been applied to fill in the dent, it is allowed to cool and solidify completely, and English body files are used to remove the excess solder and to smooth the repaired surface.

Working with body solder requires a lot of skill, so you need a lot of practice to get the hang of it. There are several downsides to using body solder that deserve your serious consideration. First and foremost, anytime you're working with a molten metal like body solder, you run the real and significant risk of getting burned. Secondly, there's the ever-present risk of fire. And thirdly, lead and melted lead vapors are poisonous—need I say more? And there's one more thing about body solder: It has been known to fall out of the repaired area when traveling on rough and bumpy roads. This was particularly true of side repairs such as on doors and quarter panels.

In the early days of auto body repair, there wasn't any choice—lead body solder was the only game in town. But thanks to technology, things are quite a bit different today. There are numerous plastic-based body fillers and repair materials available that are vastly superior in every way to lead body solder, so why take a step backward to do your repairs the hard way?

Bondo

Bondo is a brand name for a line of body repair products manufactured by the Bondo Corporation of Atlanta, Georgia. However, due to its popularity over the years, like the Band-Aid, Bondo has fallen into misuse as a generic term for plastic auto body filler. While many popular auto body fillers are available, including Duramix Fiberglass Filled Polyester Putty, 3M Premium Lightweight Body Filler, Black Knight Body Filler, Gorilla Hair, Tiger Hair, and others, there is only one Bondo brand, so choose your terminology and your filler brand accordingly.

I favor using fiberglass-reinforced body fillers, but it's purely a matter of personal choice. These fillers contain strands of chopped fiberglass mixed in with the plastic compound. I prefer them because the fiberglass strands endow the body filler with additional strength that, in my opinion, is good for any repair.

All of the plastic body fillers, including the fiberglass reinforced ones, work in the same way. The base plastic compound is mixed with a small amount of hardener. When these two materials are mixed together, a chemical reaction begins that starts to cure or harden the plastic compound. While still in a plastic state, apply the body filler to the dented surface with a flexible spatula. For best adhesion to the car's surface, remove paint from the area being repaired and drill a few small holes to give the body filler something to grip onto. The amount of hardener used affects curing—and working—time. The more hardener used, the faster the body filler cures and the less time you'll have to work with it. I tend to go a little heavy on the hardener because I work fairly fast. If you've never used body filler before, mix up a couple of test batches to get a handle on how fast it cures with varying amounts of hardener.

After the filler has cured and is completely hardened on the repaired area, remove the excess material using a coarse file called a "cheese grater," then sandpaper of increasingly fine grits to get the surface smooth. The only way to tell if the surface is really smooth is by running your hand and fingers over it; there is substitute for the sense of touch. If you feel any high, low, or rough spots, they will most certainly be visible when the car is painted, so they have to be addressed and corrected at this stage of the restoration.

Small pinholes caused by bubbles in the body filler as it was being applied are inevitable. Some people simply add more body filler and take it down again, hoping to fill in the original bubble holes. Unfortunately, the result is usually that more holes from the new layer of filler are introduced to the repair site.

The correct way to finish the body filler repair is to apply a thin layer of lacquer glazing putty over the repaired area and let it dry thoroughly. The key word here is to apply a *thin* layer; you don't want to have a huge buildup of putty here—you merely want to fill in the air bubble pin holes.

When the putty is thoroughly dried, you can sand it down, again letting your hand be your guide until you get a uniformly smooth and even surface.

When sanding contoured areas like the lower quarter panels where they curve in, I frequently wrap the sandpaper around a piece of old automotive heater hose to make a flexible sanding block. This permits me to follow the contour while still maintaining contact with the area to be sanded through the curve.

4-Wheel Jive

The cars of the late 1940s and early 1950s became favorite vehicles of customizers who frequently molded in the fender seams to the body using lead solder, which was the only material available during that period. These molded seams gave these cars a smooth appearance, and they collectively became known as "lead sleds" because of the lead body solder that was used.

Sheet Metal

Some body restoration repairs require replacing or patching the body metal with new sheet metal. This is most frequently the case with the bottoms of doors and quarter panels that have rust damage. Quickly repairing such damage using plastic body fillers is not the right way to fix these problems, and the repair will have to be done again very soon as the rust continues to spread.

Replacing a panel's sheet metal requires some special tools that include a MIG welder and associated gear, a metal nibbler (hand or pneumatic) for cutting the sheet metal without deforming it, flanging pliers, and a bending brake, among other items. Unless you're skilled and experienced in working with sheet metal, you may be better off farming out repairs of this kind to an auto body repair facility. For difficult panel repairs of curved areas where a new panel must be fabricated entirely from flat steel sheets, special tools like an English wheel and a pneumatic planishing hammer may be required. These two tools will cost approximately $1,000, and you'll still have to learn how to use them; this takes a lot of practice before you will achieve the results you're after. Other specialized tools like metal shrinkers and stretchers may also be required to form new inner trunk lips, fender lips, and other complicated replacement parts.

When rust has rotted away the bottoms of the doors, you may be able to purchase a replacement door skin rather than fabricating a repair patch from sheet metal. Because the door skins are made to fit the door frame correctly, it's a fairly simple matter to drill out the spot welds that were put in on the assembly line to attach the skin to the frame, remove the old skin, and install the new skin, using the MIG to produce new tack welds.

However, before installing the new skin, be sure to arrest the rust from causing further problems by coating the door frame and inner door surfaces with Eastwood Rust Encapsulator or POR-15 Rust Preventive Paint.

Fiberglass

I've also seen successful repairs of quarter panel rust damage done with fiberglass. Although this is a bit unorthodox, it does indeed work and is undetectable if done correctly.

First, the rust is removed completely, grinding away at the damaged area until bare metal is exposed. Next, fiberglass resin is applied to the area, and fiberglass cloth is cut and applied over the resin. More resin is applied to thoroughly saturate the fiberglass cloth on both sides of the repair area, smoothing the cloth to conform it to the panel's contours.

When the fiberglass resin has cured completely, the area is smoothed using abrasives. This repair works best when the fiberglass cloth is applied to the inside of the panel, rather than the outside, because any depression on the outer surface can easily be built up with additional resin or body filler to bring it to the correct height, whereas applying the fiberglass cloth to the outside of the panel requires grinding it down to make it flush with the panel's surrounding metal. Another advantage of doing the repair from the inside of the panel is that it can be smoothed a bit and then primed and painted with flat or satin black so it unobtrusively blends in with the rest of the panel. From the car's exterior, it looks perfect; only some very keen eyes looking at the inside of the panel will detect that it was repaired.

3M Weather Strip Release Agent is excellent for removing old weather stripping and its adhesive. Be careful when using it, however, because it readily removes lacquer-based paint as well. An inexpensive set of weather stripping tools makes removal of the old weather stripping much easier.

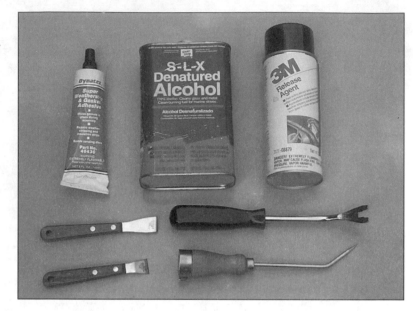

Weather Stripping

Weather stripping is the rubber material you find on the inside frames of your vehicle's doors, hood (on Corvettes), and trunk. The weather stripping functions like a gasket to seal the passenger compartment from the elements and keeps rain, snow, and drafts from entering the car. It also keeps the trunk dry and seals the engine compartment. So weather stripping serves some very important functions for your vehicle.

Like every other aspect of the restoration, make sure you take a lot of photos of the original weather stripping so you have a reference for the spacing and positioning when you install the new rubber.

Weather stripping is attached to your vehicle with adhesive and usually with some hardware fasteners such as screws or clips. Removing the hardware fasteners is fairly straightforward as long as you use the appropriate screwdriver(s), pliers, or pry tools as required. Removing the old weather stripping and its adhesive is a bit more involved.

Pit Stop

Be sure to have plenty of ventilation when using both the Release Agent and the Weather Strip Adhesive. Both of these compounds have harmful, noxious fumes. You should also use eye protection when using the aerosol Release Agent to keep it out of your eyes. Both of these products are also flammable, so take the appropriate precautions to prevent fire.

The 3M company makes an excellent aerosol Weather Strip Release Agent that quickly softens weather strip adhesive and permits the weather stripping to be removed without pulling the paint from the car. If your vehicle has lacquer paint, be careful not to get the release agent on any other areas; it will rapidly remove the lacquer as well.

You can use a narrow-blade putty knife to remove any caked-up weather strip adhesive after the Release Agent softens it up. Companies like Steele Rubber Products (see Appendix A) have complete weather strip kits for thousands of vehicles as well as individual weather strip components. Other marque-specific parts suppliers also offer weather strip kits for particular years, makes, and models, so shop around for the best deal before you make your purchase.

3M also makes Weather Strip Adhesive in black and yellow colors. You'll be able to determine which color is correct for your restoration when you remove the old weather stripping.

Generally, you won't install new weather stripping until after the car is painted. However, we'll discuss what installing new weather stripping involves now for the purposes of continuity.

When you install new weather stripping, work on a small area at a time. Run a generous bead of adhesive on the body-contact side of the weather strip and put it in place, working the piece a little at a time to make sure that it is correctly aligned and straight. As a reference, refer to the photos you took before removing the old rubber.

I use strips of masking tape to hold the weather stripping in place while the adhesive cures. This ensures that the new rubber will bond to the body exactly where I want it to be.

Install any screws or clips as you work your way around the door, hood, or trunk. These retainers also help keep the weather stripping where it should be while the adhesive sets up.

Stripping the Car for Fun and Profit

Well, actually this heading is a misnomer. What you're really going to be doing is stripping to save money, and you may have fun while you're doing it.

Essentially, you'll be taking off just about anything that would need to be masked when the car is painted if it isn't removed. That means big items like the bumpers and grill as well as the smaller stuff like hood ornaments, outer door handles, accent moldings, windshield wipers and wiper arms, and so forth. The less masking that needs to be done, the less time it will take for the car to get into the paint booth; based on an hourly rate plus material, this should result in a lower cost to have the car painted.

Prepping for Paint

I also recommend stripping the old paint off the car yourself if you can do it. You can choose from a couple of methods: You can use a chemical stripper or abrasives. There are ups and downs to both methods.

Chemical strippers work well, but they're messy. You brush the stripper on, let it set for a few minutes, and then use a putty knife or paint scraper to remove the stripper and the paint. The stripper literally dissolves the paint and turns it into a gelatinous mass that can be pushed off the vehicle using a scraper. If the car has several layers of paint on it, it may require a couple of additional applications of stripper to get everything off until you're down to the bare metal.

The downsides of chemical strippers are that their vapors are harmful, they're messy, and they can seep into crevices that you won't be able to reach; down the line, this can result in further seepage that will ruin your new paint.

Although it goes fairly fast, abrasive paint stripping is more labor intensive than chemical stripping. I use 3M abrasive discs for removing paint using my air-powered orbital sander because the coarse discs remove paint aggressively, and they last much longer than sandpaper discs.

On the downside, abrasive stripping is messy and noisy. You'll be creating an unbelievable amount of dust as you remove the paint, which, in turn, settles on everything in your garage shop. And because this dust is airborne, be sure to wear a respirator or at least a dust mask and eye protection. If you're using an air-powered sander, you might also want to invest in a pair of hearing protectors to shield your ears from compressor and sander noise.

You can go a step further after you strip the paint by masking off all the trim that couldn't be removed easily. This would include the windows and windshield, all of the windshield molding, door lock keyholes, and just about anything else that constitutes bright work, glass, rubber or other items that you don't want to get paint on. Take your time and be careful with your masking. The better your masking job is, the less time required to clean up overspray after the car emerges from the paint booth.

Without a professional facility and the right equipment, the chances for a successful paint job are significantly diminished. A professional body shop is equipped with a paint booth, which is essentially a sealed room with circulating fans and filters to remove and trap dust to keep it from settling on the new paint being sprayed onto the vehicle. In most states it is illegal to paint a vehicle outside an EPA-approved paint booth, and you can get a hefty fine for doing your painting in your garage.

The paint booth also keeps the resulting paint particles from overspray from circulating freely in the atmosphere. My friend Carl Bessey painted his 1976 Corvette in his garage, using overspray sheeting to form a makeshift tent around the car while he did his work. Even with the tenting, the neighborhood was treated to generous clouds of orange dust and the noxious vapors of automotive base coat and clear coat. Because he has considerable skill with a spray gun, the paint job came out surprisingly nice considering the circumstances under which it was applied. Suffice it to say he was not voted "good neighbor of the year" on his block.

A professional-grade respirator is absolutely essential when painting a vehicle, and it can be expensive. A painter's overall suit and good eye protection are also mandatory items, as well as a pro-caliber spray gun, paint mixing and filtering equipment, and a compressor that can put out a constant volume of air for sustained periods.

When all of these things are considered, having your collector vehicle painted at a body shop probably sounds like a pretty good idea now, doesn't it?

Hit the Roof—Convertible Tops

While convertibles are colloquially called 'ragtops,' the material used for these tops is anything but rags. The fabric that is used is high quality canvas with an extremely tight weave and is usually treated with water repellent.

Installing a new convertible top can be extremely tedious and frustrating, especially if the aftermarket top you purchased doesn't fit the way it should. Surprisingly, the quality control in manufacturing these replacement aftermarket convertible tops is often absolutely atrocious—the fit can be anywhere from bad to truly terrible. Bob Turnquist, the owner of Hibernia Automotive Restorations, one of the largest and most respected professional restoration facilities in the country, told me the fit of the replacement tops they ordered over the years was so poor that he now has a full-time top specialist on staff who custom sews all the tops they need for their restorations.

I've also heard similar complaints from other hobbyists about the difficulty they've encountered installing their tops and the poor fit of the finished job. For these reasons, you may want to go to a professional upholstery and convertible top shop to get a comparison quote for having them do the entire job as opposed to you purchasing an aftermarket top and struggling with it yourself. You may find that the few hundred dollars more that it will cost for the shop to make the top and install it is a far better value in the long run over the headache you may encounter doing the job yourself.

Pot Metal, Plating, Bright Work, and Lenses

Here we're talking about all that nice, bright, shiny stuff on the car that isn't painted. Typically, these pieces are made of chrome-plated *pot metal*, stainless steel, chrome-plated steel and polished or brushed aluminum as well as plastic lenses on parking, tail, and turn-signal lights.

Pot Metal

Pot metal is usually used for hood ornaments, make and model scripts, emblems, and badges on vehicles. Pot metal is nonferrous so it doesn't rust; it is susceptible to pitting, however.

Brake It Down

Pot metal is a low-grade nonferrous alloy composed of copper and zinc used for die-casting.

Pits in pot metal can sometimes be successfully filled in using silver solder and then buffed to a uniform shine. In most instances, however, it is easier to replace pitted pot metal emblems or badges, and if the pitting and corrosion is very advanced, there really is no other choice. Fortunately, reproduction parts are readily available from numerous sources such as Trim Parts, Inc.

Frequently a pot metal emblem will also have some painted components. If the chrome plated section is in good shape but the painted areas are worn or faded, these are easy to refurbish using model paint such as Testor's Enamel.

The first task is to remove the old paint. You can use paint stripper or #0000 steel wool; in this instance, I would opt for the stripper because it is nonabrasive and won't scratch the surrounding chrome plating. Whenever using stripper, thinner, or other flammable solvents, take the proper precautions against fire and be sure that you have adequate ventilation.

When all of the old paint has been removed and the part is thoroughly dry, use a fine-point artist's brush to apply the model paint. The trick here is to apply the paint very wet by adding it in drops and let it flow across the area to avoid brush marks.

Stainless Steel

Stainless steel trim normally only requires some buffing and polishing to bring back its original luster. Noxon, Brasso and other quality metal polishes do a great job on stainless, as well as polishes specifically made for this metal. There are also polishing rouges that are used with buffing wheels to really bring up the luster almost to a chrome-like finish.

Light dents and dings in stainless trim can usually be removed using a pointed body hammer and a small anvil. A series of small, light taps on the inside of the trim piece take the dent or ding out better than larger, more forceful hits, which can result in pock marks on the inner surface. After the dents or dings are removed, buff the part to bring up the shine.

Occasionally, stainless steel trim also has some painted accents, such as a satin or flat black dividing strip along the center of a piece of trim molding. As with the pot metal parts, the old paint on the stainless trim should be completely removed using stripper or very fine steel wool. After the paint is removed, the part should be buffed and masking tape carefully applied on the edges of the area to be painted. To ensure good masking, run your fingernail down the edge of the tape to press it flat against the molding. Use additional masking tape as needed to keep the paint from getting on other undesired areas of the part.

Paint doesn't adhere well to stainless steel and, as a result, a coat of self-etching primer should be applied first and allowed to dry. The primer etches itself into the surface of the stainless steel, forming a bond that provides a foundation for the finish paint to "bite" into. Two or three light coats of the satin or flat black paint should be applied next, allowing each to dry before applying the successive coats. Several light coats provide a more uniform finish than a single heavy coat, and there is less chance for getting runs in the paint when spraying it on lightly.

After the paint has thoroughly dried, remove the masking tape and the part is ready to roll.

Aluminum

Aluminum is also occasionally used for trim on vehicles, and the 1957 Chevrolet's tail fin appliqué illustrates this use well. Aluminum is a durable metal that doesn't rust, although it does oxidize and becomes dull due to exposure with the atmosphere and the elements. Like stainless steel, aluminum can be buffed to clean it up and restore its luster.

Busch's Aluminum Wash is excellent for cleaning and brightening aluminum trim. The wash is sprayed on from the trigger bottle, allowed to sit for a few minutes, and then rinsed off. Rarely, a little help from an old toothbrush may be required to work the wash into any crevices or corners to remove the stubborn stuff.

Busch also manufactures an excellent aluminum polish that rapidly cuts through oxidation and produces a brilliant shine that rivals that of chrome. Busch Aluminum Wax & Sealant for polished uncoated aluminum surfaces is excellent for removing swirl marks, and it provides improved corrosion resistance while polishing up to a mirror-like luster.

As with stainless steel, various rouges are also available for aluminum from The Eastwood Company and others for use with buffing and polishing wheels.

Chrome

Aside from polishing chrome to bring its luster up, there isn't too much you can do to correct pitting, deep scratches and rusting on chromed parts like bumpers other than replacing them or having them rechromed.

Because of increasingly strict government regulations to protect the environment, the prices for chrome plating have soared over the last couple of decades. The prices are so high in some parts of the country like the Northeast that, in fact, it is frequently a toss-up as to whether you should have an existing part rechromed or just purchase a new reproduction part. Bumpers are an excellent case in point. I recently asked for a price quote on rechroming the dual rear bumpers and one-piece front bumper for a 1969 Corvette from a rechroming house in Pennsylvania. The quote came back at $850 for the three pieces. In addition, the shipping to and from my home to the factory would be approximately $75 each way, bringing the total up to $1,000.

Conversely, Mid-America Direct (see Appendix A) offered new reproduction bumpers for $349.99 each, and the shipping charge figured in at $39.99, for a total of $1,089.96. So, for an extra $90 I purchased three brand-new bumpers that were delivered directly to my door. And I still have the original bumpers that I can sell at a swap meet easily for at least $300. So, from this example, you can see that rechroming doesn't always make the best economic sense.

Some specialty houses rechrome bumpers as their main business, and you can frequently save some money by going to a specialty house rather than to a local chroming company. But you'll also have to factor in the cost of shipping the bumpers to and from the chromer, plus the effort and material required to pack them.

The same holds true for smaller chrome parts such as window cranks and door handles; more often than not it is cheaper to purchase replacement parts than to have the originals rechromed. Of course, there are parts for which you won't be able to find replacements easily, and you'll opt to have these pieces replated as required. But be sure to shop around from a number of plating companies to get the best value.

Lenses

The clear, amber, or red lenses found on backup, tail, parking, and turn-signal lights often become dull due to exposure, countless car washes, and dirt and grime. But, unless they are suffering from deep scratches or cracks, these units can usually be saved and made to look as good as new with a little effort.

Use a mild dishwashing liquid to wash the lens—do not use an abrasive cleanser, however. You may find an old toothbrush to be useful for getting the caked-on grime out of the edges or corners of the lens while washing it. Rinse it and let it dry thoroughly. Gently rub out light scratches with fine metal polish such as silver polish. Deeper, more stubborn scratches can often be removed by rubbing them with toothpaste on your finger, followed by fine metal polish after rewashing the lens to remove toothpaste residue.

Environmental Issues

By its very nature, the restoration process produces a lot of waste byproducts. It is your duty as a citizen of Planet Earth to dispose of these waste materials in an ecologically responsible manner; this is especially important because many of these byproducts are toxic.

Gasoline, oil, grease, solvents, and other petroleum-based chemicals should be taken to recycling centers and never simply thrown out as regular garbage or, worse yet, dumped onto the earth itself. Most municipalities have recycling centers that will accept petrol-chemicals as well as paints, automotive batteries, and other hazardous waste materials that pose an ecological or health threat.

Most of the larger automotive parts stores will accept your old batteries and used motor oil for recycling without charge.

Automobile tires are a major waste problem because they don't readily biodegrade. In many municipalities, you can dispose of your old tires legally; for a small fee, the city may send a truck to pick up your tires and charge a couple of dollars per unit for their removal; other municipalities may waive this fee entirely if you drop off the tires at the recycling center. Most of the larger tire centers will also accept your used tires for a small disposal fee.

After stripping the old paint from your vehicle, use a shop vacuum with a clean filter to pick up the debris and clean your shop. Be sure to bag this waste material tightly and check with your local authorities to find out if any special disposal is required for stripped automotive paint waste, especially if you've used liquid paint stripper.

The Least You Need to Know

♦ There are several ways to remove dents and dings, including suction, air pressure, slide hammers, and paintless removal methods.

♦ Weather stripping keeps the elements from entering the passenger compartment.

♦ Stripping old paint from the vehicle can be done by chemical or abrasive means.

◆ Pot metal was frequently used for die-casting hood ornaments, badges, and emblems on collector vehicles.

◆ Sometimes it makes more economic sense to replace a part rather than have it replated.

◆ All hazardous waste materials resulting from the restoration process must be disposed of in an ecologically responsible manner.

Chapter 21

Inner Beauty

In This Chapter

- Restoring the seats, dashboard, and clock
- Working on the electrical system
- Recarpeting your vehicle
- Replacing headliners, door panels, and visors
- Refurbishing old parts early
- Paying attention to detail

You'll be spending most of your time in the interior of your collector car (hopefully), so making it look good is of prime importance. A good-looking interior in which everything functions as it should makes driving a collector vehicle an absolute joy.

Inner Beauty

While a collector car may look beautiful from the outside, nothing takes the shine off the apple like a ratty interior. And there's really no excuse for your interior to look any less attractive than the rest of the car. After all, you've spent countless hours and made a sizeable investment in the motor, body, running gear, and outer appearance of the vehicle, so now is no time to get cheap with the interior.

Spend a couple of dollars more to get professional-quality hog-ring pliers (left) rather than the cheap amateur ones (right). The professional pliers require less effort and make attaching hog rings much easier.

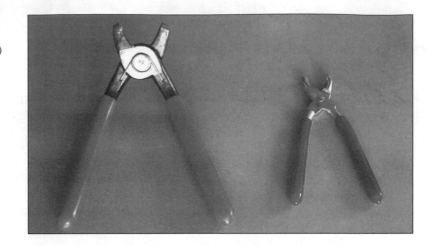

Seats and Such

If you think about it, the seats—particularly the driver's seat—get the majority of the car's interior wear, an unenviable fate they share with the carpeting. Every time the car is driven, the covering of the driver's seat is subjected to friction as the driver gets in and out of the car, and its springs and foam cushioning are compressed and decompressed. It also gets the added abuse of the driver bouncing up and down as a result of road irregularities that get past the suspension. There is no question about it: The seats take a beating.

Depending on the age, condition, and mileage of the project vehicle, the seats may merely need to be recovered; or they may require new foam padding and frame repairs. To do either or both of these restoration jobs, you'll need the right tools.

Seat covers are usually held onto the seat frames with *hog rings*. You can frequently obtain complete seat cover installation kits from suppliers of products for restoring specific marques, and these kits usually save money over purchasing the components individually. For example, if you purchase a seat cover installation kit for bucket seats, it typically contains enough springs, listings (tubes of fabric sewn into the back of the seat cover to accept listing rods), clips, hog rings, and s-clips to install both seat covers; sometimes a clip installation tool is also included, and this makes the installation much easier.

> **Brake It Down**
>
> **Hog rings** are "C"-shaped metal rings that are used to secure seat upholstery on the seat back and frame. Special pliers are used to squeeze the hog rings shut.

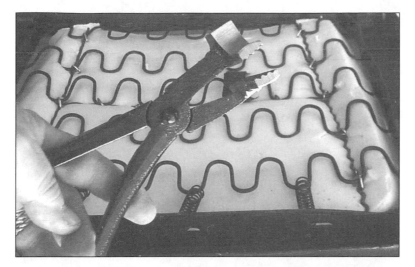

Fabric stretching pliers like these make it easier to pull the fabric tightly around the seat frame. Seat covers are expensive items, and having the right tools gives you a better shot at doing a professional-looking job.

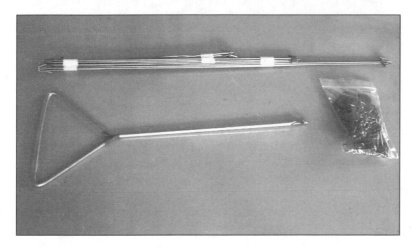

A typical installation kit includes all the listing rods, various clips, and hog rings needed to install the seat covers on a pair of bucket seats. The clip installation tool with the triangular handle makes pulling spring clips through the upholstery foam and locking them a simple task; this can be daunting if you try to do it barehanded. You can also fashion a functional clip installation tool by bending a wire coat hanger. While it won't look as elegant, it should function properly.

To install new seat covers, you must remove the seat(s) from the car by moving the seat back on its track so you can access and remove the bolts that hold the track to the floor of the car. Next, move the seat all the way forward to access and remove the rear track mounting bolts. At this point, you should be able to lift the seat(s) out of the car. If you have power seats, be sure to disconnect the wiring harness coming from the floor that attaches to the clip on the seat's connector.

Any side and rear moldings on the seat(s) should be removed next, and these are usually attached with Phillips screws. After the moldings are off the seat(s), you should be able to see the hog rings and clips that hold the seat cover(s) on. Be sure to take reference photos before you start using needle-nosed pliers to remove any of the clips or hog rings.

When all the clips and hog rings have been removed, you can peel the seat cover away from the upholstery foam and the seat frame. At this time you'll want to determine whether you need to replace the foam and springs in the seat. Generally speaking, the springs don't need to be replaced unless they have suffered rust damage. Simply replacing the foam rubber cushioning is the only requirement for restoring a comfortable ride to the seat.

Overdrive

One sign of a truly professional upholstery job is straight, uniform seams. To achieve this, make sure the inner hem of the seat cover seam faces down toward the bottom of the seat frame as you install the seat cover(s). Hems that alternate up and down the length of the seam cause unevenness and make it look like an amateur installation.

If the foam is still supple and resilient when you poke your finger into it and doesn't crumble when you touch it, chances are pretty good that it's still serviceable. If it doesn't bounce back from a poke or it crumbles while you handle it, it needs to be replaced.

You'll find that working on the seat(s) is much easier if you use a workbench as a support. Good lighting is another asset when reupholstering your seats. By all means, while the seat covers are off, take care of any rusting on the seat frame or springs using the appropriate products to arrest it and prevent it from recurring.

Pulling the seat cover fabric until it is taut and then trying to load a hog ring into the pliers can be frustrating. Use a rubber band to hold the hog ring in the pliers so it is ready for use as soon as you need it. Simple tricks like this one help make the job go faster and easier, so learn to be creative and think "outside the box."

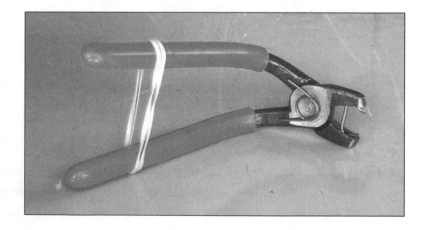

The average hobbyist can do a good job of reupholstering his or her seat(s) with no prior experience. The most important things to remember are to take your time and work the fabric slowly, a little at a time, to avoid rips and tears. With leather and Naugahyde/vinyl upholstery in particular, it helps to work in a warm, ambient temperature of seventy degrees or better. Colder temperatures cause the material to stiffen and lose elasticity. I have also used a hair dryer several times to warm the seat cover material, which makes it easier to stretch over the frame and around corners.

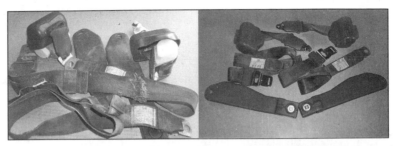

Don't forget your seat belts. If your vehicle was equipped with them when it left the factory, you are legally required to have them in the restored vehicle as well. Restoring seat belts is usually beyond the capabilities of the hobbyist and is best farmed out to specialists like Ssnake-Oyl Products (see Appendix A for contact information). The unrestored units are at the left, and the belts at the right are what they looked like after Ssnake-Oyl was finished with them.

The Mad Dash

The dashboard is, for all intents and purposes, your command center. It contains the gauges that tell you the condition of your motor, it can alert you to problems with the lubrication, cooling, or electrical systems, and it tells you how much fuel you have, how fast you're going, and how far you've gone. That is quite a bit of information from a neat pod positioned in front of the driver, wouldn't you say?

The dash is also usually the location for such creature comforts as the heater, defroster and air conditioning or vent controls, the radio, cigarette lighter and the clock as well as for such requisite safety equipment as the windshield wiper controls, headlight switch, remote outside mirror controls and other such devices.

On older collector vehicles, the dashboards were made of unpadded steel painted to complement the car's color scheme. In the mid-1960s, manufacturers started to pad the dashboards as a step toward improved driver and passenger safety. Along with the padding, some problems were introduced as these padded dashes frequently exhibited a tendency to crack due to exposure to UV light, hot summer heat, and the elements.

If you have an older all-steel dash, it should be a fairly straightforward matter to remove all of the knobs, trim, glove box, and support brackets so that the front of the dash can be removed. Remember to take photos while you're disassembling it, and make drawings of where the wiring sockets plug into the gauges and their color codes. On some vehicles, it may be necessary to drop the steering column by removing the column support bolts in order to remove the face of the dashboard. Some vehicles also have individual gauge "pods" that can be removed as a separate unit rather than removing the dash all in one piece.

Your factory shop manual will have a wiring diagram, just don't depend on it to be 100 percent accurate for your vehicle. Running changes during production and particular options combinations may not be reflected in the wiring diagram and they're very "schematic" representations, with elaborate traceries of lines and obscure symbols for switches and other components.

When you've disconnected everything from the dash, including the defroster and heating and air conditioning/vent ducting, you should be able to remove the upper dash panel itself. These panels are usually held in place with sheet metal screws that attach the panel to the bracing. When the screws are removed, the panel can be removed for cleaning and refurbishing or repainting as needed. Reassembling the dash is the reverse of removal, so be sure to check your photos for reference.

You may have additional options for some of the padded dash panels. You may elect to replace the panel entirely, in which case the same procedures described above for unpadded steel panels apply. But you may also be able to purchase an upper dash pad skin for your car model. These skins are actually molded caps that fit over your existing dash pad, and they cover any cracks or blemishes in the pad itself. They are held on with interior adhesive and can usually be ordered in the required color or dyed with aerosol interior dye to the correct color. Installing these dash pads is very easy, although I recommend installing them in an ambient temperature of seventy degrees or higher; a hair dryer or heat gun may also come in handy for making the dash cap a bit more flexible during installation.

Gauge restoration, such as refacing a speedometer or tachometer, is not for the average hobbyist and should be sent out to a professional gauge restoration house. Marque-specific restoration parts suppliers usually offer gauge restoration services in their catalogs, but be sure to compare prices first to get the best deal.

Often, dashboards will have some trim appliqué, usually made of stainless steel or aluminum. The same products and techniques discussed Chapter 20 also apply to inside metal trim.

Older cars have painted wood grain treatments that are best reproduced by someone with experience (a *lot* of experience) with the technique.

Do Collector Car Clocks Ever Work?

The short answer to this question is, "no." At least, most of the time they do not work. There are exceptions where an original vehicle clock (we're talking pre-quartz movement here) still works, but they are the rare birds, indeed.

Unless you're a clocksmith, you should not attempt to repair your collector vehicle's clock yourself. Although occasionally only cleaning and lubrication are required to get it ticking again, the problems are usually more deep rooted. The problem could be a burned-out motor, a shot relay, or perhaps worn gears. These problems are beyond the ability of most hobbyists to diagnose and repair, even if the parts were readily available, which they probably are not.

Rather than going through the time and expense of having your antiquated vehicle clock repaired and restored, you may want to consider having it converted to a modern, reliable, and accurate quartz movement.

The nonfunctioning electric clock from this 1969 Corvette probably hasn't worked since 1969, so it was replaced with a direct-fit quartz-movement clock from Rogers Corvette Clocks.

Several clock and gauge restoration specialists advertise in *Hemmings* and *Old Car Weekly*, so these are good resources for finding someone to repair or upgrade your clock. And most of the marque-specific parts suppliers offer clock and gauge repair and restoration services as well, so check their catalogs, too. As always, shop around for the best price before you send your clock or gauges out to be refurbished although, frankly, no one expects the clock to work and you're better off spending your money on other more important things like gauges.

Wiring and Electrical Issues

For reasons that I don't quite comprehend, the thought of working on an automotive electrical system is terrifying to most hobbyists. There's no logical reason for this fear, however.

Automotive electrical systems are essentially closed-loop systems, meaning that every device and component in the system has a positive connection and a negative connection. When a switch is turned on, such as the windshield wiper, the connection is closed so the current flows to the device to power it. When the switch is turned off, the loop is opened and no power goes to the device.

Most post-1949 vehicles use negative ground electrical systems. This means that the metal of the frame, engine, and body all function as ground or negative connection for all the electrical connections. This arrangement greatly simplifies the vehicle's wiring circuits. For example, the cigarette lighter only requires one "hot" or positive wire going to its heater element; the metal of the dashboard socket it sits in provides the negative connection.

The vast majority of cars use negative-ground electrical systems; however, the Ford Motor Company used positive ground wiring until the 1960s and so did Dodge up to the early 1950s.

There are some exceptions, however—most notably, Corvettes, Avantis, Bricklins, and perhaps a few other vehicles that have bodies made of fiberglass or other nonmetallic materials. In these vehicles, the motor and chassis are still the negative ground terminals, but most of the interior electrical connections require discrete ground wires in addition to the positive leads because the body isn't electrically conductive.

Pre-1955 vehicles generally had six-volt electrical systems, but twelve-volt systems have been in use since then. Along with the changeover to higher voltage electrical systems, the vehicles' wiring was also upgraded at about that time, doing away with the cloth and resin-coated insulation on wiring and going to plastic and rubber insulation. This upgrade greatly reduced the incidence of shorts and electrical fires.

Fuses are your automotive electrical system's safety valves that prevent current overloads and damage from malfunctioning devices. When the current exceeds the fuse's capacity, the fuse element melts, thus opening the loop in the circuit.

If you don't want your pride-and-joy collector car to turn into a lump of burned slag, don't replace fuses with a higher amperage rating to keep them from blowing. A blown fuse is a symptom of a major problem that you need to find.

These are three types of automotive fuses. The glass-tube type of fuse at the left was used through the early 1980s, whereas the flat plastic fuses at the center and right are usually found on later-model vehicles.

When a fuse blows, it is an indication that something isn't right in the electrical system. The problem could be a *short circuit* caused by a hot wire touching a ground, a faulty relay, or a defective device itself.

A few simple tools are all that you'll need to find and fix most electrical and wiring problems. A low-voltage circuit tester and multimeter are the two main tools, and you should have some electrical tape, a crimping tool and crimp connectors, a wire stripper, razor blade, and scissors on hand. A soldering iron and rosin-core solder will come in handy sometimes, as will an electrical faultfinder, if you have one. The faultfinder is a pricey item, however, that you can do without for most jobs.

Brake It Down

A short, also called a **short circuit,** is a defect in an electrical circuit that permits the current to take a short path or circuit rather than following the prescribed path. A short frequently results in the burning out of related circuits and/or the failure of the device. Fuses are used in automotive electrical systems to protect against damage from short circuits.

I also suggest getting a battery load tester. These are relatively inexpensive devices (under $50) that test the true condition of your battery by applying a load to it that simulates actual use. Most of these devices can test both six- and twelve-volt batteries, and you can use it to test the batteries of your "normal" vehicles as well.

Pit Stop

Never replace a burned-out fuse with one of a higher rating. The purpose of the fuse is to prevent further electrical damage from occurring to the circuit it is designed to protect or to the vehicle itself. Using a higher rated fuse completely negates the protection the originally rated fuse was designed to provide. Locate and correct the source of the problem, and then replace the fuse with one of the correct rating.

Solving most electrical problems requires some logical thinking and a little detective work, but it all boils down to tracing the circuit to find out where there's a hole in the loop that shouldn't be there. When you find the hole, you've found the problem.

For example, let's say that the windshield wipers of your collector vehicle aren't working. Bear in mind that the basic diagnostic procedures I'm outlining here apply to any type of automotive electrical problem.

First, make sure that the battery is charged and connected. This may sound elementary to the point of being simple, but when you take things for granted you're not being a good electrical detective.

When the battery and its connections check out, move on to the next step: checking the fuse for the wipers. If the fuse is burned out, it indicates a problem in the circuit or with the wiper motor itself. Replace the fuse with one of equal value, but do not turn on the wipers.

Open the hood and locate the snap-on connector to the wiper motor and disconnect it. Most vehicles require the ignition switch to be in the "on" or "accessory" positions for the wipers to operate, so turn the key to put the switch in the "on" position, and turn the wipers on. If the replacement fuse blows at this point, there is a good likelihood that the problem is in the wiper switch or in the circuit that goes to the switch, so investigate these problems next. If the fuse does not blow, the switch and wiring are okay up to that point. In other words, there are no shorts in the circuit.

Use your low-voltage circuit tester to locate the hot contacts of the wiper motor harness. You can clip the negative lead to clean, unpainted metal on the firewall or engine for grounding and with the switch turned on touch the tip of the tester to the contacts. The one or ones that cause the tester to light up are the hot contacts. This establishes that you have a good wiper circuit from the switch to the wiper motor; hence, the problem is the wiper motor itself. You can verify this easily by reconnecting the harness connector to the motor—the fuse should blow immediately, confirming that the motor is the culprit and needs to be repaired or replaced.

A multimeter with an audible continuity test feature is highly useful for locating breaks in automotive circuits. If the circuit is okay, you will hear an audible beep when you touch the meter's two leads to the end of a circuit when it is closed. If you don't hear a beep, there is a hole in the loop; check the continuity along the circuit to find out where it is broken.

Rugs over Rust?

The only thing in your vehicle's interior that gets more of a workout than the driver's seat is the carpeting. You can get form-fitted replacement carpeting in the correct color and pile for almost any vehicle, both from marque-specific suppliers and from automotive carpeting specialty manufacturers like Auto Custom Carpets, Inc. (www. accmats.com). Replacing the carpeting in your vehicle isn't difficult to do, but it's labor-intensive.

First, you must remove the seats—both front and back—from the vehicle. Next, remove the sill-plate moldings, which are usually fastened with Phillips screws. The front kick panels should also be removed at this time. Now you're ready to start pulling up the old carpeting.

Some vehicles have a layer of jute padding, also known as underlayment, under the carpeting to provide additional temperature and noise insulation; on other vehicles, the carpeting may have its own underlayment bonded to it. I prefer to use replacement carpet that already has its own jute padding bonded to it because this saves time and work, but this is a personal preference.

Hidden treasure: When replacing the carpeting in a 1969 car recently I came upon three quarters, a dime, and an S&H Green Stamp—not a bad haul. You never know what you're going to find when you work on an old car or truck.

When you remove the old carpeting and padding, you'll probably find some change and other small items that were dropped over the years. And don't be surprised if you find rust on the floor panels under the carpet—this isn't an uncommon discovery in older vehicles. By all means, address the situation using either POR-15 or Eastwood Rust Encapsulator to prevent further rust damage. If the floor pans are severely rusted, you may have to weld in replacement panels. (If they are that badly rusted you probably would have discovered that when you were doing your under car-frame inspection earlier in the restoration.)

These are two types of automotive carpeting plugs or fasteners. The left one is made of rubber and has a spear-shaped head that keeps it in place. The one on the right is made of plastic and, when the plunger is pushed in, the tip of the plug expands to prevent it from pulling out of the hole.

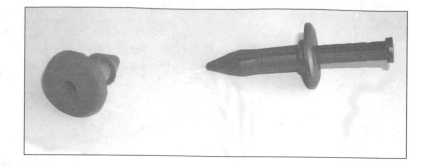

Plugs often hold carpeting to the firewall in the upper foot-wells. These plugs are usually rubber, but they can also be made of plastic. The plug is inserted through the carpeting into a hole in the foot-well. These plugs, in addition to carpeting adhesive, keep the carpet in place.

Pit Stop

Be sure to have adequate ventilation when using this aerosol carpet adhesive because the fumes can make you lightheaded and give you a nasty headache if you inhale too much of it. It is also highly flammable, so don't smoke or have any open flames around when using it.

Proceed with your carpet installation by working from front to back. Put the carpeting and/or underlayment in place to check the fit before you glue anything down; some trimming may be necessary, and this can be done with a utility knife or heavy shears. When you're satisfied with the fit, peel the carpeting back and spray some carpet adhesive on the floor panels rather than on the carpeting or backing itself. Be generous with the adhesive and give it a couple of minutes to set up before you press the carpeting in place.

Headliners, Door Panels, and Visors—Oh, My!

Removing and replacing a headliner can be a tricky proposition, especially if you've never done it before. While the procedure is basically the same for all vehicles, there are some variations depending on make, model, and design.

All of the upper headliner molding and trim should be removed first, followed by the A-pillar moldings and rear window moldings. With these pieces out of the way, you should be able to remove the bow fasteners to free the headliner suspension bows and, ultimately the headliner itself. Be sure to photograph the bow fasteners as well as the headliner and take close-ups of the seams and stitching and the orientation of the bows. These photos will come in handy when you install the new headliner.

Headliners are available for most vehicles from restoration parts suppliers and marque-specific parts houses. You can also have one fabricated by a local automotive top and upholstery shop.

While a single person can easily handle taking the headliner out, installing a new one is a two-person job. A second set of hands to provide support while you position the bows and secure them makes this job easier. The important thing is to take your time and do the job right. Haste makes waste, and putting a tear or a hole in a new headliner is not the objective here.

Door panels are generally held in place with screws and clips. Frequently, the screws may be hidden by an arm rest, lower panel carpeting, or trim, so having an assembly manual or a shop manual for your particular vehicle comes in handy for locating the position, number, and type of fasteners used.

You will need a handle clip removal tool for removing the window crank, vent crank, and inner door handle. These tools cost less than $10 and are readily available at the local NAPA or other automotive parts stores. These handles are held in place with a spring clip, which prevents the handle from being pulled off the mechanism's splined shaft. These clips are all but impossible to remove without one of these tools. When it is time to reinstall these handles, simply insert the clip in the handle, position the handle on the shaft, and give the handle a sharp rap with the heel of your hand or a soft mallet to seat it.

Depending on the door panel, you may be able to recover or refurbish it. For some door panels, replacement may be the only option. Be aware, however, that some replacement door panels are shipped "bare bones;" that is, they are devoid of any trim or accent pieces, so you may have to recycle the original door panel trim or order new replacements for these items as well. Don't forget about armrests, too. Detachable armrests are not usually supplied with the replacement door panels, either, so you may have to purchase them separately from the same supplier from which you buy the door panels.

Other interior trim such as sun visors and their mounting hardware, the rear view mirror, coat hooks, passenger assist grips, or other passenger compartment items might need to be restored.

Cracked steering wheels are frequently encountered in older vehicles that have plastic or hard rubber-rimmed steering wheels. These cracks can be repaired using epoxy-based putty and complete steering wheel repair kits that include the putty, a file, and other items including detailed instructions. These are available both from POR-15 and The Eastwood Company. Having used both, I can attest that they are similar and they both produce excellent repairs.

You may also opt to replace the steering wheel with a correct replacement unit, or perhaps to upgrade to something a little snazzier like an aftermarket wheel from Grant or LeCarra.

A Stitch in Time

The old saying, "a stitch in time saves nine," is also true of restoration work. Replacing a part can often be avoided if the original part is repaired or refurbished as soon as any damage is discovered, rather than allowing it to continue deteriorating. A case in point is the upholstery on a rear seat. I know someone who bought a restoration project car that was in fairly decent shape. The interior, in particular, was very well preserved for a vehicle as old as this one is. The front seat definitely needed to be recovered, but the rear seat had almost no wear on it at all, and only had a slight rip at the front seam where the threads had pulled apart. Certainly, this rip could have easily, quickly, and inexpensively been repaired by a local upholstery shop had Steve tended to it immediately. Instead, he took the seats out of the car and put them against the wall in his garage, where they soon became catch-alls for other parts that were taken off the car. By the time Steve got to the interior restoration, the rear seat had a couple of major tears and a big stain from some part that leaked grease or oil on it. So Steve had to shell out some major bucks to have the seat reupholstered, when initially a simple, inexpensive repair was all it needed.

The Least You Need to Know

- ◆ You spend most of your time in the car's interior.

- ◆ Of the interior components, the driver's seat and carpeting get the most wear.

- ◆ Original collector car clocks seldom work.

- ◆ Diagnosing and fixing automotive electrical problems is not difficult if the circuit is traced logically.

- ◆ Aerosol carpet adhesive is hazardous to your health and is highly flammable.

- ◆ Attention to small details sets great restorations apart from mediocre ones.

Part 5

Ready to Roll

Well, congratulations! You've not only seen the light at the end of it, you're out of the tunnel now. Time to get in, turn the key and enjoy the fruits of your labor—well, almost. There are still some things you'll want to do, like getting your pride and joy appraised and insured, considering your registration options, driving it or transporting it in a trailer, going to cruise nights and car shows, learning about car clubs and things you can do to protect your investment.

Making It Legal

In This Chapter

- Getting your vehicle appraised
- Insuring your restored vehicle
- Comparing rates, coverage, and mileage caps
- Getting a special historic registration
- Varying driving restrictions

You've seen the light, and you're almost out of the restoration tunnel. Now it's time to get your restored vehicle insured and legally registered so you can start enjoying the fruits of your labor. Insuring and registering a collector vehicle is different from doing the same for a normal, everyday car. This chapter covers the things you need to know in order to insure and register your car.

The Law of the Land

Regardless of the state you live in, the following things are required to legally drive your collector car:

- The minimum liability insurance required by your state
- A valid registration certificate and license plates
- A valid driver's license

Assuming that you already have a valid driver's license, you're already one-third of the way there. Let's discuss how you should go about getting the other two items on the list.

Because it is over 25 years of age, this 1933 Dodge street rod was legally registered in New Jersey as an historic vehicle, as indicated on the license plate. Check with your state's Division of Motor Vehicles to learn whether your collector vehicle is eligible for a special registration such as this.

Having Your Vehicle Appraised: What's This Jalopy Worth?

You've spent endless hours of labor and a lot of money to turn what started out as a heap into this beautiful collector's item. Having invested such so much time and money in this vehicle, the first thing you should do is get its value appraised.

You can check the pages of *Hemmings, Old Car Weekly,* and other such publications to find appraisers who advertise. You can also check your phone directory's yellow pages to locate a local appraiser.

There are professional appraisers' organizations such as the American Society of Appraisers that certify members and substantiate their qualifications. These organizations have directories of qualified appraisers in specific subjects.

When choosing an appraiser, check his credentials to establish that he has passed the certification or licensing criteria that might be required by your state, and ask him for references. As part of your standard research, check with the local Chamber of Commerce and your state's Better Business Bureau to find out whether any complaints or grievances have been made against the appraiser.

Appraisers generally offer their services on a set-fee basis, plus any travel expenses they may have incurred. Frequently, the travel expenses can include compensation for the time spent in transit. For the purposes of illustration, let's say that you've engaged an appraiser who lives an hour (60 miles) away from your location. The appraiser quotes you the following rate:

Flat fee appraisal for one collector vehicle: **$150**

Transit compensation (1 hour each way @ $50): **$100**

Mileage including tolls (120 miles @ .50/mi): **$60**

Total Appraisal Cost: **$310**

Some appraisers also give you an appraisal based on photos and/or a video that you supply of the vehicle; this is often the case with appraisal services located in states other than the one in which you reside. Generally, these appraisers supply you with a guide sheet of the type of photos and how many they require to render their services, or their criteria for your vehicle's video. Comparatively speaking, these "appraisals done at a distance" are usually less expensive than having an appraiser travel to your location to evaluate the vehicle, but they also are less rigorous and subject to challenge in the event of a loss.

In addition to checking the restored vehicle's overall appearance and condition, most appraisers will also request copies of receipts for parts, services, and materials used in the restoration because they frequently factor these expenses into the appraised value.

Of course, there is no guarantee that these expenses will have any significant impact on the final appraised value. Remember the anecdote I recounted earlier about my friend, who spent $37,500 restoring her 1941 Plymouth, "Harry," that had an appraised value of $7,500.

An accurate appraisal by an accredited appraiser is a valuable document for several reasons:

> **Overdrive**
>
> Shopping for price when considering appraisers and insurers is good, but be sure to compare apples to apples. Make sure that the services provided are identical among various sources before comparing their prices.

- ◆ It establishes what the vehicle is worth in its current condition. This is very important if the vehicle is involved in an accident or a catastrophe like fire or flood.

- ◆ From the appraised value, the cost for any collision damage, repairs, or replacement parts can be calculated in real-world values rather than "guesstimates."

- ◆ It gives you a firm basis for insuring the vehicle at full value. The appraisal is an objective, third-party assessment of what the restored vehicle is worth, not a subjective value that you put on it.

◆ An appraisal certificate may help you get your asking price if and when you decide to sell the vehicle because you can prove its appraised value rather than placing some "pie in the sky" arbitrary value on it.

While your pride and joy may be worth a million bucks to you sentimentally, you have to be practical and get a real-world appraisal on it so you'll know its actual value.

Finding a Collector Car Insurer

Again, the pages of *Hemmings* and *Old Car Weekly* as well as marque-specific and general collector car magazines often advertise insurance companies that specialize in providing coverage for collector vehicles. The Internet is also a terrific place to find an insurer for your collector vehicle; while writing this chapter, I searched "collector car insurance" on Ask Jeeves, and I received more than 15 choices. Further refining or varying the search criteria to locate "antique vehicle insurance," "muscle car insurance," "street rod insurance," and so on would probably turn up search results that fit your requirements even better.

Now bear in mind that while liability insurance may be the only insurance your state requires, you'll definitely want additional insurance to protect your investment from such perils as collision, fire, and theft. With this thought in mind, be sure to inquire whether the company offers a "comprehensive" insurance package that includes this additional coverage in addition to liability. Most companies do offer comprehensive packages that save you money over purchasing each of these coverages individually.

Brake It Down

As the name implies, the **replacement value** is an auto insurance term that indicates the amount it would cost to replace the vehicle with one of the same year, make, and model in the same condition. This is an arbitrary insured value on a vehicle that is usually determined by a certified appraisal and other factors such as current auction selling prices for similar vehicles. The replacement value might not reflect the actual investment that you have in the vehicle, however—only the amount it would cost to replace it.

When purchasing such additional coverage, the vehicle's *replacement value* must be established. This value is usually based on a certified appraisal of the vehicle, and it is often also in conjunction with the prices of comparable vehicles have recently sold at auction.

Brake It Down

As the name suggests, the **agreed value** is a collector vehicle insurance term that denotes the value of a vehicle as agreed on by both the vehicle owner and the insurance company. Agreed value is usually applied to such vehicles as street rods and customs that are unique and for which no formal valuation guidelines are established. The receipts for parts, labor, services, and supplies used to bring the vehicle into its present form are often factors that come into play in establishing the agreed value.

Custom vehicles such as street rods are generally unique; as a result, establishing a firm replacement value is not as straightforward as it is for a true restoration, such as for a stock 1965 Mustang Convertible. For these specialty vehicles, collector insurance companies frequently offer an *agreed value* policy. The value of the policy is based on an amount that both the owner of the vehicle and the insurance company agree upon.

Because collector vehicles are highly regarded by their owners, they are often driven limited distances and with great care. More often than not, owners of collector vehicles are mature, responsible individuals who are interested in protecting the investments they have made in their vehicles. Collector vehicle insurers therefore feel that insuring these vehicles is a relatively safe bet and, consequently, the insurance premiums are generally very low compared to the equivalent coverage for everyday, "normal" vehicles. Following is an actual advertisement I found in one of the collector periodicals:

> **Example Quote**:
>
> $20,000 street rod
>
> $100,000 liability and uninsured motorist coverage
>
> 3,000 miles per year
>
> $250 annual premium for agreed value coverage/zero deductible

This particular example quote was for Los Angeles, California; the rate you pay for your collector vehicle insurance may be even lower, depending on your location. As with everything else relating to your collector vehicle, shop around for the best price and coverage.

Mileage Caps

Several collector car insurance companies stipulate *mileage caps* as a term of their coverage. These caps are usually 2,000-3,000 miles a year, but for a slightly higher rate, these caps can be extended to higher figures. If you anticipate driving your collector vehicle more than the standard cap on the policy, you should ask for a higher cap or a policy with no mileage cap. It's a good idea to compare rates from several companies, as the quotes can fluctuate quite a bit with higher caps or on no-cap policies.

> **Brake It Down** _____
>
> **Mileage caps** are maximum mileage amounts that a collector vehicle can be driven during a calendar year under the terms of the collector car insurance. For example, a collector vehicle policy with a 2,500 mileage cap can be driven a maximum of 2,500 miles in a calendar year. If this mileage is exceeded and the vehicle is in an accident, the insurance company can deny coverage and compensation because the exceeded mileage cap violated the terms of the policy.

Because most hobbyists only use their collector vehicles for recreational pursuits such as going to car shows or cruise nights, a 3,000 mile cap policy is just fine for the majority of cruisers, especially those in parts of the country where winters are cold and inclement. However, in climates where the weather is fair all year around, a higher cap policy or an unlimited mileage policy may be the smarter way to go if you anticipate using the vehicle for all 12 months.

Special Historic Registrations

Using my home state of New Jersey as an example, a collector car or truck can be registered as an historic vehicle if it is at least 25 years old. It doesn't matter if it is a "survivor," a stock restoration, a custom or a modified vehicle; if it has reached the quarter-century mark, it qualifies as an historic vehicle in New Jersey. Other states have similar provisions, so check with your state's Division of Motor Vehicles to find out what they are. Again citing New Jersey, there are several significant and worthwhile advantages to registering a collector car or truck as an historic vehicle:

- There is a low one-time registration fee of $41. There is no charge for registration renewal for as long as you own the vehicle.

- The vehicle is exempt from motor vehicle inspections and compliance to emissions standards.

♦ Insurance coverage on historic vehicles is only a fraction of what it is on "normal" vehicles.

In addition to "historic vehicle" registration, New Jersey also has a "street rod" registration. Owners of modified antique automobiles manufactured before 1949 and registered in a New Jersey street rod club, an affiliate of the National Street Rod Association, Inc., are eligible to apply for street rod plates that cost $15. Vehicles registered as street rods are required to pass a motor vehicle safety inspection in New Jersey.

New Jersey "street rod" plates are also available for modified vehicles made before 1949, provided that the owner is a member of a NSRA-sanctioned street rod club. Vehicles registered as street rods are not exempt from motor vehicle inspections in the Garden State.

In New Jersey, four photos of the vehicle (both sides plus the front and the back) must accompany the application for either historic or street rod registrations. The requirements are different in other states, however.

Some states also offer other specialty registrations such as "antique vehicle," "special interest vehicle," "street rod," and possibly others. To find out what your registration options are for your particular area, contact your state's Department of Motor Vehicles.

"Vanity plates" are also available in New Jersey, even for historic vehicles such as this highly customized 1976 Corvette. Check with your state's DMV to find out what registration and license plate options are available for you. As of this writing, the registration fee for vanity plates on a historic vehicle in New Jersey is $91.

Driving Restrictions

New Jersey and most other states have stipulations for the use of collector vehicles registered as historic, street rod, or other specialty designations. These stipulations are generally restrictions on how and when the vehicle can be used and for what purposes. For example, here in the Garden State, the restrictions for motor vehicles at least 25 years old and having a specialty registration may be "owned as a collector's item and only used for exhibition and educational purposes by the owner." What that means, essentially, is that it's okay to go to cruise nights and car shows, parades and other such public exhibitions, or to drive your collector vehicle to a school or other location for the purposes of using it as an educational tool. It's not acceptable to use the vehicle as a daily driver to get you to and from work or the grocery store. Bear these restrictions in mind when using your collector vehicle; you may wind up with a summons and fine if you're found to be in violation of the DMV's restriction.

The Least You Need to Know

◆ A certified appraisal of your restored collector car is useful for insuring and selling the vehicle.

◆ Insuring your restored vehicle for either replacement value or agreed value is a very good idea.

◆ Compare rates, coverage, and mileage caps from several collector car insurers to get the best deal.

◆ Most states offer special registrations for historic, antique and specialty, custom, or modified vehicles.

◆ The registration options and driving restrictions vary from state to state.

23

Trailer Queen or Street Machine

In This Chapter

- ◆ Looking, but not touching
- ◆ Examining trailers
- ◆ Driving your collector car

Now that your restoration is finished, you have to decide whether you're going to transport your vehicle with a trailer or drive it to and from shows and cruise nights. This chapter covers the pros and cons to both. We also discuss some basic tips on collector vehicle etiquette and on keeping your pride and joy looking great while you're driving it.

Trailer Queen or Street Machine?

The decision to trailer or drive your restored collector vehicle is a personal one that only you can make. As I noted earlier in this book, there is no way you can keep a 100-point car perfect if you drive it; for this reason, transporting the vehicle in a trailer is the choice that some owners make.

Brake It Down _____

Trailer queen is a slang term, often with demeaning connotations, for a collector car that has been restored and is never driven. These cars are transported to shows in or on trailers and usually have almost no miles on the odometer. However, this term doesn't apply to racecars, which put many harsh miles on the odometer on the racetrack and in a significantly more demanding environment than ordinary street driving.

Others prefer to drive their vehicles, and for many hobbyists, the joy of driving their restored vehicle is the big payoff for the hours of hard work that went into restoring the vehicle. While there's a lot of upkeep as far as cleaning and appearance maintenance goes with a "driver," it's often a labor of love that these owners gladly perform after they cruise.

A Thing of Beauty to Behold—Look but Don't Touch

Most of what I'm going to say here is just plain common sense, but over the years I've found that a surprising number of people lack it seriously, especially when it comes to car shows and cruise nights.

First and foremost, whenever you're at a car show or a cruise night, by all means enjoy looking at and inspecting all of the great collector vehicles; however, do it with your eyes—not your hands. The first rule of collector car etiquette is to never touch someone else's vehicle. It is not only rude, it's uncalled for, and it shows disrespect for the property of others. Put yourself on the other side of the fence and you'll appreciate why you wouldn't want fingerprints all over your highly polished, expensive paint job.

Secondly, if you have small children or grandchildren that you take to collector car events, teach them to respect other people's property as well. I'm often appalled when I see small children, accompanied by oblivious parents, waving their ice cream cones or cotton candy around at car shows. It's also very disheartening to see people pushing strollers or carriages around shows and cruise nights, especially when they try to squeeze between the rows of cars on exhibition—the chance of them bumping into a collector car and causing a scratch is a very real possibility. Youngsters on bicycles, skateboards, scooters, and roller blades also represent potential disasters around collector vehicles.

Whenever you're near collector vehicles, be especially mindful of zippers and buckles on your clothing as well as purses, key chains, and cell phones that may cause scratches if they come into contact with the paint.

Trailer Types

Trailers can be divided into two categories: vehicle transport trailers and accessory trailers. Let's examine each of these categories in more detail.

There are two basic types of vehicle transport trailers: open and enclosed. Open trailers have no sides or roof, so the vehicle is exposed while it's on the trailer. Open trailers are less expensive than enclosed trailers but they offer less protection from road debris and the elements.

I know a couple people who have open trailers, and they only use them to keep the mileage of their collector cars down when the show they're going to is a considerable distance away. Both of these guys have heavily padded, weatherproof car covers that they keep on their cars while in transit on the trailers.

Overdrive

Hauling a car on an open trailer with a car cover flapping in the 60mph wind is insane. Even the most velvety soft, finely fitted and generously padded cover will act like fine sandpaper after a hundred miles, burnishing the paint and causing irreparable harm. If you're going to haul on an open trailer, leave the car uncovered.

An enclosed trailer costs more than an open unit, but the extra expense is worth it because enclosed trailers offer additional benefits. In addition to sheltering the vehicle from inclement weather and pebbles or other roadway debris while it is being transported, enclosed trailers can also function as storage units for the collector vehicle when it's not in use, thus freeing up garage space for other uses. Enclosed trailers also frequently have compartments for keeping your polishing cloths and other detailing supplies and equipment.

I recommend using a car cover even if you have an enclosed trailer, because it will keep stray dust particles from settling on the car while in transit or storage.

Surprisingly, auto transport trailers do not always come with ramps; they must often be purchased separately, and you can usually get one from the vendor from whom you purchase your trailer. While steel ramps are usually offered, I recommend purchasing aluminum ramps for a couple of reasons. First, they're lighter than steel, which makes them easier to handle. Secondly, they won't rust, and they don't require any painting or other maintenance.

Accessory trailers are great for stowing gear such as pop-up shade tents, chairs, picnic coolers, and other items that your vehicle may not be able to accommodate in its trunk.

If you intend to trailer your collector vehicle, a pair of quality ramps is essential. These lightweight units from Oxlite Manufacturing (see Appendix A for contact information) weigh only twenty-seven pounds each and have a load capacity of five thousand pounds.

This accessory trailer is painted to match the collector vehicle that tows it, including the flame motif. These are great for hauling the car show gear that won't fit into the collector vehicle itself, in this case a 1927 REO street rod with a rumble seat instead of a trunk.

These accessory trailers are readily available, and you can find ads for them in *Hemmings, Old Car Weekly,* and other collector hobbyist publications. Some folks get quite creative with their trailers, giving them paint jobs that complement the tow vehicle and maintain the overall theme.

An accessory trailer is usually defined as having one axle with one wheel attached to each end of the axle. These conventional trailers attach to the tow vehicle at a single point, with the hitch on the trailer connecting to the ball on the tow vehicle.

Here's a prime example of some creative thinking. The owner of this accessory trailer used an old Coca-Cola refrigerator box as the basis, welding a couple of soda-shop stools on the platform to complete the nostalgia theme. The chrome five-spoke mag wheels on the trailer match the ones on the collector car tow vehicle, too.

Conversely, a single wheel trailer has only one wheel. The trailer attaches to the tow vehicle using a special hitch that attaches at two points to the vehicle instead of just one.

Single wheel trailers fell out of favor and are no longer being manufactured because they are very unwieldy when disconnected from the tow vehicle, and they don't handle well at speeds over 45–50 mph. Also, because they are small, they can be very difficult for the tow vehicle's driver to see. For certain, they are a rare curiosity, so if you encounter one at a collector car event, be sure to check it out.

Tips for Driving Your Collector Car

Having been involved in this hobby for over a decade now, I've learned some useful things along the way that I'm happy to share. These helpful tips should increase the enjoyment of driving your collector car and help keep it looking good and running well.

◆ Before going on a cruise night or to a car show, check the weather forecast. While you'll almost inevitably get caught in an unforeseen shower sooner or later, there's no point in heading out when the chances for rain are already stacked against you. A bottle of Rain-X in the glove box is also a good idea, as older windshield wipers often leave something to be desired.

◆ Keep a waterproof car cover in the trunk just in case you do encounter a shower. As an alternative, you can also use clear plastic overspray sheeting to shield against rain.

◆ Always check your oil and tire pressure before taking your car out for a cruise. Battery electrolyte, the radiator's coolant, and the automatic transmission fluid level should also be checked as a matter of routine and replenished as required.

- A custom fitted "bra" will help to protect the nose of your car from pebble chips. Get one that attaches with Velcro, because these are easy and fast to put on and remove.

- Stay in the right lane and observe the speed limit. Collector cars attract enough attention just by being on the road. You certainly don't need a speeding ticket, so don't set yourself up as a target for the local constabulary.

- Keep your road observation skills sharp. Look ahead to safely avoid puddles and potholes.

- There are plenty of bad drivers on the road, so drive defensively and don't assume that the other guy sees you. Keep your headlights on to increase your visibility even during daylight hours.

- Driving your collector car requires your full attention. Don't engage in distractive behavior like talking on your cell phone or trying to dig a CD or cassette out of the case while the car is in motion. Pull over to the side of the road if you must engage in such activities.

- Courtesy on the road is especially important when you're driving your collector car. Keep a safe distance between you and the car in front of you and signal your intent to turn well in advance.

- Always make sure that you have a jack, lug wrench, and a fully-inflated spare tire in the vehicle, or at the very least, a can of tire inflator; you never know when you're going to get a flat.

- Standard equipment that should be in your trunk includes the following: jumper cables or a "hot box" for jump-starting the car, a basic tool kit that includes pliers, wrenches and screwdrivers, a flashlight, a quart of oil, and road flares or reflectors.

The Least You Need to Know

- You should never touch someone else's collector car.

- Enclosed trailers offer more protection than open trailers, and they can also be used for storing the collector vehicle when you're not taking it to shows.

- Rope or bungee cords will prevent a car cover from flying off while towing a collector car on an open trailer.

- Collector vehicles attract enough attention by themselves; don't set yourself up for a summons by speeding.

Chapter 24

Car Shows and Cruise Nights

In This Chapter

- ◆ Attending national, regional, and local shows
- ◆ Selecting car show winners
- ◆ Getting trophy fever
- ◆ Bringing gear
- ◆ Cruising in your vehicle
- ◆ Participating in cruise nights and having fun

You are justifiably proud of your restored collector vehicle, and you're eager to show it off. There are no better venues to exhibit your pride and joy at than car shows and cruise nights, which we discuss in this chapter.

It's Time to Show and Cruise

Sometimes it's difficult to distinguish between car shows and cruise nights. That's because trophies and door prizes are frequently presented at both events. While cruise nights are very casual events, car shows—at least for the most part—have some formal structure and registration requirements. And car shows can be local, regional, or national events. Let's find out more about them.

National, Regional, and Local Shows

National shows open to all marques are generally hosted by large organizations such as the Antique Automobile Club of America (AACA) and the National Street Rod Association (NSRA). While national shows are usually held once a year, these organizations also sanction regional shows that make it easier for members of local chapters to enter their vehicles without traveling across the country.

There are also marque-specific shows held on national and regional levels, such as Corvettes at Carlisle and the Oldsmobile shows. With many of these regional shows, the top winners are frequently invited to attend the national show to vie for top honors in the country. Needless to say, the competition is very tough and the vehicles entered always represent the cream of the crop.

There are other major shows held at locales such as Pebble Beach, Meadow Brook Hall, and Amelia Island that also attract the best restorations. These, too, are very high-end shows that are entered by well-heeled collectors.

The vast majority of us, however, enter and attend the local shows the most. Frequently sponsored by a local car dealership, merchant, chamber of commerce or a service organization like the Lion's Club, Rotary, or Knights of Columbus, they are often organized and hosted by a local car club with the proceeds going to some worthy charitable cause or organization. Local shows are generally a lot of fun, with DJ music and lots of activities going on all day.

These local shows are frequently very close to home and usually held on a Saturday or Sunday from the spring through late autumn, although some may also be held on weekday evenings. Registration for these shows is normally under $20, with a discount offered for advance registration. In addition to having a spot reserved for your vehicle on the day of the show, you also have a chance to win a trophy award.

When you enter the show, along with your windshield placard that has your show entry number on it, you often receive a numbered ticket for the door prize drawings. These door prizes can be just about anything from a novelty item, such as a pair of sponge dice to hang from your rear-view mirror, to something really useful like a tool set or a gift certificate for dinner for two at a local restaurant.

Frequently 50/50 drawings are held during local car shows. Of the collected proceeds, the winner receives 50 percent of the money, and the other 50 percent is donated to the cause or charity for which the show is being held.

Various activities throughout the day keep things moving. Events like the fan belt toss, spark plug changing contests, tug of war, dice roll, pedal car and tricycle races, bubble gum blowing contests, and automotive trivia contests help to pass the time and ensure that there's plenty for the entire family to do or watch while at the show.

Elvis has left the building and entered the car show. Elvis impersonators often provide entertainment and—more often than not—comic relief at local car shows.

Other popular entertaining diversions are the Elvis Presley and Marilyn Monroe look-alike contests, Elvis impersonators, car-related karaoke, and *flamethrower* contests.

This early 1950s car is shooting flames out of its exhaust. Flamethrower contests are fun to watch, but I suggest observing them from a distance rather than close up. Having a fire extinguisher on hand nearby is an absolute must.

Brake It Down

Flamethrowers are ignition devices—usually spark plugs—that are inserted into the exhaust pipes and, when activated, ignite unburned exhaust gases and shoot flames out of the tail pipes. The carburetors of flamethrower cars are usually set to run quite rich, thus providing plenty of unburned fuel vapor for the ignition devices. Flamethrowers, popular during the 1950s and 1960s, are rarely seen today because they are not safe vehicle modifications. Nevertheless, they are quite entertaining to watch and evoke memories of simpler, less complicated times.

Local shows often have vendors selling parts, novelties, and automobilia, and sometimes swap meets are ancillary events that are held in conjunction with the show. These swap meets offer excellent opportunities for selling surplus parts from your restoration or finding items you still might need.

Overdrive

Many car shows require proof that your collector vehicle is covered by insurance. Another frequent requirement is that it is equipped with a U.L. approved fire extinguisher.

When registering for a show, you'll have to decide what category your vehicle fits best in. Some local shows simply break their classes down into makes: Ford, Chevrolet, Pontiac, Plymouth and so forth, with separate classes for cars, trucks and motorcycles.

Other show registrations offer many different classes that help to narrow down where your vehicle belongs. Here's an example of the classes available on the registration form from a recent local show:

[ ] Preservation Class	[ ] Mustang 1964–1973
[ ] 1900–1916	[ ] Mustang 1974–Present
[ ] 1917–1929	[ ] Factory Muscle Cars (non-Mustang/Camaro/Firebird)
[ ] 1930–1936	[ ] Foreign Cars
[ ] 1937–1942	[ ] Foreign Sports Cars
[ ] 1945–1951	[ ] Street Rod/Modified Pre-WWII
[ ] 1952–1957	[ ] Modified Post-WWII
[ ] 1958–1964	[ ] Special Interest
[ ] 1965–1970	[ ] Monster Trucks
[ ] 1971–1978	[ ] Motorcycles & Scooters 1900–1978
[ ] Model-T	[ ] Kiddie Cars (gas, electric, pedal) No Fee
[ ] Model-A	[ ] Display—Farm Tractor No Fee
[ ] Classics	[ ] Display—Fire Engines No Fee

[ ] Pre-WWII Commercial	[ ] Display—Stationary Engines—No Fee
[ ] Post-WWII Commercial	[ ] Modified Commercial—1977 All Years through 1977 under Post-WWII
[ ] Corvette thru 1967	[ ] Corvette 1968–Present
[ ] Camaro/Firebird 1967–1981	[ ] Camaro/Firebird 1982–Present

Brake It Down

Street stock is a show designation that is used for vehicles that are essentially stock, with some minor bolt-on aftermarket accessories such as mag wheels or chrome valve covers. The criterion is usually that such modifications can be removed and the vehicle returned to pure stock in one-half hour or less.

Other shows, both general and marque-specific, may offer additional classes such as stock, *street stock*, modified, custom, and *wash-and-show*.

Brake It Down

Wash-and-show is a show designation that is used for vehicles that are essentially drivers. Generally, the car is washed, sometimes polished, and the interior vacuumed before entering it in the wash-and-show class. In this class the hood stays closed because the engine compartment is not inspected and the undercarriage is not checked. This class is also known as the "lazy man's show class" because it takes only minimal effort to get the car presentable for this class.

Judge Not, Lest Ye Be Judged

Regardless of the show, some form of evaluation is used to select those who win trophies and those who do not. There are four major methods used to select winners at car shows, and here's what each entails.

Points-System Judged Shows

The points system is used at all truly judged shows. Judges who are formally trained or at least very familiar with the particular type of vehicle they are judging thoroughly inspect all of the vehicles in their class. A formal judging sheet is used to record point values for various components such as the engine, chassis, body, paint, glass and so forth. Points are deducted from the perfect score values in each of these categories if some imperfection or flaw is found. Thorough judging can involve more than one judge and can take some time. These judged shows are the most serious, and if you're a winner, they can make you feel great. On the other hand, if, for some reason, your car doesn't measure up to snuff, they can be depressing and disheartening.

Some (but not all) shows make the judging sheet available to you at the end of the show so you can see where your vehicle is lacking. This can help you make the necessary improvements or corrections so you'll have a better chance of garnering an award next time. Many hobbyists feel that judged shows are the equivalent of an automotive proctology exam.

This is an actual judging sheet from the Antique Automobile Club of America for junior cars.

(Copyright 2001 AACA)

Subjective Selection

This is a much more relaxed means of selecting vehicles for trophies and awards at car shows. As the name implies, the selection method is subjective; in essence, this means that a vehicle appeals to a person who selects it on some subjective level. This could mean that the selection person is a Mustang fan, or perhaps he met his girlfriend and took her on a date in a vehicle like this. It could also mean that the color strikes his fancy, or the vehicle has cool graphics or sharp wheels or any other kind of subjective criteria. Winning an award at a show in which subjective selection is used is the equivalent of a coin toss in determining who gets a trophy and who goes home empty-handed.

Peer Judging

In peer-judged shows, the show entrants themselves select the show winners. When you register for such a show, you receive a ballot with your goody bag. You use this ballot to vote for the car that you feel is the best, and the one that deserves to win top honors. All other show entrants also have ballots. Generally, you are asked not to vote for your own vehicle, but this rule is frequently ignored.

Sometimes these ballots have several categories, such as: best street rod, best Mustang, best Corvette, best truck, best muscle car and so forth, and these are used to determine the winners in each of those categories.

When the votes are tallied, the vehicle that has the most takes first place, the runner-up takes second, and so on. There is also a trophy for best overall or best of show, and this is generally awarded to the vehicle that tallied the highest number of votes regardless of category.

People's Choice

Unlike peer judging, where the entrants select the winning cars by voting ballots, people's choice shows involve the spectators voting on the cars they consider the best; the entrants do not vote at all. This is very subjective because often spectators don't really know what they're looking at; they have no idea about the rarity of a vehicle or the hours of work and expense that went into making it look as it does today. Ballot box stuffing is also highly prevalent at such shows.

Overdrive

A comfortable chair and an umbrella or sun canopy make spending the day at a show a lot more enjoyable. Bringing a cooler with sandwiches and beverages rather than buying food and drinks from the show vendors saves you several dollars.

Trolling for Trophies

Winning a trophy is validation and confirmation that you've done a laudable job on your collector car. You've cut the mustard, made the grade, and brought home the gold. It feels good to win, and winning your first trophy is likely to etch itself into your memory as deeply as your first girlfriend or boyfriend.

For many hobbyists, this trophy lust lives on as long as they're involved in the collector car hobby. Others become jaded after a few years, and they don't even bother entering shows; these folks also frequently turn down a trophy they win at a cruise night. What could provoke such crazy behavior? With a couple of hundred trophies lining the rafters of my garage, I can personally tell you that trophy storage becomes a problem over time. And they're dust collectors, as well. After a while you may come to the realization, as I did, that the real trophy is the one with four wheels on it that you can drive, and not some gold-plated piece of plastic mounted on a marble base. But that's my perspective on it. You're new and fresh and excited to be in this hobby, so let me give you some pointers on how to successfully troll for trophies.

The trophies are all lined up on the table as the show moderator prepares to call out the winning car numbers and classes over the microphone. The thrill of winning your first trophy is one that you won't soon forget.

- ◆ **Talk up your car.** Don't be afraid to point out your vehicle's interesting and unique features to show spectators and passers-by; you don't know who may be a selector or who may have influence on the selection. You can mention interesting things like, "It took me three years to complete the restoration and I have put more than 1,500 hours into it," or, "There are five coats of base, five coats of color, and seven coats of clear," or whatever else is interesting. Be sure to ask these folks if they have any questions—getting a trophy is often a public relations exercise, so have your best people skills working for you at the show.

◆ **Show Your Pictures.** Remember all the prerestoration photos you took way back when? There's no better place to display your restoration photo album than at a car show. Seeing what the car looked like before you restored it gives the viewer a deeper appreciation and understanding of the huge investment of time, labor, and money it took to turn what began as a heap into a collector's item. You can and should be justifiably proud to show off your photos at shows.

Getting a trophy at the 2nd Annual Benefit Car Show sponsored by the No Dice Cruisers Car Club was a virtual no-brainer: Every preregistered entrant was guaranteed a trophy, a goody bag full of stuff, and free soda and doughnuts throughout the day. Here's a bunch of last minute entrants in line to register the day of the show.

◆ **A Sign of the Times.** Having a sign or placard that extols the features and virtues of your vehicle is helpful for letting people know what's special about it. Flash Cards (visit www.mv.com/ipusers/motion/ for more information) is a company that specializes in producing self-standing, full-color signs for collector cars that include color photos of the vehicle, the owner's name, and the important specs.

You can also get color "trading cards" from Flash Cards that are cards with color photos on one side and black and white shots on the back with pertinent facts about the vehicle. These are great for distributing at car shows as "souvenirs" to enthusiastic spectators. Once again, you never know who may have the ear of someone in charge of trophy awards, so shake hands, kiss the babies, and give them the five-cent tour of the vehicle, smiling all the while.

My friend Roy had this black Plexiglas sign made that listed the details of his 1936 International truck street rod, and he displayed it at shows in front of the vehicle. Roy passed away unexpectedly while I was writing this book, but he lives on in my memory and I wanted to include him here.

"Little Miss Lizzy"

'36 INTERNATIONAL C–SERIES
OWNER: ROY F. MERKEL
MANALAPAN, NJ

CAB: CHOPPED, CHANNELED
SUICIDE DOORS
ALL STEEL (EXCEPT FENDERS)

POWER: 350 CHEVY /400 TURBO TRANS

SUSPENSION: MUSTANG II IFS

FRAME: HAND BUILT 2X4 TUBING

BED: HAND BUILT 5X5 DIAMOND PLATE
OAK RAILS

WHEELS: 5 SPOKE CRAGAR S/S

REAR: 9" NARROWED FORD POSI REAR
– 3:55 GEARS

PAINT: DUPONT CANDY APPLE HOT PINK

♦ **Influence Peddling.** While I don't condone this practice and I've never engaged in it myself, I know for a fact that it does go on, and I know some trophy-hungry people who have done it whenever they could. What it boils down to is the practice of making donations of money, goods, or services to exert favorable influence on the powers that be with the objective of getting a trophy.

As with everything else in life, it takes all kinds of people to make the world go around. And, just as often, it's not what you know, but who you know. Bear in mind, however, that some people can't be bought, and it's not an ethical thing to do, either.

It's easy to get caught up in trophy fever, especially when you're new to the hobby. Regardless of how nice your car is, you won't always win a trophy, so don't set yourself up for a disappointment. The objective is to have fun, so don't get blinded by the flash of a trophy—all that glitters isn't gold. It's the good times and the nice folks you meet that matter, not the trophies.

Hauling Your Gear

I touched on accessory trailers in Chapter 23, but I didn't discuss their uses to any greater extent there.

If you intend to go to a lot of shows, there are several items that will make sitting out in the sun all day a bit more comfortable. Admittedly, this gear takes up space, and depending on your vehicle, your trunk and back seat may not be able to accommodate it. If this is the case, you may want to consider an accessory trailer.

In addition to the foldable canvas chairs that are popular at car shows, lightweight aluminum pop-up shelters are also nice to have because they provide shade from the blistering summer sun. Shows held on blacktop surfaces like shopping center parking lots can be especially hot and uncomfortable, so having a shelter to provide some shade is indeed a good thing.

Many people stock large cooler chests with food, bottled water, and soda, and these chests require lots of space as well. I also know a few folks who bring small charcoal grills or hibachis with them so they can cook their own hot dogs and hamburgers.

And don't forget that other items like detailing supplies, boom-box stereos, portable TVs, Nintendos, and DVD players you may elect to bring along all have to be hauled, so an accessory trailer could make your life easier. You'll find ads for accessory trailers in *Hemmings*, *Old Car Weekly*, and *Street Scene* magazine, among others.

Cruising the Venue

Just cruising in your collector vehicle can be a lot of fun by itself. You don't have to be going to a car show or a cruise night to enjoy driving your collector vehicle. While such events give some hobbyists an excuse to take their collector vehicle out for a spin, I personally never needed an excuse.

Depending on the particular era your vehicle is from, you may want to purchase some cassettes or CDs of music from that period to give appropriate auditory complement to your cruising. You don't have to go far (unless you want to, of course)—a short jaunt to the local McDonalds or Tasty Freeze can be a cruise in itself.

A popular thing that I've often done with my friends is to organize brunch and dinner cruises. We pick a restaurant that offers a Sunday brunch buffet, agree on a central meeting spot that's convenient for everyone, and embark on our cruise from that spot to the destination restaurant. After brunch, we all depart for our prospective destinations.

Wearing her poodle skirt, 10-year-old Elizabeth Merkel is ready to go cruising in her dad's cool street rod truck.

The dinner cruises work in the same way, but they take place later in the day and they don't necessarily have to be on Sundays. Friday and Saturday evenings are good times to schedule dinner cruises with your friends.

The nice thing about the Sunday brunch cruise is that the restaurant charges a fixed price for the buffet, so each individual or couple can pay their own check. On dinner cruises, we usually divide the total check by the number of people in our party equally and add on the gratuity, although some folks may prefer to have individual checks.

Brake It Down

A **poker run** is a cruise that has five stations designated as part of the cruise. At each of these stations, you select a card and that card is recorded on your score sheet. At the end of the poker run, the cruiser with the best hand wins a prize. It's lots of fun and it gives you another opportunity to enjoy your collector car.

Most restaurants are delighted when a group of collector cars park in their lot for a brunch or dinner cruise, because it attracts a lot of attention and brings in more potential customers. Some restaurants will even offer a discount to anyone who shows up in a collector vehicle.

Organizing *poker runs*, scenic cruises through the countryside, and even adventure cruises can all add to the enjoyment of the collector car hobby and give you extra opportunities to take your car out and enjoy it.

Cruise Nights and Car Hops

Cruise nights are great fun. These are informal events usually hosted by and held at local fast food restaurants, ice cream shops, or shopping centers. Unlike car shows, there is no registration fee, and you're not required to enter in a special class or division. Cruise nights are no-pressure events that are designed so both participants and spectators can have fun enjoying an assortment of collector vehicles.

A typical cruise night has a DJ spinning tunes (frequently "golden oldies") and making announcements of drawings for door prizes, asking trivia questions, or informing everyone of upcoming shows and events. The hosting food vendor may issue discount cards to cruisers so they can save money on food or beverages.

Some cruise nights also hold 50/50 raffles for the benefit of a charity or other good cause, and frequently dash plaques and trophies may be awarded. For the most part, cruise nights are relaxed and informal, so you can get there whenever you want and leave at any time.

This little fellow is obviously enjoying the cruise scene in his 1937 Ford Cabriolet stroller. The collector car hobby is truly a family activity that can be fun for all.

Carhops offering curbside service were very popular during the 1950s and the 1960s, and many cruise nights sponsored by fast food restaurants are bringing them back into vogue. I know of a local burger and fried chicken restaurant that has teenagers on roller-blades come right to your car and affix a tray to the window. These waiters- and waitresses-on-wheels take your order and deliver your food and drinks right to your car. This particular place offers a 20 percent discount to anyone who comes in a collector vehicle, even if it isn't during a cruise night, which is a good incentive to go there.

Of course, many hobbyists prefer not to eat in their collector vehicles, so they can eat at the counter or an outside table. They still get the collector vehicle discount, however.

Cruise nights, like this one hosted by the township itself in Freehold, New Jersey, are held on the last Thursday of the month. This cruise night regularly attracts hundreds of collector cars of every description from stock vintage vehicles to muscle cars to wild street rods and customs. You never know what you might see at a cruise night, but you're sure to have fun looking.

Are We Having Fun Yet?

The whole point of the collector car hobby is to have fun, and that should always be first and foremost in your mind. This is a hobby—a pastime that's supposed to give you relaxation, recreation and entertainment—in short, fun.

While it's only natural to jump into car shows and cruise nights with both feet at first, pace yourself and don't set up such a hectic schedule that it becomes work—you'll burn yourself out in a hurry if you do that. When my wife and I first got involved in this hobby a decade ago, we went to cruise nights five nights a week and car shows every weekend—and it was loads of fun, at least for a while.

But everyday demands of life can't be neglected, and there are chores that need to be done. Don't let your cruising time interfere with taking care of business. It's easy to overdose if you go to too many events too soon, so remember: Too much of anything is not good.

Enjoy the hobby and take your time to smell the roses—you'll find that you'll have more fun that way, and you'll continue to enjoy this hobby for many years to come.

The Least You Need to Know

- ◆ Collector car shows are held on national, regional, and local levels.

- ◆ Points-system judged shows are the most competitive.

- ◆ Newcomers to the collector car hobby often get trophy fever.

- ◆ Going on casual cruises alone or with friends can be very enjoyable.

- ◆ Cruise nights are relaxed and informal events that are a lot of fun for participants as well as spectators.

Chapter 25

Collector Car Clubs

In This Chapter

- Bringing people together
- Joining local clubs
- Fostering common interests
- Displaying your club membership
- Organizing fun club activities

Some people decide that they want to be "lone wolves"—they don't want to join and belong to any car clubs, preferring to come and go as they please without having to attend meetings or other club functions. Many others, however, want to belong to a car club to spend time with other people who share their interests.

This chapter focuses on collector car clubs to give you a good idea of what to expect from club memberships.

Marque-Specific Car Clubs

Marque-specific car clubs restrict their membership to owners of specific car makes. The benefit of joining a marque-specific club is that everyone in the club shares an interest in the same marque that you do. This can be invaluable for getting maintenance tips, tech advice, securing any parts you need, borrowing specialized tools and fixtures, and more. The common interest also helps to further your knowledge and enjoyment of your particular marque.

There are national and regional marque-specific clubs that you can join. Many clubs are listed in *Hemmings* and *Old Car Weekly* as well as magazines dedicated to specific marques. The Internet is also an excellent way to find a marque-specific club.

To give you a very small sample of the marque-specific clubs that are out there, here are some of the results that a general search for "car clubs" on the Internet returned:

American MGB Association

www.mgclub.org
Phone: 1-800-723-MGMG or 773-878-5055
E-mail: info@mgclub.org

North America's oldest and largest club for all MGBs, MGB-GTs and Midgets. A nonprofit organization founded in 1975, it offers color magazines, e-magazines, technical advice, member recommendations on service, body and parts sources, registration of your MG, a tradition of service, and free member classified ads that appear in the *Octagon* magazine and on the AMGBA website.

Ford Galaxie Club of America

www.galaxieclub.com
Phone: 870-743-9757
E-mail: director@galaxie.com

The Ford Galaxie Club of America is open to owners of Galaxies from 1959 to 1974 and dedicated to the restoration, preservation, and enjoyment of these Ford passenger automobiles. The main goal of the club, which has over 1,800 members worldwide, is to unite 1959 to 1974 Galaxie owners the world over and to preserve the name Galaxie and its association as one of the first muscle cars of the 1960s in perpetuity.

National Firebird & T/A Club

www.firebirdtaclub.com
Phone: 773-769-6262
E-mail: info@firebirdtaclub.com

This is North America's largest and oldest club for all years of Firebirds, including the Trans Am, GTA, Formula, and Firehawk. Established in 1984, it offers color magazines, e-magazines, technical advice, member recommendations on service, body and parts sources, registration of your Firebird and TA, a message board area, a tradition of service, and free member classified ads that appear in the *Eagle* magazine and on its website.

Corvette Club of America
www.corvetteclubofamerica.com
Phone: 270-737-6022
E-mail: info@corvetteclubofamerica.com

The Corvette Club of America is dedicated to preserving America's sports car, the Chevrolet Corvette. The club is the fastest-growing national Corvette club in the country and members can enjoy Corvette pictures, news about shows and events, memorabilia for sale, technical how-to articles and more in the bi-monthly magazine, *Corvette Capers*, and on its website.

Local General Car Clubs

Some "general" car clubs are also worthy of your consideration because they welcome owners of all makes and models; some specify the age threshold for the vehicle at 25 years old or older, while others don't impose such a requirement.

Membership requirements vary from club to club, and each club has its own rules and bylaws. Many clubs are incorporated as nonprofit organizations, and these clubs are often very civic-oriented. Such clubs may sponsor car shows or cruises, and any funds generated are donated to charitable causes.

Going to a couple of local car shows and asking participants about car clubs is an excellent way to find out about clubs that are active in your area. Cruise nights are another great way to meet members of local clubs, and don't forget checking out the Internet to locate potential clubs, too.

Common Interests and Camaraderie

Probably the strongest "glue" that makes car clubs work and keeps them together is the common interest bond they generate among their members. This is true of the "general" clubs as well as the marque-specific ones. It's a good feeling to be among others with the same common interests because it generates a synergy that, in turn, creates friendships and a strong "esprit de corps" (team spirit).

There is generally some formal structure to car clubs, although some are more casual than others. Usually there is a requirement to pay dues, and this may be a single annual payment or a monthly collection taken up at meetings. Dues are used to pay the expenses of running the club, such as postage, printing, insurance, and so forth. Minutes of the meetings are usually kept, and a newsletter is frequently published and mailed to members to keep everyone abreast of club business and upcoming events.

Be aware, however, that you might have to do some "club shopping" to find one that's right for you. I discovered another club while driving down a main highway about 15 miles away from my home on a Friday night. This particular club was hosting a cruise night at a fast food restaurant, and everyone appeared to be having a good time. Several people were line-dancing to "Be-Bop My Baby All Night Long," so I decided to pull in to find out more about this club. As I drove my '33 Dodge street rod into the parking lot, a couple of club members directed me to a parking spot and came over to introduce themselves as soon as I got out of the car. This club started to look better by the minute and I immediately felt welcome and at home with this group.

My wife, Liz, and I joined the club and became very active members. Within the first two years, we were both elected to officer positions and we made some very good friends; two couples became our closest and dearest friends. The common bond of the collector cars fostered the camaraderie and lasting friendships. That's one of the best things about this hobby—the friends you make.

Three amigos—(left to right) the author, Ken McBrearty, and Roy Merkel (deceased) clowned it up for the camera at a car show in 2001. We all joined the same club and became close friends over the years, and eventually left that club and founded the No Dice Cruisers car club.

(Photograph by Liz Benford)

Drag Plates and Club Colors

The club I belonged to had black satin jackets with the club name and logo on back. We also had T-shirts and everyone proudly wore this apparel whenever we went to car shows or cruise nights. We were all proud to be members of what was one of the biggest car clubs in our state at the time.

We also had *drag plates* on our vehicles. Drag plates are important to club members because they proclaim your membership to anyone who is following your collector vehicle.

When you become a member of a club that fits your interests and personality, it's only natural to be proud of being part of such an organization. Wearing club colors and putting a drag plate on your vehicle identifies you as a member and it makes you feel good.

Brake It Down

Drag Plates are rectangular metal plates suspended from the rear of a club member's vehicle that have the club name and logo on them. They identify the vehicle and its driver as a member of that club.

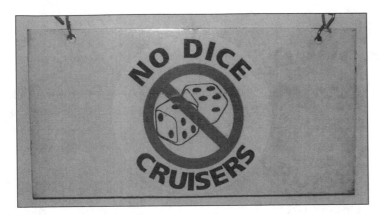

This is a drag plate from the No Dice Cruisers car club in New Jersey.

Poker Runs, Rallies, Brunch Cruises, and More

When you're considering joining a club, ask about their activities and how frequently they stage them. The following are some of the fun things that clubs often organize:

♦ **Poker Runs.** These are road rallies that require you to follow a predetermined course with five stops along the way. At each of these stops, you pick a card. The fifth stop is the end of the course, and your hand is recorded at that time. The person with the winning poker hand wins the prize, trophy, money, or whatever the top award may be. Poker runs are a lot of fun, and they give you an opportunity to drive your collector vehicle, too.

♦ **Rallies.** Rallies are timed courses that must be driven over a predetermined route. The objective is to make the best time while still observing the posted speed limits. Along the way, there are several checkpoints where your time is recorded. The car with the best time wins, and awards are usually also given to the second and third place cars.

♦ **Brunch Cruises.** Clubs often have Sunday brunch cruises to restaurants that offer a fixed-price brunch buffet. These are a lot of fun for all family members, and the restaurants frequently offer "cruiser discounts" to club members.

♦ **Mystery Cruises.** These are fun cruises to unknown destinations. Only the road captain knows where the final destination is, so these cruises are basically follow-the-leader caravans.

♦ **Holiday Parties.** Most clubs sponsor holiday parties for their members. Some-times these parties are held at restaurants, while other times they are held in rented halls. Everyone is usually asked to bring a gift to be exchanged with other members after picking a name or number from a hat, and frequently toys and other items are collected for donations to the needy. Santa almost always pays a visit to these parties, and sometimes Elvis shows up, too!

♦ **Cruise Nights.** Many local clubs host cruise nights that are sponsored by fast food restaurants or other local merchants. These are fun social events and they're a great way to raise public awareness of the club and attract new members. They often hold door prize drawings and 50/50s. Some cruise nights also award trophies, and discounts for food and beverages at the sponsoring eatery are commonly given to cruisers.

♦ **Car Shows.** Almost every club sponsors and hosts a car show at some time in its life. While organizing a show takes a lot of time and hard work, it can be an en-joyable and rewarding event if everyone in the club pulls together to make it hap-pen smoothly. The proceeds from these shows are usually donated to worthwhile causes, although some of the proceeds may also be used for the club treasury to fund other events throughout the year.

The Least You Need to Know

♦ Marque-specific clubs bring people with interests in your particular marque together.

♦ Many national clubs also have regional chapters that you may want to join.

♦ Wearing club colors and having a drag plate on your vehicle identify you as a proud member of your car club.

♦ When you go on a mystery cruise, you never know where the destination is until you arrive there.

♦ Car clubs often sponsor cruise nights and car shows to raise public awareness and to raise funds for worthy causes.

Chapter 26

Protecting Your Investment

In This Chapter

- Cleaning and detailing your vehicle

- Preparing for winter storage

- Choosing among garages, trailers, portable shelters, car bubbles, and car covers

- Storing your car in a climate-controlled facility

This chapter explores the various things that need to be done and what you'll need to protect your investment through the cold, harsh winter.

Protecting Your Investment

You have invested a great deal of time and money in your collector vehicle, so it only makes sense that you want to take the necessary steps to protect your investment. This includes such items as cleaning, detailing, prepping, and storing the vehicle so it stays clean and well-preserved while it isn't being used.

There are several things you can do to protect and preserve your vehicle, and there are many good products out there to help you achieve this end.

Details, Details, Details ... Cleaning and Detailing

Cleaning and detailing your collector vehicle is the first thing you should do anytime you won't be using the car for any length of time. By putting it away clean and fully detailed, it's ready to use as soon as the covers come off. Think of cleaning and detailing as a way to make a car that already turns heads even more attractive.

There are many brands of products for cleaning, waxing, and detailing your collector car. I have had truly excellent results with car care products from Ibiz (see Appendix A for contact information), and they are my personal favorites. Having used Ibiz products for over a decade, I have no intention of switching to anything else (remember, don't fix what isn't broken). These products are head-and-shoulders above everything else I've tried, and they deliver consistent results.

4-Wheel Jive
The horizontal egg crate grille was a styling feature introduced on the 1941 Cadillac and is still in use today.

Just as you did during the restoration process, you'll work front to back in detailing the vehicle. First, concentrate on the engine compartment. Lift the hood, and be sure to use a fender apron or towels to avoid belt buckle scratches while you leaning over to work on the compartment. It's also a good idea to take off your jewelry to avoid scratching the finish, too.

Spray Nine

While there are several good "industrial strength" cleaners for degreasing engines, I personally prefer to use Spray Nine (see the Appendix A for contact information). Hose down the entire engine compartment with clean water and spritz Spray Nine liberally on areas that have grease, oil, or road grime on them. If you've cleaned your vehicle after every cruise or car show, this muck should be minimal.

The valve covers and the front of the engine block around the timing cover are the usual areas that need attention due to oil seepage, especially if the gaskets are old. Be sure to give the Spray Nine enough time to work—spray it on and let it sit for approximately five to ten minutes before rinsing it off. A soft one-inch wide paintbrush (an old toothbrush also works well) helps the cleansing and speeds things up a bit if you have any caked-on grime.

Spray Nine cleanser and degreaser is great for cleaning up the engine compartment. A good quality hose nozzle helps to direct the spray pattern and pressure precisely. Detailing swabs and brushes are ideal for getting into crevices and corners to remove dirt, wax, and polish.

When you're finished with the Spray Nine, hose the engine compartment down to rinse it clean and let it drip dry. Use your air compressor with an air nozzle to blow away the puddled water on the intake manifold and other areas. This helps to minimize rusting caused by pooled water.

While the engine compartment is air-drying, you can work on the rest of the car. Remove your fender aprons and close the hood. You'll come back to complete the engine compartment detailing when the rest of the car is finished.

> **Pit Stop**
>
> Avoid getting the Spray Nine on any chrome-plated parts because it's strong stuff and can cause pitting; the same goes for getting it on polished aluminum, which it will dull.

Washing the Exterior of the Car

Your next task is to wash the exterior of the car thoroughly. It's important that you use a quality car wash concentrate or car shampoo. Never use household dish detergent or household cleansers. It's preferable to work in the shade, if possible, because the hot sun will dry the car unevenly and leave you with streaks later.

Wet down the entire car and use a soft sponge to apply the suds, working in a circular motion to clean the surface of the vehicle. I prefer to use natural sea sponges rather than the synthetic sponges because they're softer, and I don't like using a chamois because of its tendency to hold dirt that can cause scratches. Be sure to equip your hose with a good nozzle that permits you to adjust the spray and pressure. A large plastic bucket is also better to use than a small pail, because it will hold more sudsy solution.

After thoroughly sudsing the entire car, rinse it using moderate hose pressure. Terry cloth towels are best for drying because they're soft and thirsty, although some people prefer to use those soft rubber "water blades." Even if you use a water blade, you're still going to need a towel for some of the drying, and I'm not a big fan of the squeegee, which, essentially, is a water blade. Switch to new dry towels as the ones you started with become water soaked.

Ibiz makes a full line of car care products for both the exterior and interior, and they carry a 100 percent satisfaction guarantee. They also make soft circular applicator pads.

Protecting Your Clean Car

Now that your car is nice and clean, it's time to apply a protective wax; carnauba wax offers the best protection from UV and acid rain. The Ibiz car wax contains montan wax, which is a fossilized carnauba wax, the best you can get. A little of this stuff goes a long way, so it's really economical. What I like best is that it doesn't take any of the paint off, and it gives the car's surface a mirror-like shine.

You can apply the Ibiz car wax directly to the car's surface or put it on a polishing cloth. Because this wax is 100 percent nonabrasive, it's safe for all automotive finishes including enamel, lacquer, and clear coat. I find it's best to work the wax in a circular motion doing about a two-by-three-foot section at a time. When you reach the end of this two-by-three-foot area, the portion you did first will be dry and you can wipe it off with a clean cotton cloth or soft terry towel. Work your way around the car until you have waxed it all. You'll find that the Ibiz wax gives you a super slippery finish that reduces friction and eliminates swirl marks. This wax can also be applied using a buffing wheel, although I prefer hand waxing. You can use detailing swabs or brushes to get the dried polish out of the corners or other places that cannot be comfortably reached with the cloth or towel.

The chrome and other brightwork, emblems, and trim are the next items to get attention. Use a good metal polish and a soft cloth, working the polish in smooth strokes with a soft cloth. When it is dry, wipe it off with another smooth cloth. As with the wax, you should remove any dried polish remaining in crevices or corners using detail swabs or a small detail brush.

The wheels and tires come next on the agenda. Your car may have painted steel wheels with chrome trim rings and center caps, aluminum wheels, or mag wheels—perhaps even wire wheels. Regardless of what kind of wheels you're running, they must be cleaned, and your tires must be dressed.

Overdrive

Don't discard your old toothbrushes when they are worn. They make excellent brushes for cleaning and detailing hard-to-reach places on your collector car, such as wire wheels, the back of your tire valve stems, and so forth.

Busch Chrome Wash and Aluminum Wash are both great for quick and easy wheel cleaning. The aluminum polish is excellent for polished aluminum pieces, and the wax and sealant is great for protecting unpolished aluminum parts like an intake manifold.

I use Busch Chrome Wash and Aluminum Wash (see Appendix A for contact information) on the wheels of my collector vehicles, and I've found it to be great. I spray the appropriate wash on the wheel, wait approximately five minutes, and then hose it off. Dirt, road tar, sap, brake dust, and grime literally rinse away with minimal, if any, brushing. One of my vehicles has custom-made chrome wire wheels, and while these are difficult to clean by hand, it's fast and easy using the chrome wash. The aluminum wash also works well and does a nice job of cleaning up polished, brushed, or anodized aluminum wheels; it also works well on magnesium wheels. Their aluminum polish and wax and sealant are also great for keeping your aluminum wheels and parts looking good.

When you're finished working on the wheels, it's time to apply some tire dressing to make that black rubber shine. While I prefer the Ibiz Tire and Rubber Finish, several other good tire dressings are available at your local auto supply store, and they all work pretty well. The difference between them is how long they keep the tires looking shiny and wet, and the Ibiz dressing lasts quite a while.

Touch Ups

The engine compartment should be dry, so take the opportunity to inspect the valve covers, intake manifold, thermostat housing and other areas for faded or chipped paint, and touch them up with the appropriate color for your make and model. These paints are readily available at most auto parts stores, and they're usually sold in aerosol cans. The problem with aerosols is the inherent overspray they produce. To get around this problem, I use a small disposable "artist" brush for doing touch ups rather than spraying. Shake the can, then thoroughly spray about one-half inch of paint into a small jar (baby food jars are ideal) for dipping the brush. If you have any rusted bolts, this is a good time to touch them up with paint, too.

A little satin black paint (available at the local hardware store) can be brushed on the firewall, inner fenders, radiator braces, or other black areas that require touching up. If you wish, you can use Rust-Oleum satin black or Eastwood Satin Black Rust Encapsulator on any rusted bolts or braces to conceal the rust and prevent it from recurring, too.

Moving on to the interior, I recommend working from the rear forward, and from top to bottom. It's a good idea to start your interior detailing by emptying everything from the rear deck and rear seats, as well as from the ashtrays, map pockets and door pockets if you have them (I keep change and parkway toll tokens in my ashtray). A good vacuuming is in order, and a shop vac with several nozzles of different sizes usually does a better job than a house vacuum cleaner. Vacuum the rear deck, seats and carpeting and the backs of the seats, under the seats and the floor foot panels, rockers, and kick panels. Then proceed to do the headliner and the front seats, floors, rockers and kick panels.

A wipe-down of all the trim and panels including the door panels and dash, trim moldings, and windshield pillar posts is next. While you may be tempted to use something like Fantastic or another spray cleaner, I advise you not to; Windex works well and it isn't as harsh as the spray cleaners.

For any plastic or vinyl interior parts, you can also purchase a vinyl/leather cleaner and protectant at your local auto supply. Household spray cleaners don't offer any UV protection and, in fact, will cause the plastic material to deteriorate more quickly.

If you have leather seats and a leather-wrap steering wheel, these are the next items on the list. I personally don't like to use saddle soap to clean my leather buckets, because I think it removes too much oil from the leather; other hobbyists I know disagree, so it's your own call here. I use Ibiz Sheen because it does a good job and it saves me time and effort because it cleans and protects with the same application.

Cleaning Glass and Lenses

The last detailing tasks are to clean the glass and gauge lenses; again, Windex works just fine for these jobs. To avoid washing off the vinyl treatment, however, I suggest spraying the Windex on a soft cotton cloth rather than directly on the inside of the windows and windshield, so there's no overspray. Get the cloth fairly wet, wipe down the windows in a circular motion, and use a soft dry cloth to finish the job. Do the same thing to your gauge lenses.

Prepping for Winter

Storing your collector car for the winter doesn't simply mean driving it in the garage, throwing a car cover on it and forgetting about it until the spring. There are several things that should be done to store the car properly, and neglecting to do so will have adverse effects on the vehicle.

Be sure to check your cooling system to make sure it has sufficient antifreeze—replenish it as required. It's a good idea to have enough antifreeze in the system to protect it to 50 degrees below zero. Make sure that you have the engine running as you add antifreeze, and keep it running long enough for it to reach normal operating temperature. This allows the thermostat to open completely so the antifreeze circulates throughout the engine rather than simply topping it off in the radiator.

It's also a good idea to leave the windows cracked about one-half inch to let fresh air circulate; this keeps the interior dry and smelling fresh. You may also want to add an air freshener. I don't recommend leaving a hanging-type air freshener in it for the duration of the winter storage, however. The aroma would permeate the rugs and upholstery, so take it out of the car after a few days or a couple of weeks at the most.

There are two schools of thought about whether you should have a full tank of gas or an empty tank when you store the car. Like many other hobbyists I've spoken with, I contend that a full tank of gas with an added stabilizer is much better than an empty tank, which is subject to rusting from condensation, like the fuel line itself. It stands to reason that if the tank and fuel lines are already filled with gasoline, there's little if any room left for condensation and subsequent rust to occur.

Those proponents of storing the vehicle with an empty tank cite that there is a greatly reduced risk of fire if there is no fuel in the car. I'm not careless around my collector cars, so the fire risk outweighs the very real risks of condensation and rusting that will occur with an empty tank.

You can purchase gasoline stabilizer from the local auto supply stores to stop the additives in the gas from forming varnish that gums up the carburetor or fuel injection systems.

I don't suggest changing the oil when you put the car into storage because it is likely to gather moisture from condensation, which is produced by temperature changes.

Overdrive

Be sure to top off all the other fluids, such as power steering fluid and brake fluid in the master cylinder, to cut down on condensation.

Instead, you should add some additional oil to intentionally overfill the crankcase. This keeps the crankshaft submerged in oil, thus protecting it and the upper sides of the oil pan from any rust that could result from condensation. Be sure to put a note on the car to remind yourself to drain the oil, replace the filter, and refill it with the proper amount of fresh oil in the spring before you start the vehicle for the first time after it comes out of storage.

The battery can be left in the car or taken out, depending on your personal preference. Either way, make sure that each battery cell is filled up to the full mark.

If you take the battery out of the car, store it on wood, such as two-by-fours or ¾-inch plywood, rather than on the concrete floor itself or on a steel shelf. I recommend using a trickle charger such as a Battery Tender, which is available from Eastwood and other suppliers, to keep the battery fully charged for the duration of its storage. The nice thing about the Battery Tender is that it automatically shuts itself off when full charge has been reached, and then turns on again as the battery starts to discharge from standing.

If you leave the battery in the car, I still suggest keeping a Battery Tender connected and plugged in to keep the battery fully up-to-snuff.

Storage preservatives can also be added to the motor if you desire. Available at the local automotive part stores, these preservative sprays can be sprayed into the carburetor or into the cylinders after removing the spark plugs. They are useful in areas of the country where there is a lot of humidity and condensation occurs often.

Overdrive

Chrome and other bright work can be protected from rusting or oxidizing by applying a thin coat of vegetable cooking oil to it. The vegetable oil won't harm paint the way petroleum-based oils will.

Garages and Portable Shelters

Most people have unheated garages with concrete floors, and these are fine for storing collector cars as long as a few precautions are taken.

The correct way to store your vehicle is to jack it up and let it rest on jack stands. The important thing here is to put the stands on the axles or control arms, rather than the on the car's frame. The reason for this is to keep the suspension "loaded" with the weight of the car. If you place the jack stands under the frame, the suspension will dangle at full extension, and this is not good for the car itself or the suspension components.

Putting the car up on jack stands gets the weight of the car off the tires so they don't develop flat spots. It also puts more distance between the floor of the garage and the car, thus preventing additional condensation from occurring and providing additional air circulation to help dry off any condensation that does occur.

I also recommend putting some carpeting under the car as an added condensation-prevention measure. I've used discarded commercial-grade carpeting that has a rubber backing, and I find that it is good for cutting down on floor-to-chassis condensation. I acquired several square yards for free from a banquet hall that was being remodeled, and the contractor was only too happy to load it into my trunk to make additional space for other refuse in his dumpster.

Mice seek the warmth and shelter of garages as cold weather approaches, and they can fit into openings as small as a nickel. Mice love car interiors and often make their nests in them, burrowing into the seats or pulling out the stuffing to line their nests. I've also found that, for some reason, mice like engine compartments; I've found nests in the air cleaners of several collector cars when they came out of storage. Rats share the same pesky characteristics of mice, but on a larger scale.

Portable shelters are an alternative storage solution that you may want to consider if you don't have room in your garage for your collector car and don't want to pay monthly rent to store your vehicle elsewhere.

Portable shelters like this pointed-roof Cover-It Car Shelter from North American Outdoor Products are inexpensive and provide excellent protection from the elements.

(Photograph courtesy of North American Outdoor Products)

North American Outdoor Products (see Appendix A for contact information) manufacturers a line of Cover-It portable shelters that are available in rounded styles or house styles (pointed roofs) in a wide range of sizes in addition to fabricating custom shelters for special requirements. The single-vehicle shelters cost about $300; they're easy to erect and quite durable. They featured zippered doors to keep out the elements, and they can be anchored on cement, gravel, or earthen surfaces.

Whenever you're using an outdoor shelter, you should take some additional precautions to ensure safe storage of your vehicle. I recommend putting a waterproof vinyl tarpaulin on the floor of the shelter and using carpeting on top of the tarp as extra moisture shielding. Again, elevating the vehicle on jack stands while keeping the suspension loaded is also a good idea.

Even though the car is in a shelter, it is still vulnerable to critter damage—more so, in fact, because the pests may be able to burrow under the shelter to gain access. Because the shelter is outside, other critters like raccoons and skunks may also find its interior to be a comfy place to stay during the winter months, and your vehicle's upholstery and other interior components may make comfy nests and provide some snacks at the same time.

There are a couple steps you can take to thwart these pests and keep them at bay. Traditional spring-loaded traps usually get rid of mice, rats, squirrels, and chipmunks if baited with peanut butter—all of these creatures find peanut butter irresistible for some reason.

You may also want to consider a more humane way of keeping these critters out of the shelter and away from your collector car by using one or two ultra-sonic pest repellers. These are available from better hardware stores and mail order sources like The Sharper Image and Brookstone. These battery-powered devices emit an ultra-sonic noise that such creatures find very irritating and uncomfortable. Because of this, they will give the source of the sound a wide berth. The batteries usually last a month or two before they need to be replaced.

You can also get bottles of fox urine from farm and agricultural supplies that you can put around the perimeter of the shelter to ward off these backyard pests. Because foxes are predators, the pests will think there is a fox nearby if they smell the urine and avoid what they perceive as dangerous turf. The downsides to fox urine is that it smells, it's more expensive than the nine-volt batteries required by an ultra-sonic pest repeller, and it must be re-applied after each rain, snow, or heavy dew to maintain its repellent power.

Car Bubbles and Car Covers

Another viable storage alternative is to purchase a car bubble from Jim's Car Capsules (see Appendix A for contact information). As the name implies, this inflatable zippered envelope provides a controlled environment for storing your collector car and also helps to keep pesky critters out. These car capsules are available for both indoor and outdoor storage. Made of a heavy-gauge plastic, the capsule's perimeter has a zipper.

An inflatable car capsule from Jim's Car Capsules is an ideal solution for providing a controlled storage environment. The unit shown here is actually an indoor car capsule, but we shot it in my driveway to give you a better look; the heavier outdoor capsules are silver in color and are UV resistant.

(Photograph by Liz Benford)

To use the capsule, the basemat is positioned on the ground (or floor of the garage or trailer—they're also ideal for use in the Cover-It Portable Shelters), the car is driven onto the basemat and the upper plastic portion is then pulled over the car and zipped up. A 12-volt fan is then inserted into the inflation duct at the front of the capsule and powered on, thus inflating the capsule. A battery tender provides the power for the fan, or a car battery can power it if electrical outlets aren't available for the tender. Under normal use, a fully charged automotive battery powers the fan for a full week before it needs recharging.

If you live in California, Arizona, or another region of the country where winters, and the weather in general, is mild year-round, all you need is a soft car cover. There are several good covers available from many manufacturers, and the best of these soft covers have a soft flannel backing with a heavier cloth top-side. I also recommend using such a cover even when storing your car in your garage because they help keep dust and other debris off the car while it's being stored.

Storage in Trailers

If you already own an enclosed vehicle transport trailer, you can use it for storing your collector car as well. If you don't own one, you may want to consider purchasing one, because in addition to storing your vehicle, you can also use it for transport if you wish.

CAUTION | **Pit Stop**

Don't drain the oil from your engine when putting the car away for storage. Doing so will increase the possibility of internal rusting due to condensation. Instead, store it with the oil in the engine and change the oil and filter as soon as it comes out of storage.

Depending on how much property you have and your zoning ordinances, you may want to invest in a cargo trailer or overseas shipping container as a storage solution for your collector car. You can get used trailers and cargo containers for a reasonable price when they've reached the end of their cargo-bearing lives; in most instances they are still quite serviceable as vehicle storage containers. I have a couple of 45-foot trailers to house my collector cars at the rear of my property, and I had the wheels removed from these trailers so they can sit on the ground. Moving the cars in and out of the trailers is easily accomplished using a pair of Oxlite aluminum ramps.

If you don't have a garage or trailer in which to store your car, you should seriously consider purchasing a high-quality all-weather car cover. The amount of protection the cover provides is directly proportional to its price. A high-end, custom-fitted all-weather cover will set you back $300–$400, but it is well worth the investment.

A good all-weather cover like this one from Auto Chic is the ticket when enclosed storage isn't available. The cover has a soft fleece inner surface and a moisture-resistant outer layer that lets the car "breathe" while still protecting it from the elements.

(Photograph by Liz Benford)

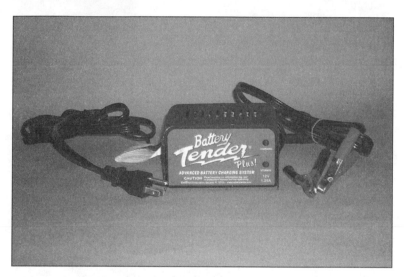

A Battery Tender is a trickle charger that keeps your collector car battery fully charged while it's in storage. The Battery Tender automatically turns off to prevent overcharging, and turns itself on again as needed. For approximately $50, it's a great investment and no collector car hobbyist should be without one.

Climate-Controlled Storage

Another option you may wish to explore is storing your collector car in a climate-controlled facility. While this is more costly than the other options we've explored, it has several benefits that are worth considering.

This vintage Cadillac is stored along with a dozen other collector vehicles in a climate-controlled facility at Hibernia Auto Restorations (see Appendix A for contact information) in Hibernia, New Jersey. The facility is alarmed, insured, and has video surveillance 24/7 as well as an air filtration system and fire protection. Vehicle maintenance and Battery Tenders are also part of the storage package, which costs approximately $300 per month for the average vehicle.

The cost of storing your vehicle in a climate-controlled facility can be justified by the benefits it provides:

◆ The temperature and humidity are controlled to remain consistent all year long. This keeps condensation and subsequent rust at an absolute minimum.

◆ The facilities are secured and insured, so there's no worry about your vehicle being stolen or damaged.

◆ The air is usually filtered in these facilities to prevent dust, and the facility also frequently furnishes a protective car cover to keep the vehicle looking its best.

◆ The vehicles are maintained to keep them in good working order. The vehicles are often "exercised" on a monthly basis; people take them for a short ride to keep their fluids circulating and to prevent them from getting "garage sores" from remaining stationary for long periods.

◆ The storage facility is vermin-proof, so damage from animal pests is a not an issue.

◆ Knowing your vehicle is safely stowed away and in the good hands of a professional facility gives you peace of mind.

The Least You Need to Know

◆ Cleaning and detailing should always be performed before a collector vehicle is put into storage.

◆ Adequate vehicle preparation should be done before winter storage.

◆ Garages, trailers, and portable shelters are all viable options for collector vehicle storage.

◆ A collector vehicle should be stored with the suspension "loaded" to prevent flat spots on the tires and other problems.

◆ Climate-controlled storage facilities offer many benefits that can justify their fees.

Well, that wraps it up. I certainly hope you've enjoyed reading this book at least as much as I enjoyed writing it and that you've found it to be helpful. On a parting note, I wish you a happy restoration and a most enjoyable, fun-filled experience in the collector car hobby.

—Tom Benford

Services, Suppliers, and Internet Resources

In this Appendix you'll find the complete contact information for the service providers, parts, tools, products, and periodicals I mention throughout the text of this book. It should prove to be a handy reference for you during your restoration efforts.

Collector Car Funding and Financing

Capital One Auto Finance
401 West A Street, Suite 1000
San Diego, CA 92101
Phone: 1-800-689-1789
Fax: 1-888-412-7543
E-mail: comment@capitaloneauto.com
Web: www.capitaloneautofinance.com

Classic Car Financial
P.O. Box 10720
Bedford, NH 03110
Phone: 603-262-2006
Fax: 603-424-2117
E-mail: dmcmanus@classiccarfinancial.com
Web: www.classiccarfinancial.com

Premier Financial Services
47 Sherman Hill Road
Woodbury, CT 06798
Phone: 203-267-7700
Fax: 203-267-7773
E-mail: info@whynotlease.com
Web: www.whynotlease.com

Gettysburg Financial
4699 N. Federal Highway, Suite 110
Pompano Beach, FL 33064
Phone: 954-444-9680
Fax: 561-218-5727
E-mail: pat@gettysburgfinancial.com
Web: www.gettysburgfinancial.com

Classic Auto Loans
1251 S. Federal Highway #123
Boca Raton, FL 33432
Phone: 561-305-6900
Fax: 561-892-0156
E-mail: info@classicautoloans.com
Web: www.classicautoloans.com

Registered Automotive Importers

Automotive Importers
1730 South First Street
Yakima, WA 98909
Phone: 509-248-4700
Fax: 707-839-1662
E-mail: sales@stevehahns.com
Web: www.hahnsauto.com

Autosport Design
203 West Hills Road
Huntington Station, NY 11746
Phone: 516-248-0066
Fax: 516-248-4422
E-mail: car-sales@autosportsdesign.com
Web: http://www.autosportdesign.com

European Auto Repair Center
6845 SW 59th Place
Miami, FL 33143
Phone: 305-661-2939
Fax: 305-662-2105
E-mail: rramjit106@aol.com

Sunshine Car Import
745 NE 19th Place
Cape Coral, FL 33903
Phone: 941-458-1020
Fax: 941-458-4410
E-mail: scarimport@aol.com
Web: www.sunshine-car-import.com

Western Cascade
6440 South 143rd Street
Tukwila, WA 98168
Phone: 206-243-2667
Fax: 206-439-7833
E-mail: karen@westerncascade.com
Web: www.westerncascade.com

Supplier Contact Information

ADP Hollander
14800 28th Avenue N, #190
Plymouth, MN 55447
Phone: 1-800-825-0644
Web: www.hollander-auto-parts.com

Has an assorted interchangeable part manual in print and on CD-ROM.

Auto Chic, Inc.
6-B Hamilton Business Park
85 Franklin Road
Dover, NJ 07801
Phone: 1-800-351-0605
Web: www.autochic.com

Offers car covers.

Busch Enterprises, Inc.
908 Cochran Street
Statesville, NJ 28677
Phone: 704-878-2067

Specializes in metal care products.

Contemporary Corvette
2705 Old Rogers Road
Bristol, PA 19007
Phone: 1-800-367-8388
Web: www.contemporarycorvette.com

This is a 1968-present Corvette boneyard.

Craftsman Automotive Tools
All Sears stores nationwide
Web: www.craftsman.com

Offers automotive hand tools, air compressor, hand-held abrasive system, roll-about tool chests, and air tools.

Custom Autosound Manufacturing, Inc.
808 W. Vermont Avenue
Anaheim, CA 92805
Phone: 714-535-1091
Web: www.customautosound.com

Offers retro-look and stealth car audio systems.

The Eastwood Company
263 Shoemaker Road
Pottstown, PA 19464
Phone: 1-800-345-1178
Web: www.eastwoodcompany.com

Has hydraulic floor jacks, jack stands, restoration supplies, assorted hand and air tools, Rust Encapsulator paint, Diamond Cad paint system, self-etching primer, work lights, digital automotive multimeter, Battery Tenders, dent repair systems, battery jumper box, sandblast cabinet, buffer, tumbler, MIG welding gloves and welding supplies, English wheel, pneumatic planishing hammer, assorted shop supplies, and equipment.

Garden of Speedin', Inc.

4645Q Ruffner Street
San Diego, CA 92111
Phone: 1-800-668-6743
Web: www.gardenofspeedin.com

Offers parts locator guides in print and CD-ROM formats.

Hibernia Auto Restorations, Inc.

52 Maple Terrace
Hibernia, NJ 07842
Phone: 973-627-1882
Web: www.hiberniaautorestorations.com

Offers comprehensive collector car restoration services such as engine rebuilding, body restorations, interiors, and so forth.

Hobart Welders

600 W. Main Street
Troy, OH 45373
Phone: 1-800-626-9420
Web: www.hobartwelders.com

Hobart manufactures auto-dimming MIG welding helmets and welders.

Ibiz, Inc.

750 E. Sample Road, Building 7, B7
Pompano Beach, FL 33064
Phone: 1-800-FOR-R-WAX
Web: www.ibiz-inc.com

Manufacturers of car care products include car wax, interior car products, car wash, and more.

Jim's Car & Bike Capsules

13930 Fruitville Road
Sarasota, FL 34240
Phone: 877-227-8957
Web: www.carcapsules.net

Has inflatable indoor and outdoor car capsules in various sizes.

Lincoln Electric
22801 St. Clair Avenue
Cleveland, OH 44117-1199
Phone: 1-800-833-9353
Web: www.lincolnelectric.com

Manufacturers of home and professional MIG welders and welding accessories.

Kanter Auto Products
76 Monroe Street
Boonton, NJ 07005
Phone: 1-800-526-1096
Web: www.kanter.com

Offers engine overhaul kits, brakes, shocks, and other automotive restoration parts and accessories.

Mid-America Direct
#1 Mid America Place
P.O. Box 1368
Effingham, IL 62401
Phone: 1-800-500-8388
Web: www.madirect.com

Offers new reproduction Corvette chrome bumpers and other Corvette restoration parts and accessories.

North American Outdoor Products
Cover-It Shelters
17 Wood St.
P.O. Box 26037
West Haven, CT 06516
Phone: 1-800-514-1572
Fax: 203-931-4754
Web: www.coveritshelters.com

Has round-top and house-type portable car shelters.

Oxlite Manufacturing, Inc.
1800 Rees Street
Breaux Bridge, LA 70517
Phone: 1-800-256-2408
Web: www.oxlite.com

Offers high-capacity, lightweight aluminum trailer ramps.

Spray Nine Corporation
251 North Comrie Avenue
Johnstown, NY 12095
Phone: 1-800-477-7299
Web: www.knightmkt.com

Has a spray cleanser and degreaser available in various sized bottles.

Ssnake-Oyl Products
114 North Glenwood Boulevard
Tyler, TX 75702
Phone: 1-800-284-7777
Web: www.Ssnake-oyl.com

Offers seat belt refurbishing services.

Steele Rubber Products, Inc.
6180 Hwy 150 East
Denver, NC 28037
Phone: 1-800-544-8665
Web: www.steelerubber.com

Offers weatherstripping, pedal pads, and other automotive rubber products.

Trim Parts
2175 Deerfield Road
Lebanon, OH 45036
Phone: 513-934-0815
Web: www.trimparts.com

Offers pot metal reproduction trim parts, emblems, and lenses.

Vette Brakes & Products
7490–30th Avenue North
Saint Petersburg, FL 33710-2304
Phone: 1-800-237-9991
Web: www.vettebrakes.com

Has steering, suspension, and brake products for Camaros, Firebirds, Corvettes, and other marques.

Vintage Air
10305 I.H. 35 North
San Antonio, TX 78233
Phone: 1-800-862-6658
Web: www.vintageair.com

Has direct-fit and custom-fit aftermarket air conditioning systems for vintage and collector cars.

Internet Resources

www.hemmings.com—the online version of *Hemmings Motor News*

www.oldcarsweekly.com—the online version of *Old Cars Weekly*

www.carsandparts.com—the online version of *Cars & Parts* magazine

www.autorestorer.com—a source for restoration information and service and parts providers

Glossary

Although all of these terms were defined throughout the text of the book, I've included them as a glossary here for quick and easy reference. These terms are all you need to know in order to "talk the talk" in the collector car hobby. Enjoy!

Agreed Value   As the name suggests, the agreed value is a collector vehicle insurance term that denotes a vehicle's value, which is agreed upon by both the vehicle's owner and the insurance company. Agreed value is usually applied to such vehicles as street rods and customs that are unique and for which no formal valuation guidelines are established. Frequently, the receipts for parts, labor, services, and supplies used in bringing the vehicle into its present form are factors that come into play when establishing the agreed value.

Air Springs   An air spring is a type of airbag, rather than a metal spring, that is used to support the vehicle and control its ride motions. Air springs, also known as air suspension, can deliver excellent driving comfort over a wide range of vehicle loading because they can be made very soft for a lightly loaded condition, and their pressure automatically increased to match any load increase.

Alternator   The alternator is a device that converts rotational energy to AC current, provides energy for the vehicle's electrical system, and also recharges the battery. The alternator uses the principle of electromagnetic induction to produce voltage and current. Before the advent of the alternator around 1963, DC generators were used on automobiles.

Automobilia Accessories, advertising specialties, brochures, or other memorabilia items that specifically relate to the automobile. These items can include sales brochures, owners' manuals, key chains, ashtrays, tin signs, gas pump globes, and other items of similar nature.

Bias-Ply Tires Once the conventional and predominant automobile tires, bias ply tires have cords in their plies of structural fabric that are at an angle (the bias angle) to the circumferential centerline. The carcass is constructed of adjacent layers of fabric that run continuously from bead to bead. A typical passenger-car tire has two plies of fabric with cords running at an angle of 30–40 degrees to the circumferential centerline.

Binders This is a slang term for a car's brakes.

Box Girder Frame A chassis frame that uses side rails connected by cross members only at the front and back is referred to as a box girder frame because the side rails and front and rear cross members form a rectangular box.

Brake Fade When brakes get extremely hot, they are less effective at stopping. Two reasons for this "fade" in braking power are that the brake shoe or pad material loses its ability to grip as it gets hot, or that moisture in the brake fluid actually boils, thereby creating air bubbles that reduce the pressure at the wheel. Lower brake pressure results in less stopping power.

Breaker Points Early automotive distributors are equipped with a mechanical switch that has two contact points. When closed, these two points supply current to the primary windings of the coil; when they open, the energy is transferred to the coil's secondary windings, which amplify it to supply the high energy needed to fire the spark plugs. Also simply called points, they eventually wear out and must be replaced as part of a routine tune up. With the advent of electronic ignition, breaker point distributors became obsolete.

Bright Work Bright work is a collective term for the chrome, stainless steel, pot metal, or aluminum trim on a vehicle. The name stems from the fact that these pieces are bright (as opposed to painted).

Camshaft The camshaft is the shaft in the engine, which is driven by gears, belts, or chain from the crankshaft. The camshaft has a series of cams, or lobes, that open and close intake and exhaust valves as it turns.

Carson Top This is a solid, removable roof that is usually covered in a soft material and used on some roadsters, cabriolets, and phaetons.

CID CID is an abbreviation for cubic inch displacement, which is a measurement of the volume of an engine's cylinders that denotes the total volume of the engine's combustion chambers. Essentially the larger the CID, the more horsepower the engine can produce.

Classic Car   The Classic Car Club of America (CCCA) defines a classic car as "a fine or distinctive automobile, either American or foreign, built between 1925–1948 in limited numbers. They are also sometimes called full classics or Classic with a capital "C."

Coil Spring   A coil spring is a spiral of elastic steel that is used in many sizes for different purposes throughout a vehicle, most notably as the springing medium in the suspension system.

Concours d'Elegance   This term refers to a car show of the very finest vehicles, or a vehicle that is up to *concours* standards. Typically, *concours* shows and levels of restoration center on such outstanding and high-end marques as Bugatti, Talbot-Lago, Duesenberg, Delahaye, Isotta-Fraschini, and others of similar type are found at these prestigious shows.

Cooling System   The cooling system removes heat from the engine by the forced circulation of coolant and thereby prevents the engine from overheating. In a liquid-cooled engine, it includes the water jackets, water pump, radiator, and thermostat.

Coupe   A coupe is a two-door closed body type that is typically distinguished from a two-door sedan by a sleeker, shorter roof and longer trunk.

Crankcase   This is the metal case that encloses the crankshaft. In most engines, the oil pan and the lower portion of the cylinder block form the crankcase.

Crankshaft   This is the main shaft in the engine that contains one or more cranks, or "throws," that are coupled by connecting rods to the engine's pistons. The combustion process creates reciprocating motion in the rods and pistons, which in turn is converted to a rotating motion by the crankshaft as it revolves.

Cylinder Block   The cylinder block is the basic part of the engine to which other engine parts are attached. It is usually a casting and includes engine cylinders and the upper part of the crankcase.

Decked   In customizing terms, a decked car is one that has had the chrome details and trim removed from the trunk and smoothed over.

Distributor   As the name implies, the distributor delivers the spark to each cylinder to initiate combustion. The distributor typically contains the breaker points and cam, centrifugal and vacuum advance mechanisms, and a shaft driven by the camshaft. The coil generates high voltage and is passed to the distributor, which uses a rotor to supply this current to each spark plug through insulated wires.

Double-Ending   This describes an auction that charges a "buyer's premium" (commission) and a "seller's premium" (commission) when the auction ends successfully. The auction company collects a commission from both parties at the end.

Drag Plates   Drag plates are rectangular metal plates suspended from the rear of a club member's vehicle that have the club name and logo on them. They identify the vehicle and its driver as a member of that club.

Drive Train   The drive train consists of the components that connect the power produced by the engine to the vehicle's drive wheels. The drive train typically consists of the clutch in a manual transmission or the torque converter in an automatic transmission, the transmission, the drive shaft, and universal joints used to connect the drive shaft to the rear differential and the drive axles that actually propel the vehicle when the transmission is engaged.

Fat Fendered   This is a nickname for 1935 to 1948 Fords that were wide and rounded in appearance.

Flamethrowers   Flamethrowers are ignition devices—usually spark plugs—that are inserted into the exhaust pipes, and when activated, ignite unburned exhaust gases and shoot flames out of the tail pipes. The carburetors of flamethrower cars are usually set to run quite rich, thus providing plenty of unburned fuel vapor for the ignition devices. Popular during the 1950s and 1960s, flamethrowers are rarely seen today because they are not safe modifications to make to a vehicle.

Float   The float is a part of the carburetor that meters the fuel coming into the carburetor from the fuel pump and ensures that a steady supply of gasoline is available for the engine, even when making sharp turns or going up steep hills.

Fordor   This is what Ford called its four-door cars in the 1930s and 1940s.

Four on the Floor   This is a colloquial term for a four-speed manual transmission with the shifting lever mounted on the floor rather than on the steering column.

Frame-Off Restoration   This is a restoration project in which the entire vehicle is completely disassembled with all parts cleaned or replaced as necessary in order to meet the original factory specifications as closely as possible.

Frame-Up Restoration   This type of restoration is not as detailed as a frame-off, but it involves restoring the paint, chrome, interior, and mechanicals to original specifications without completely disassembling the car.

Frenched   Headlights and taillights are said to be frenched when they are recessed and smoothed into the body panels.

GTO   This stands for Gran Turismo Omologato, which is Italian for Grand Touring Homologated. The name was originally applied to the famed 1962 Ferrari 250 GTO and noted that enough of the vehicles had been built for FIA-sanctioned (Fédération Internationale de l'Automobile) GT racing. Pontiac later used the term for the vehicle that launched the American muscle car phenomenon. The FIA stipulates that a certain number of cars must be built in order for the car to be homologated and permitted to race.

Gullwing Doors   Gullwing doors are hinged to open vertically rather than horizontally. The name came about because, when open, the doors resemble a seagull in flight with wings spread. The Bricklin had electrically-operated gullwing doors.

Harmonic Balancer   Also sometimes called a vibration damper, a harmonic balancer is a cylindrical weight that is attached to the front of the crankshaft to reduce the torsion (twisting) vibration that occurs along the length of the crankshaft in automotive engines.

Kit Car   This refers to a reproduction of an existing automotive design (for example, 1932 Ford Coupe) that is sold in various stages of production to allow the builder to complete and customize it. Kit cars are very popular with the street-rodding set.

Ladder Frame   A chassis frame that uses side rails connected by cross members throughout its length is called a ladder frame because the cross members form the "rungs" that are attached to the side rails, thus resembling a ladder.

Leaded Gasoline   This refers to gasoline that has tetraethyl lead or other lead compounds added to it to increase its octane rating and reduce its knock or detonation tendencies. American cars manufactured since 1975 or foreign-made vehicles exported to the United States since 1975 require unleaded gas and are equipped with catalytic converters to reduce exhaust emissions.

Leadsled   A leadsled is a lowered, late-forties car with molded body seams that are usually done with lead solder.

Leaf Spring   A leaf spring is composed of one or more long, slightly curved flexible steel or fiberglass plates. Several plates of diminishing lengths are mounted on top of one another and clamped together. Shackles attach leaf springs to the vehicle's frame.

Mags   This is an abbreviation for magnesium wheels. Mags are lightweight wheels that usually have a five-spoke design made of magnesium or magnesium/aluminum alloy. These wheels are attractive and give the car a custom look. Pontiac introduced the first factory mag wheels in 1962.

Matching Numbers   In the most correct sense, this means that the car's vehicle identification number (VIN) matches with the partial VINs on the engine and the transmission. To be a true "matching numbers car," the engine identifier and the transmission identifier also match the options on the build sheet. The codes for the other major components such as the rear end, radiator, and alternator should also match. Many other items plus individual components (that is, heads, block, intake manifold, etc.) also have date codes either cast or stamped into them, and these should match as well.

MIG Welder   Also called a wire welder, MIG stands for metal inert gas. A MIG welder uses electric current to create a high-energy electric arc. Welding wire is fed through the tip of the welding gun, and an inert gas (usually argon) flows out of the tip of the gun to displace the air around the area being welded. Because there is no air, the weld is fast and smooth with little or no slag produced. MIG welders are a body shop's favorite tool for performing sheet metal repairs, and heavy-duty MIG units can be used for welding thicker metal such as chassis rails.

Mileage Caps   Mileage caps are maximum mileage amounts that a collector vehicle can be driven during a calendar year under the terms of the collector car insurance. For example, a collector vehicle policy with a 2,500-mileage cap can be driven a maximum of 2,500 miles in a calendar year. If this mileage is exceeded and the vehicle is in an accident, the insurance company can deny coverage and compensation because the exceeded mileage cap violated the terms of the policy.

Mill   This is an old slang term for a car's engine.

Monoleaf Spring   This is a leaf spring with a single, long, slightly curved, flexible plate, usually made of fiberglass or an epoxy resin.

Nitrocellulose Lacquer   This is a type of automotive paint that was used through the early 1980s. Because of its noxious vapors and high toxicity, the Environmental Protection Agency (EPA) outlawed it for use in the United States.

Nitrous Oxide   Also simply called nitrous, nitrous oxide (N_2O) is commonly known as laughing gas. Nitrous is often used in drag racing to boost engine performance for short periods. When burned, N_2O releases nitrogen and oxygen; the released oxygen permits more gasoline to be burned, thereby resulting in the boost in power.

No Reserve   This is an auction term that means the vehicle being sold at auction will go for whatever the high bid on it is; no preset bid threshold must be met. There is always a minimum starting bid; however, this may also be waived at the seller's discretion.

NORS Parts   NORS is an abbreviation for New Old Replacement Stock. NORS parts are original boxed parts that were made many years ago, and, although they may not be 100 percent correct, they are usually more desirable than reproduction parts because many parts used on the assembly line were never sold as replacement parts. The original manufacturer produced and offered separate parts, perhaps slightly different in appearance because of design changes, for replacement purposes. Because the original manufacturer produced them around the time the car was still new, they are also scarce and command high prices.

NOS Parts   NOS is an abbreviation for New Old Stock. NOS parts are original parts in their original boxes (as opposed to reproduction parts) that have been stored for several years. A NOS part is identical to the part used on the assembly line. Because of their originality, NOS parts are usually scarce and command the highest prices.

O-ring   An O-ring is a type of sealing ring, usually made of rubber, silicone, or a similar flexible material, that is shaped like the letter "O." The O-ring is compressed into adjoining grooves to provide a seal. O-rings are commonly used to seal the fittings of automotive air conditioning systems.

Pitman Arm   The pitman arm is a lever connected to the steering box sector shaft that moves from side to side to steer the front wheels.

Pot Metal   Pot metal is a low-grade nonferrous alloy composed of copper and zinc used for die-casting.

Rack-and-Pinion Steering   This is a steering system with a pinion gear on the end of the steering shaft that mates with a rack (sort of like a geared wheel opened up and laid flat). When the steering wheel is turned, the pinion also turns, thus moving the rack to the left or right. This movement is transmitted through the tie rods to the steering arms at the wheels.

Rag Joint   This is a colloquial term for the flexible steering coupler disc, usually made of layers of canvas that are sewn together, that connects the steering shaft to the steering box. The canvas helps to prevent vibration and shocks caused by roadway irregularities from being transmitted to the steering wheel.

Ragtop   Ragtop is a slang expression for a convertible. Early convertibles through the 1950s used canvas for the tops, hence the name "ragtop."

Replacement Value   As the name implies, the replacement value is an auto insurance term that indicates the amount it would cost to replace the vehicle with one of the same year, make, and model in the same condition. This is an arbitrary insured value on a vehicle that is usually determined by a certified appraisal and other factors, such as the current auction selling prices for similar vehicles. However, the replacement value might not reflect the actual investment you have in the vehicle   only the amount it would cost to replace it.

Replicar   A replicar is a replica of a real car that was made at an earlier time. Popular examples include the Shelby Cobra replicars produced by several companies. While these replicars are often expensive, their price is frequently just a drop in the bucket compared to what an original version of the vehicle is worth in the current market.

Reserve   This is an auction term that means the buyer has set a minimum price that he will accept for the vehicle at the auction. If this minimum (the reserve) is not met, the auctioneer will ask the seller if he or she wants to waive the reserve and accept the final bid; if the seller declines to accept it, the vehicle is not sold.

Ring Man   This is the name for an auction employee who calls out bids and points to the bidder so the auctioneer knows from whom and where the bid came from. It is the ring man's job (there are usually several scattered throughout the buyers area) to keep the pace of the auction fast and to build the bidding frenzy, urging bidders to keep bidding higher. Though a ring man may act friendly, he is not your friend; his job is to drive the price up so the seller gets the most money for the vehicle and the auction gets the biggest commission, at your expense.

Runabout   A runabout is a small, light two-seat car. The term was mainly used to describe American cars that were small, very basic and inexpensive. The runabout was the predecessor to the roadster.

Running Chassis   Also sometimes called a "rolling chassis," this refers to an automobile's frame, engine, transmission, suspension, gas tank, steering system, drive train, brakes, wheels and tires, and cooling system. In effect, it is the complete car without the body attached to it.

Rust   Rust is any of various powdery or scaly reddish-brown or reddish-yellow hydrated oxides formed on iron and iron-containing materials (such as steel) by low-temperature oxidation in the presence of water. The chemical name for rust is ferric oxide (Fe_2O_3).

SAE   SAE is an abbreviation for the Society of Automotive Engineers, a professional engineering organization that publishes research papers and defines various standards of measurement for the American automobile industry.

Salvage Yard   Junkyard, boneyard, and auto parts recycling yard are all slang names for a salvage yard. As its name implies, parts and assemblies are salvaged from wrecked or junked cars for resale, thus giving the parts a second shot at life rather than being turned into scrap metal.

Shackle   The term shackle refers to a swinging support that attaches to the car's frame on one side and to the leaf spring on the other side. It is used to accommodate the change in the spring's length as it deforms in response to the wheel's up and down motions as it encounters bumps and other irregularities in the road.

Shill Bid   This is a false auction bid placed by the seller's friend, accomplice, relative, or even himself using another name to increase the bids against you to drive the price up on the vehicle.

Shoe Box   This is a slang name for the squarish-shaped 1955, 1956, and 1957 Chevrolets.

Short   Also called a short circuit, a short is a defect in an electrical circuit that permits the current to take a short path or circuit rather than following the prescribed path. A short frequently results in the burning out of related circuits and/or the failure of the device. Fuses are used in automotive electrical systems to protect against such damage from shorts.

Single Wheel Trailer   A single wheel trailer is an accessory trailer that has only one wheel supporting it.

Slush Box   This is a slang term for an automatic transmission. An automatic transmission uses transmission fluid (the "slush") and hydraulic pressure to engage the drive train rather than the metal gears used in a standard manual transmission.

Street Stock   Street stock is a show designation that is used for vehicles that are essentially stock with some minor bolt-on aftermarket accessories such as mag wheels or chrome valve covers. The criterion is usually that such modifications can be removed and the vehicle returned to pure stock in one-half hour or less.

Suicide Door   A suicide door has the hinges at the rear of it, rather than at the front. Suicide doors were popular during the 1920s and 1930s.

Three Deuces   This is a slang term for an engine equipped with three two-barrel carburetors. This configuration is also called a tri-power setup, or a six-pack.

Torsion Bar   A torsion bar is a long, straight bar fastened to the frame at one end and to a suspension part at the other. It is, in effect, an unwound coil spring that absorbs the energy that road irregularities produce by twisting. The torsion bar's main advantage over the coil spring in a front suspension is that it provides an easy means of adjusting suspension height.

Trailer Queen   This is a slang term, often with demeaning connotations, for a collector car that has been restored and is never driven. These cars are transported to shows in or on trailers and usually have virtually no miles on the odometer. This term doesn't apply to racecars, however, because they put many harsh miles on the odometer on the race track and in a significantly more demanding environment than ordinary street driving.

Transverse   This term indicates something that is situated or lying across, crosswise, or at a 90-degree angle to the perpendicular. Cross members are transverse beams.

Tudor   Tudor is what Ford called its two-door cars in the 1930s and 1940s.

Unibody Construction   Also called unitized construction, this describes a car that is engineered so that the body, floorpan, and chassis form a single structure. This results in a vehicle that is generally lighter and more rigid than one using traditional body-on-frame construction.

VIN   This is an abbreviation for Vehicle Identification Number. The VIN is the car's identification that carries its serial number, model, year of manufacture, and basic equipment information, and it is stamped onto a metal plate that is attached to the vehicle. Since the late 1960s, the VIN plate has been required by law to be affixed to the top of the dashboard to make it visible from the outside of the vehicle.

Wash-and-Show   Wash-and-show is a show designation that is used for restored vehicles that are essentially drivers. Generally, the car is washed, sometimes polished, and the interior vacuumed before entering it in the wash-and-show class. In this class, the hood stays closed because the engine compartment is not inspected; the undercarriage is not checked either. This class is also known as the "lazy man's show class" because it takes only minimal effort to make the car presentable for this class.

Wet Sanding   Wet sanding is a finishing technique that uses very fine grit sandpaper dipped in water to remove the "orange peel" surface of a newly painted car. The water acts like a lubricant so that only very small amounts of paint are removed with each stroke and the remaining finish is smooth and ripple-free. Wet sanding is always done by hand.

Index

U-V

W-X-Y-Z